Further and Higher Education Partnerships

SRHE and Open University Press Imprint
General Editor: Heather Eggins

Further and Higher Education Partnerships

The Future for Collaboration

Edited by
Mike Abramson
John Bird and
Anne Stennett

The Society for Research into Higher Education
& Open University Press

Published by SRHE and
Open University Press
Celtic Court
22 Ballmoor
Buckingham
MK18 1XW

and 1900 Frost Road, Suite 101
Bristol, PA 19007, USA

First published 1996

A catalogue record of this book is available from the British Library

ISBN 0 335 19597 0 (pb) 0 335 19598 9 (hb)

Library of Congress Cataloging-in-Publication Data

Further and higher education partnerships / edited by Michael
    Abramson, John Bird, and Anne Stennett.
        p. cm.
    Includes bibliographical references and index.
    ISBN 0-335-19598-9 (hardcover). — ISBN 0-335-19597-0 (pbk.)
    1. University cooperation—Great Britain. 2. Continuing
education—Great Britain. 3. Postsecondary education—Great
Britain. I. Abramson, Michael, 1946- . II. Bird, John, 1944- .
III. Stennett, Anne, 1938- .
LB2331.5.F87   1996   95–47027
378.1'04'0941—dc20   CIP

Typeset by Graphicraft Typesetters Limited, Hong Kong
Printed in Great Britain by St Edmundsbury Press Ltd
Bury St Edmunds, Suffolk

Contents

List of Contributors

Mike Abramson, Head of Combined Honours, University of Central Lancashire, Preston.

Stephen Bigger, Head of Student Recruitment, Westminster College, Oxford.

John Bird, Principal Lecturer in Sociology, University of the West of England, Bristol.

Peter Brophy, Librarian, University of Central Lancashire, Preston.

Peter Chambers, Vice Principal, Bradford and Ilkley Community College.

Kate Clarke, Senior Assistant Registrar for Academic Quality, University of Hertfordshire.

Jim Gallacher, Research Fellow, Glasgow Caledonian University.

John Hilborne, Assistant Director, Quality Assurance Group, Higher Education Quality Council.

Peter Lines, Dean of Engineering and Director of Academic Quality, University of Hertfordshire.

James Lusty, Pro-Vice Chancellor (Students), University of Central Lancashire, Preston.

Colin Mellors, Pro-Vice Chancellor, University of Bradford.

Sofija Opacic, Research Officer, National Union of Students.

Alan Roff, Deputy Vice Chancellor, University of Central Lancashire, Preston.

John Selby, Franchise Co-ordinator, Coventry University.

Norman Sharp, Higher Education Quality Council, Scottish Office.

Anne Stennett, Professor Emeritus, Bath College of Higher Education.

Stephen Ward, Further Education Liaison Co-ordinator, Bath College of Higher Education.

List of Abbreviations

AfC	Association for Colleges
APEL	accreditation of prior experiential learning
APL	accreditation of prior learning
ASC	academic subject category
BITC	Business in the Community
BTEC	Business and Technical Education Council
CATS	credit accumulation and transfer scheme
Cert.Ed.	Certificate in Education
CGLI	City and Guilds of London Institute
CHE	College of Higher Education
CLA	Copyright Licensing Agency
CNAA	Council for National Academic Awards
COSHEP	Committee of Scottish Higher Education Principals
CPVE	Certificate in Pre-Vocational Education
CVCP	Committee of Vice Chancellors and Principals
CVE	Continuing Vocational Education
CVU	Council of Validating Universities
DES	Department of Education and Science
DENI	Department for Education of the Northern Ireland Office
DFE	Department for Education
DipHE	Diploma in Higher Education
EBP	education business partnership
FE	further education
FEC	further education college
FEDA	Further Education Development Agency
FEFC	Further Education Funding Council
FEI	further education institution
FEU	Further Education Unit
FHE	further and higher education
FSG	funding subject group
FTE	full-time equivalent

GCE	General Certificate in Education
GCSE	General Certificate in Secondary Education
GNVQ	General National Vocational Qualification
HE	higher education
HEFCE	Higher Education Funding Council for England
HEFCW	Higher Education Funding Council for Wales
HEI	higher education institution
HEQC	Higher Education Quality Council
HMI	Her Majesty's Inspectorate
HNC	Higher National Certificate
HND	Higher National Diploma
ISI	Institute for Scientific Information
IT	information technology
JANET	Joint Academic Network
LEA	local education authority
LINCS	Local Integrated Colleges Scheme
NFER	National Foundation for Educational Research
NRA	National Record of Achievement
NUS	National Union of Students
OCN	Open College Network
OFSTED	Office for Standards in Education
PCFC	Polytechnics and Colleges Funding Council
RSA	Royal Society of Arts
SACCA	Scottish Advisory Committee on Credit and Access
SCONUL	Standing Conference of National and University Librarians
SCOTCATS	Scottish Credit Accumulation and Transfer Scheme
SCOTVEC	Scottish Vocational Education Council
SHEFC	Scottish Higher Education Funding Council
SOED	Scottish Office Education Department
SQMS	Scottish Quality Management System
SWAP	Scottish Wider Access Programme
TEC	Training and Enterprise Council
TVE	technical and vocational education
TVEI	Technical and Vocational Education Initiative
UCAS	Universities and Colleges Admissions Service
UDC	Urban Development Corporation

Introduction

Mike Abramson, John Bird and Anne Stennett

This book explores key aspects of cross-sector academic partnerships in the United Kingdom that emerged in the late 1980s, and boomed in the early 1990s, as an initial response to the radical changes in the funding and structure of post-compulsory education and as a device to meet government demands to increase participation in the higher education experience. As partnerships have matured, however, less pragmatic and longer-term rationales have been developed, which have the potential to withstand the bewildering vagaries of government policy. Among these newer rationales is the commitment to widen participation in higher education to tradition-ally under-represented groups (and so to create *genuine* mass higher edu-cation) and a growing understanding that the intrinsic worth of partnership lies in institutions being able to do together what they cannot do separately.

The earliest, and still the most common, form of association is that be-tween further education institutions (FEIs) and higher education insti-tutions (HEIs), and takes the form of an academic franchise. Within this arrangement, the whole, or part, of a course developed and owned by one institution (the HE franchiser) is delivered by another (the FE franchisee). Currently, most universities franchise non-degree provision and lower levels of degree courses across a wide academic spectrum, but with a strong em-phasis on the part-time study mode. Progression to higher academic levels, where necessary at the host institution, is normally, but not universally, guaranteed.

It is important to note, however, that further and higher education (FHE) partnerships have now gone beyond franchising to embrace the develop-ment and delivery of joint courses, articulation agreements and 'traditional' validations of complete higher education programmes owned and taught entirely by FEIs. The potential of partnership has also been recognized in franchise agreements between schools and further education colleges, and has been extended beyond the local and regional levels to include national and, more controversially, international relationships. Moreover, a small num-ber of genuinely equal 'second generation' partnerships is now emerging, which thrive on a two-way flow of ideas, experience and expertise, and which extend the concept of partnership beyond courses to embrace strategic planning, research, staff development and curricular merger. Some mixed-economy colleges will seek institutional merger as a consequence, but the majority of the FE sector will wish to maintain and enhance a community-based autonomy, complemented by an exclusive associate college relationship with a regional HE partner.

Given that there are now upwards of 50,000 students engaged in 'off-campus' higher education, and that the proliferation of partnership activity has been a bottom-up, institution-led phenomenon, unguided by any national policy, it is hardly surprising that cross-sector collaboration has engendered much controversy and debate, focused on the issues of funding and quality. In his introduction to the recently published *Learning from Collaborative Audit*, for example, the Chief Executive of the Higher Education Quality Council (HEQC) issued a stern warning that unless institutions

> are able to bring at least the same degree of consistency and rigour to the quality assurance of their collaborative provision as they apply to the 'internal' provision for which they are wholly responsible, there must be a risk that collaboration in all its forms will come to be seen as 'second best'. Since collaboration is a means of responding more suitably and more flexibly to external demands on the system, this would be a considerable setback not only for the students and employers concerned, but also for British higher education as a whole.
>
> (HEQC 1995: 2)

At its best, the partnership debate has been a lively, healthy and open-minded contribution to the wider debate on accessibility, the nature of academic quality, the needs of students and, indeed, the essential nature or essence of the higher education experience. It has resulted in several excellent independent research reports, and has stimulated retrospective analyses from almost every official and professional body, including Her Majesty's Inspectorate (HMI), the Council for National Academic Awards (CNAA), the Business and Technical Education Council (BTEC), the Further Education Unit (FEU), HEQC, the Higher Education Funding Council for England (HEFCE) and the Association for Colleges (AfC). All of these are treated to critical scrutiny in the Appendix of this volume.

At its worst, however, the debate has exposed the cynicism, suspicion and subjectivity of academic elitists; the hidden political agenda of some lead bodies; the widespread, but ill-informed, assumptions of venality; and the shabby selectivity of some elements of the educational press, eager to sensationalize allegations of sleaze and scandal at every turn.

It is possible, of course, that these more negative aspects of the debate reveal more about the mood and morale of staff in higher education than they do about partnership *per se*. On the assumption that this is not the case, however, the aim of this collection of essays is to assist readers in reaching their own judgements as to the origins, nature, integrity and future of academic partnership. To fulfil this aim, contributions are provided which explore strategic, operational and research dimensions, and each contributor was asked to provide an objective and candid critique of his or her first-hand experience. All the contributors conclude with a retrospect of their current achievement, and, because this book deliberately seeks to look beyond franchising, they also speculate on prospects for the future.

The text is divided into three main sections and, as indicated earlier, includes, as an appendix, a detailed critical bibliography of the literature of partnership which should be of value to future researchers in this area.

Part 1 explores overall frameworks for partnership and contains eight contributions covering rationales, emerging national policy, funding, quality assurance, learning resources and the student experience. The thorny issue of international partnership is also addressed, as are the different approaches to partnership which are developing in Scotland. Part 2 focuses on four generic studies. A relatively new and deliberately modest relationship between one college of higher education and one FE college is the first case study and makes a valuable comparison with the second, which explains the development of a very large and well-established network, mostly based on the needs of part-time adult students, and made up of over twenty colleges. The third case study assesses the value of collaboration between schools and further education via an inner city compact initiative. The last study charts the delicate negotiations required to reach an agreement of association between a large mixed-economy college and a contiguous traditional university, with most benefit accruing to full-time students.

By summarizing the prospective elements of each contribution, Part 3 has the temerity to predict the future of cross-sector collaboration. It suggests that, though they will change, partnerships are here to stay and will continue to influence the reconfiguration of post-compulsory education as it moves towards a mass system in the twenty-first century.

Reference

HEQC (1995) *Learning from Collaborative Audit.* London, HEQC.

Part 1

Framework for Partnership

1

Partnership Imperatives: a Critical Appraisal

Mike Abramson

The partnership phenomenon

In recent years, cross-sector academic partnerships in the United Kingdom have grown not only in size but also in diversity. Even the dominant form of partnership, based upon the franchising of higher education provision to further education colleges, now has many significant variations. In terms of geographical range, for example, such franchises are now delivered at distances which are local, regional, national, European and even intercontinental. Franchised products vary in academic level from access to postgraduate; they are both part-time and full-time; sometimes whole courses are franchised, and sometimes parts of courses. Stemming from such further education (FE)–higher education (HE) links, new forms of association are also emerging. There is a growing trend within FEIs, for example, to franchise the lower levels of BTEC awards to local schools. New and innovative collaborative courses are also being developed and delivered, which weld together the expertise and strength of more than one institution.

Given this diversity, isolating clear or simple imperatives for partnership enterprise is no easy task. International franchising, for example, may be motivated by raw income generation, while local and regional franchises may embody an institutional mission to widen and deepen participation in the HE experience. Moreover, it is not completely cynical to regard some of the more recent FHE developments as Janus-faced: creatures which exploit public and student-centred rhetoric to mask more private and institution-centred realities (Bird and Yee 1994). Even where almost complete candour exists, the present volatility of public sector education dictates that rationales for partnership cannot be static. They evolve with the growing academic maturity of the franchisee, the strategic growth targets of the franchiser, the vagaries of government funding policy and the needs and wants of students.

Given all this, what currently provides the propellant fuel of FHE partnership? A 1992 *Access News* report concluded that closer FE–HE links are the single most important reason given by both sectors for current and proposed involvement in franchise activities (Grindlay *et al.* 1992). While somewhat tautologous in itself, this motive does hint at the only safe generic rationale that can be isolated: that of mutual benefit and mutual dividend (Morris 1993). Where franchising is based on expediency or greed, such mutuality is fragile and the association tenuous. However, where it is rooted in strategic desires to move from competitive to collaborative models of post-compulsory education, such mutuality can be vigorous and long lasting.

What follows, therefore, is an attempt to itemize and appraise the key aspects of perceived mutual dividend for all those engaged in 'mainstream' FHE partnership initiatives. It draws upon several excellent recent surveys, reports and other publications, and exploits the findings of cohort research into franchise students of the Local Integrated Colleges Scheme (LINCS). This network, one of the largest and best established in the country, comprising ten FE colleges in Lancashire and Cumbria, provides the opportunity to study level 1 of a part-time combined honours programme and guarantees progression to the University of Central Lancashire (at Preston) so that students may complete their degree in any study mode.

The new geography of post-compulsory education

In appraising its deeper roots, one recent writer sees the FHE partnership movement as 'a blend of commercial and academic imperialism' inherited from the United States. Franchising, she argues, is

> the offspring of American parents of doubtful compatibility – on the one side, *commercial franchising*, an American business world concept which expanded rapidly in the 1970s; on the other, the *community college movement* which mushroomed all over America at approximately the same time. It is clear that educational franchising in this country has inherited the characteristics of both its parents, although it is at present far readier to acknowledge the second than the first.
>
> (Woodrow 1993: 208)

For such models of collaboration to flourish in the UK, however, required a more conducive environment, which did not emerge until the late 1980s and early 1990s. Fundamental to its creation was the political agenda of the Thatcher era, which sought to drive post-compulsory education along leaner, more competitive and more entrepreneurial pathways, but which (for different reasons) was not anathema to the strategic and social missions of FE colleges and the former polytechnics.

The result was structural change highly favourable to partnership initiatives. Within higher education, the demise of the CNAA, the release of the polytechnics from local education authority (LEA) control and the removal of the binary line created the 'new' universities with their own degree awarding powers. Shortly afterwards the further education sector was also freed from

LEA governance, though without the authority to validate its own courses. These structural changes were complemented by curriculum developments, especially in the areas of modularity and credit accumulation and transfer, which made academic commodities more defined and more portable and which had the potential to strengthen the concept of a post-16 continuum of provision. More importantly, these changes were accompanied by a government directive to expand participation rates in HE rapidly, but in a cost-effective manner (Department of Education and Science 1991).

The new geography of post-compulsory education thus created both new challenges and new opportunities. Institutions *within* each sector were generally driven apart, especially at the regional level, and here competition rather than collaboration is now the expensive norm. Institutions *across* sectors, however, seeking fulfilment of complementary needs and ambitions, quickly saw more dividend than disadvantage in the formation of academic partnerships.

Partnership dividends for higher education

Of the many and various perceived dividends for HE, the following four are most frequently cited.

Direct income generation

Although rarely given as an explicit rationale it is generally assumed that HEIs must be making a profit from partnership. For obvious reasons, evidence of direct financial gain is not easily available. It is *probable* that money is being made from international franchising, as overseas students pay huge tuition fees to complete their degrees at the franchiser institution. It is also *possible*, since few explicit formulae exist, that HEIs may be excessive in their top-slicing of HEFCE funds, bid for on the colleges' behalf. However, it is more likely that most HEIs make no direct financial gain from FE partnerships, and that those which take quality assurance and administrative infrastructures seriously may be running at a direct financial loss. As one former assistant director of the HEQC has warned, 'Good quality assurance does not come cheap – but, from the franchiser's point of view (at least), it may be significantly less economical to run franchises with so light a touch on the tiller that the franchise ship runs on to the rocks' (Yorke 1993: 181).

In strictly financial terms, therefore, any dividend is best perceived as long-term and indirect.

Indirect income generation

Despite Bocock and Scott's (1994) warning that such motives 'can be exaggerated', there is no doubt that, until recently, many HEIs saw FHE collaboration as one means of achieving strategic growth targets by widening and deepening the pool of potential students. Going some way to reducing both geographical barriers and student fears of large institutions, 'distributed' delivery of higher education would, it was assumed, reach the parts that centralized delivery could not. The ten years' experience of the LINCS network suggests the correctness of this assumption, since many hundreds of mature part-timers, who would never have considered applying to university directly, have now graduated successfully. Moreover, even though the Bocock–Scott report finds only a weak correlation 'between those institutions with severe capacity constraints and those which have been most active in developing links with HE colleges' (p. 11), the prospect of student growth with less capital expenditure on teaching, library and residential accommodation at the centre did contribute to the early appeal of cross-sector partnership.

From the academic perspective, the downloading of sub-degree courses to FE may also be perceived as an indirect dividend, since it can free time for university teachers to expand provision for progressing students, develop taught postgraduate programmes and engage in more research and publication. Moreover, since the flow of academic exports is not always one way, universities have benefited from the expertise of specialist colleges in order to create unique joint courses (e.g. a BSc in forestry management) that neither partner could deliver separately. However, colleges should beware of academic asset stripping of their most popular provision. The expertise of one LINCS college, for example, was the catalyst for the creation of a completely new university department of tourism and leisure. In part, this led to academic promiscuity, divorce and the college's re-marriage to a rival HE partner!

Institutional mission to increase and widen participation in HE

If the evidence of recent surveys is accurate, there is little doubt that the strategy of bringing the product closer to the consumer has contributed significantly to increasing HE participation rates. The LINCS scheme alone has grown from 11 students in 1984–5 to regular recruitment of almost 1,000 in the 1990s; and one national projection suggests that there may be up to 50,000 partnership students throughout the country in 1995 (Bird *et al.* 1993). Given the 1992 autumn statement, however, and the ensuing period of HE consolidation, it will be interesting to monitor the accuracy of such predictions. In future, will HEIs transfer some of their own numbers to FE partners in order to sustain such local growth? Apropos of widening participation, far less empirical evidence exists and it is clear that for some full-time partnerships this is not even an express aim. Moreover, as with other recent curricular innovations, such as the credit accumulation and transfer scheme (CATS) and modularity, partnership *per se* does not, of necessity, widen participation. More can often mean more of the same.

However, partnerships which are allied to appropriate targeting and recruitment strategies do offer a higher potential to recruit traditionally underrepresented groups. Of these, people in areas of geographical isolation, such as Cumbria, East Anglia and the South West, are the most obvious examples, and for them partnership provision has been the only additional HE opportunity since the creation of the Open University (Abramson and Grannell 1989; Tunbridge 1991).

Widening participation is an explicit aim of the LINCS network, and the 1993 analysis of five cohorts (1985–90) indicates both successes and failures in this respect. Forty per cent of all cohorts, for example, lacked standard entrance qualifications, and 45 per cent fell below the traditional 'white collar line'. LINCS was also particularly successful in attracting women returners, who made up 60 per cent of all students by 1990, and whose numbers are still increasing (Abramson *et al.* 1993). However, despite many efforts, the scheme has been less successful in attracting older and retired students, the unskilled and those from minority ethnic groups. Failure to attract the last group is particularly disappointing, given that four East Lancashire colleges within the network are located in areas of high minority ethnic density. Here, the predominantly white ethos of FHE and cultural perceptions as to the value of a degree seem to outweigh the convenience of its delivery. Elsewhere, where the academic provision is deemed to be of more direct relevance to minority ethnic communities (e.g. Higher National Certificate (HNC) and Higher National Diploma (HND) in business), higher recruitment has been achieved (Morris 1993).

Enhancement of regional status and influence

Predominantly, FHE partnership has been the domain of the new universities, which have always perceived the need to maintain and enhance their regional sphere of influence. As a consequence, neighbouring HEIs are usually regarded as competitors and local FEIs are wooed as collaborators. Quick to exploit a buyer's market, some FE colleges have therefore negotiated franchise agreements with several universities, a situation which may provide short-term leverage at the bargaining table, but which also multiplies delivery systems (including those of quality assurance) by the number of HE partners. Such multiple dealing may widen student choices, but given that no standard credit framework presently exists nationally, it may also confuse progression routes and erode transfer opportunities.

Partnership dividends for further education

While these must vary with strategic aspirations, geographical location and the needs of local client groups, the following advantages are generally perceived to be of most significance.

Direct income generation

As with HE, evidence of direct profit is not readily available, although it is clear that by generating additional streams of recurrent funding, partnership activity is not likely to be loss making for the FE sector. Some direct income may accrue from full-time HE courses, especially where there is the opportunity to employ under-utilized staff and accommodation, but, as with HE, profit is best perceived in indirect terms.

Indirect income generation

Securing off-the-shelf provision, without the expense of course development and test-bedding, can be a very cost-effective method of expanding the college portfolio. This also creates the opportunity to side-step direct and sometimes expensive negotiations with external bodies such as BTEC (Warner 1992). Strategic planning frameworks and quality assurance systems are also freely imported in the same way, and have given FEIs invaluable expertise in the run up to incorporation and beyond.

Indirect income is also generated through the staff development acquired from the frequent liaison with university academics, and this in turn increases staff motivation, aids staff retention and enriches every aspect of FE teaching. Ironically, however, the best FE teachers of partnership provision are often head-hunted by the HE partner institution! Upgrading learning resources, especially the library (the most frequent condition of validation panels), also has spin-off benefits for all students within the college.

Institutional mission to serve the needs of the local community

Given a mandate of continued expansion, some college managers may see it as prudent to view the development of HE partnerships as a safeguard against a potential shortfall in the number of mainstream non-advanced further education students (Bocock and Scott 1994). However, such intentions are easily exaggerated, since the Secretary of State specifically requires the Further Education Funding Council (FEFC) to ensure that any college-based higher education is not provided 'at the expense of adequate further education provision' (Warner 1992). Hence, apart from a small number of mixed-economy colleges, the FE sector has been extremely wary of upward academic drift and has limited higher education to between 10 and 20 per cent of its total provision.

It is important to acknowledge that, far more than for even the most regional HEIs, the *raison d'être* of the FE sector has been to serve the academic and vocational needs of the *local* community. By creating additional rungs on the learning ladder, FHE partnership enhances this commitment and in so doing attracts recruitment to the college portfolio *as a whole*. Partnership provision also facilitates *internal* student progression and aids student retention. As the expansion of the LINCS network reveals, this retention is particularly noticeable among adults studying in the evening only, who have high brand loyalty but who want or need the greater intellectual challenges provided by higher education.

Enhanced institutional status and reputation

In a highly competitive post-corporate world, FEIs are as sensitive as their HE partners to the need to enhance institutional reputations. In search of this, neighbouring colleges and sometimes schools are seen as potential threats while well-publicized collaboration with HEIs is seen to attract indirect prestige. Where the regional reputation of a single university is high, and where corporate missions and aspirations are compatible, colleges may opt for an exclusivity deal and promote themselves as associate colleges of the university. Alternatively, they may decide that the reflected glory of several HEIs is more valuable. Either way, while the general public continues to perceive higher education as the country's most prestigious educational product, these strategies of association have an obvious logic.

Such strategies, however, are not without dangers. For example, they can tempt colleges into long-distance franchises which offer little real progression opportunity, especially for part-time students. More importantly, an erroneous belief in the intrinsic prestige of higher education courses can lead to an over-indulgence in the partnership feast, which skews overall college provision and makes second class citizens of those teachers not engaged in HE teaching. As previously indicated, partnership courses are not necessarily the best or most important FE provision.

Partnership dividends for students

These clearly vary with individual student needs and expectations of HE and with modes of attendance, but the following dividends are most frequently perceived.

Local delivery

The savings in time and money accruing from study closer to home are a clear and growing incentive for all students, but they are of particular importance to self-funded part-time adult returners. The LINCS survey, for example, revealed that 73 per cent of students lived within 10 miles of their FHE partner college, in comparison with 23 per cent living within the same distance of the university. Students gave this local delivery as the single most important reason for embarking on a franchised course (Abramson *et al.* 1993). However, as outlined below, this distance dividend disappears completely if students are required to progress to a less local study centre to gain a full degree award, and can lead to high rates of non-progression.

A more appropriate learning experience

For part-time adult students entering higher education through the FE route, partnership can give a better quality of learning experience, since it provides them with an invaluable half-way house in an often familiar environment. Classes tend to be much smaller than in HEIs, staff are often more accessible and students have the support of like-minded peer groups. However, this dividend can disappear when students progress to the host HEI, where they may face overcrowded facilities, impersonal teaching and a sense of isolation. Given this, it is hardly surprising that the Bristol study reveals overwhelming student support for the opportunity to complete the entire award-bearing course at the FE study centre (Bird *et al.* 1993). Given this, is it possible that the finger of doubt in the quality debate surrounding academic partnership is pointing in the wrong direction?

Making the case for the appropriateness of younger full-time franchise students is more difficult. Full-time franchises do increase the opportunities for students to find places on courses for which there is a very high national demand (e.g. business studies). Moreover, classes are often smaller and sometimes specialist accommodation and equipment compare favourably with those of HEI counterparts. In some cases, however, full-time partnership provision may be more akin to academic overspill estates, which provide little or none of the extra-curricular infrastructure of full undergraduate life (e.g. residences, student union, clubs), where library and information technology facilities are inadequate and where a full scholarly ethos is lacking (HMI 1991).

Ease of progression

FHE partnership goes some way to creating a seamless robe of post-compulsory education, but the garment is not yet perfect. For all existing college students, it clearly eases internal progression into HE by a coherent extension of the college's academic spectrum. The LINCS survey, for example, reveals that 62 per cent of all students had previously studied at their local college, with 70 per cent undertaking such courses within the previous two years (Abramson *et al.* 1993).

Where complete courses are available locally, such as HNCs and HNDs, academic and geographical progression to the host institution is not an issue. For degree franchises, however, the norm has been to franchise only first or lower levels, and herein can lie problems. Most FHE agreements, like LINCS, guarantee academic progression. Others, however, require off-campus students to jump through additional (and often demeaning) hoops, such as an interview or re-application, to secure university admission, despite the fact that they have often performed better than their on-campus counterparts. Of course, even guaranteed progression is only a dividend if it can be made a geographical (or technical) reality. Part-time evening students in West Cumbria, for example, wishing to progress in the same study mode, are hardly likely to travel to Preston, over 100 miles distant, to sustain their studies. Even much shorter distances can be a real barrier for those on low incomes, without cars, lacking adequate public transport and with remaining cultural insecurities. Moreover, multimedia solutions to progression are still in their infancy and may not be the most appropriate learning medium for mature and under-represented student groups.

Retrospect

FHE partnership in the early 1990s blossomed in a new landscape and a new climate. The landscape was formed by the incorporation of post-compulsory institutions, and it contained new freedoms but also new threats. The climate was provided by the government commitment to increase participation rates in higher education rapidly, but within a narrow resource base. Most institutions responded to these environmental changes by adopting models of collaboration rather than models of competition. Participation in HE work therefore 'has now become the norm for FE colleges' (AfC 1994: 2).

Early FHE partnerships were the brainchild of the new universities, but many chartered universities now also have relationships with schools and colleges. Franchising of access provision, HNC and HND and the lower levels of degrees remains the dominant form of collaboration, but several more mature forms have also developed, including joint course delivery, articulation agreements and full validations. Most partnership students are local, mature and part-time, but the number of full-time students studying higher education within a predominantly FE environment has also grown significantly (HEQC 1993).

Public rationales for this collaborative boom, especially those relating to international activities, have been treated with some cynicism and incredulity. Given the pressure to increase student numbers it is probably fair to assert that *initially* FHE partnerships, and in particular franchises, were a 'production-led solution to overcome the HE sector's shortage of human and physical resources' (Palmer 1992: 85). Subsequently, however, maturing partnerships have been sustained by less pragmatic motives, including a genuine belief in synergies of association and a social mission to extend opportunities to those potential students presently excluded from higher education by geography, class or culture. Hence, even if FHE partnerships develop no further they will have made a significant contribution to mass higher education in the UK by eroding remaining artificial binary lines and by 'permanently altering perceptions of the relationship between further and higher education institutions' (Woodrow 1993: 220; see also Abramson 1994).

Prospect

Given the dynamics of the government's stop–go policies, the only safe prediction for FHE partnerships is that they will remain volatile and uncertain. Clearly, the colder climate engendered by the recent freeze on HE expansion and the reduction in tuition fee levels will test the motivation and resolve of many HEIs. Moreover, because further education is still in a period of rapid expansion, 'significant tensions are likely to arise between the two sectors because they are at different stages of development' (Bocock and Scott 1994: 5).

As a consequence, it may be that those partnerships based solely upon short-term pragmatism, where there is little or no acknowledgement of the intrinsic value of collaboration, may wither and perish. It is also likely that new developments, even when based upon more deep-rooted social purposes, will be put on hold. That said, recent surveys have indicated a remarkable level of resilience to falling temperatures. The Bocock–Scott Report, for example, declares that 'an examination of the motives for developing partnerships suggests that any set back may be only short-term' since they are 'part of a more radical reconfiguration associated with the growth of a mass system' (p. 14). Similarly, the findings of an AfC (1995: 6) survey reveal that as a result of few arbitrary actions on the part of HE institutions, most 'FE/HE partnerships seem to have survived with remarkably little acrimony'.

If this optimism is well-founded, it is highly likely that FHE partnerships are here to stay. It is important to realize, however, that they will change. It will be prudent, for example, for universities to deepen rather than widen their FE relationships by withdrawing from tenuous partnerships, based upon multiple dealing, and reinforcing strong partnerships based upon exclusivity. The result will be the emergence of 'associate' or 'university' colleges akin to junior colleges in the United States or to the early polytechnics in the United Kingdom. Indeed, some colleges are already being referred to as the 'new polytechnics'.

Some monotechnic institutions, such as colleges of nursing or agriculture, may even seek *institutional* merger, to become specialist faculties or campuses of the university. Most FEIs, however, will wish staunchly to preserve a separate autonomy as providers of broad-based community provision that contains a small but significant percentage of higher education. A more popular path, therefore, may be that of *curricular* merger as CATS and modular schemes embrace the FE sector and regional credit consortia emerge. Through the Scottish Vocational Education Council (SCOTVEC) and the Scottish Credit Accumulation and Transfer Scheme (SCOTCATS), Scotland has demonstrated the value of a national credit framework in facilitating articulation agreements as the most common form of partnership (see Chapter 7) (HEQC 1995). The sensitivities over autonomy of the new universities, however, have prevented such a framework from emerging in the rest of the UK, despite pleas to the contrary (FEU 1992; HEQC 1994).

It is also clear that in the future, associate colleges will wish to complement, or even replace, first-generation partnerships (largely the product of franchising) with more equal second-generation development that acknowledges academic maturity and aspiration and celebrates the distinctiveness of HE and FE as a strength. This means that they will be seeking to deliver higher academic levels in areas of strength through franchises, joint courses and the validation of provision developed and owned entirely by themselves. It also implies an enhancement of the concept of partnership to embrace a two-way flow of ideas, expertise and experience, which includes staff development, quality assurance, research, teaching and learning. Should this occur, it will 'become increasingly difficult, as well as gratuitous' to define which components of partnership are further education and which are higher education (Bocock and Scott 1994: 20), and the slur of 'second best' degrees will disappear.

Finally, no partnership prospect would be complete without allusion to the so-called 'information superhighway' and its potential radically to re-shape the delivery of post-compulsory education. For example, in his *Case for the University of the Lakes* (1995), Dale Campbell-Savours sees a federal or distributed university, based upon the electronic library, as the ultimate solution to geographical isolation. Several other 'televersity' pilot projects are already under way. Clearly, such technological innovation will enhance college-based learning resources in the longer term, but it should be stressed that the concept of a 'virtual college' is no quick or easy panacea to the problem of student progression. It requires significant investment in equipment and staff development. More importantly, care needs to be taken to ensure that the advantages of college-base delivery of higher education, including higher levels of personal support, are not lost or forgotten amid the high-tech hype.

References

Abramson, M. (1994) Franchising, access, quality and exclusivity: some observations from recent research into further and higher education partnerships, *Journal of Access Studies*, 91, 109–14.

Abramson, M., Ellwood, S. and Thompson, L. (1993) *Five Years of Franchising: an Analysis of the Profile, Performance and Progression of LINCS Students 1985–90.* Preston, University of Central Lancashire.

Abramson, M. and Grannell, M. (1989) *Forging Higher Education Links with an Isolated Community: West Cumbria College as a Case Study.* Preston, Lancashire Polytechnic.

Association for Colleges (1994) *The Higher Education Role of Colleges of Further Education.* London, AfC.

Bird, J., Crawley, G. and Sheibani, A. (1993) *Franchising and Access to Higher Education: a Study of HE/FE Collaboration.* Bristol, University of the West of England/ Department of Employment.

Bird, J. and Yee, W.C. (1994) *From Compacts to Consortia: a Study of Partnerships Involving Schools, Colleges, and HEIs.* Bristol, University of the West of England/ Department of Employment.

Bocock, J. and Scott, P. (1994) *Re-drawing the Boundaries: Further and Higher Education Partnerships.* Leeds, Centre for Policy Studies in Education, University of Leeds.

Campbell-Savours, D. (1995) *The Case for the University of the Lakes.* Privately Published.

Department of Education and Science (1991) *Higher Education: a New Framework* (Cm 1541). London, HMSO.

FEU (1992) *A Basis for Credit? Developing a Post-16 Credit Accumulation and Transfer Framework.* London, FEU.

Grindlay, G., Mendick, H., Sims, L. and Woodrow, M.(1992) *Report of the Access News Franchising Survey.* London, ACES, Polytechnic of North London.

HEQC (1993) *Some Aspects of Higher Education Programmes in Further Education Institutions.* London, HEQC.

HEQC (1994) *Choosing to Change: Extending Access, Choice and Mobility in Higher Education.* Report of the HEQC CAT Development Project, Director D. Robinson. London, HEQC.

HEQC (1995) *Aspects of FE/HE Collaborative Links in Scotland.* London, HEQC.

HMI (1991) *Higher Education in Further Education Colleges: Franchising and Other Forms of Collaboration with Polytechnics.* (Report 228/91/NS). London, Department of Education and Science.

Morris, D. (1993) The business of franchising, *Journal of Further and Higher Education,* 17(1), 57–60.

Palmer, A. (1992) Franchised Degree Teaching: What Can Educators Learn From Business?, *Journal of Further and Higher Education,* 16(3), 77–85.

Tunbridge, I. (1991) Franchising higher education activity at Polytechnic South West, in S. Leather and P. Toogood (eds) *Franchising in Post-16 Education.* Coombe Lodge Report, 22(9), 803–7. Bristol, Staff College.

Warner, D. (1992) Classless study, *Education,* October, 330–1.

Woodrow, M. (1993) Franchising: the quiet revolution, *Higher Education Quarterly,* 47(3), 207–20.

Yorke, M. (1993) Quality assurance for higher education franchising, *Higher Education,* 26(2), 167–82.

2

Further and Higher Education Partnerships: The Evolution of a National Policy Framework

John Bird

Introduction

Over the past ten years – and especially in the past five years – collaboration between further and higher education has been high on the educational agenda. There has been what has been described as *a quiet revolution* (Woodrow 1993). That quiet revolution has included a franchising boom: a large increase, in a rather short time, in the number and variety of higher education programmes being delivered in further education. In order to discuss the development of policies on collaboration, it is first of all necessary to say something about the terminology of collaboration and about its extent and variety.

Terminology

There is no agreement over the terminology that is to be used to classify forms of collaboration. A feeling that the term franchising smacks rather too much of the commercial – of the McDonaldization of education – has not been translated into an agreed classification system which lacks an emphasis on money and commercial gain. This lack of an agreed system of classification has often clouded debate about collaboration and has, for example, made comparisons of the systems in England and Scotland difficult.

There seem to be two schemes of classification that are regularly used. The first is based upon a study of collaboration in England (Bird *et al.* 1993) and identifies – on the basis of questionnaires to FEIs and HEIs in England – the following varieties.

- Franchising, where courses designed and developed in one institution are delivered in another.

- Associate college arrangements, where partner institutions jointly plan and manage collaboration and are jointly involved in bidding for monies and resources; this often involves joint provision where one institution on its own cannot deliver a programme.
- Validation and accreditation of courses, developed and owned by one institution, by another; this can include both 2 + 2 systems where two years are completed in FE and two in HE, and foundation years where a year 0 is added to an existing HE programme.
- Access courses, where courses developed in FE are the basis for entry to HE.

Some of these arrangements have also been extended to include FE and schools; for example, where an FE college franchises delivery of a BTEC qualification to a school.

The second scheme is proposed by the HEQC (1995) and identifies the following as important.

- Articulation, where, for example, an HNC or HND in FE gives direct access to a degree in a linked HEI.
- Joint provision, where an HEI is responsible for validation and quality assurance, but provision is delivered jointly and learning resources may be pooled.
- Validation, where the FE college is responsible for teaching, learning, assessment and quality assurance within a framework of validation by an HEI.
- Franchising, where a course or part of a course developed in an HEI is delivered in FE; the FEI delivers the course as it stands.
- Subcontracting, where one institution subcontracts the delivery of a small part of a programme to another institution.

Comparing these, we can say that franchising is common in England and was most common in the earlier history of collaboration; the subsequent history has seen an increase in validation, accreditation and associate college arrangements. Franchising was never as popular in Scotland, where articulation has usually been the preferred model. Subcontracting is extremely uncommon in both England and Scotland.

Numbers and variety

It is clear from all available sources (for example, Bird *et al.* 1993; AfC 1995) that although there was collaboration between FE and HE as early as the 1960s, the major expansion was in the late 1980s and early 1990s. As the AfC report suggests, whereas in the 1960s and 1970s only 11 per cent of colleges reported having HE work, by the early 1990s this had increased to 50.9 per cent. By the early 1990s, colleges were involved in a wide range of HE work, most of which was described by them as being franchised:

degrees, HNCs and HNDs, Diplomas in Higher Education (DipHEs) and Certificates in Education (Cert. Eds), with a slight weighting towards degree provision. This provision covered a wide range of programmes: at the most popular end, business studies and science, engineering and technology; at the less popular end, humanities and teacher education (AfC 1995: 4). As indicated elsewhere (Bird *et al.* 1993), a significant part of this provision is delivered on a part-time basis, including evening study.

There are two other ways of indicating the scale of collaboration. In terms of *numbers of students* doing HE work in FE, predicted numbers (Bird *et al.* 1993) and actual numbers are reasonably close. In 1993–4, some 32,000 students were studying HE programmes in FE, and this represented something like a fourfold increase from 1990–1 figures.

In terms of *income* going to FE for such provision, there is an indication that the scale of HE provision in FE is, for many colleges, small. In 1994–5, a small proportion of colleges (9 per cent) derived more than 20 per cent of their income from delivery of HE programmes; 17 per cent of institutions derived more than 10 per cent of their income from this source; a significant proportion – some 33 per cent – derived only between 0 and 2 per cent of income from the same source. This income derives mainly from HEFCE (42 per cent) and fees (29 per cent) (AfC 1995: 6, 7). The relatively small proportions of income coming into FE for HE provision should not lead us to underestimate its significance, if for no other reason than that this source adds to the diversity of income on which FEIs can draw. Such diversity is probably advantageous, especially in times of financial restraint and uncertainty.

Finally, by way of introduction, we can say that there is also a consensus about the public rationale for collaboration (see, for example, Bird *et al.* 1993; AfC 1995). FEIs see HE work as increasingly an integral part of their work. The public rationale for such work includes accessibility of FHE, the meeting of local needs and provision for mature students. Most HEIs concur with this view. More private rationales – appropriate to individual institutions – include giving a college a competitive edge and enhancing its local reputation *vis-à-vis* other institutions. There are, therefore, contradictions between the public rhetoric, which usually favours institutional collaboration, and the more private rhetoric, which can favour institutional aggrandizement and competition. Whether it is the public or the private that is pre-eminent, both FE and HE are especially concerned about the funding of collaboration and about the vagaries of student finances and student numbers.

Stages in the history of partnerships

The history of FHE partnerships has yet to be written. This is surprising because the development of such collaboration provides an interesting example of the development of educational policy; in particular, how far policy develops without the knowledge, understanding and intervention of policy-makers in government and related institutions (funding and quality councils, HMI and suchlike). It will be useful to provide a preliminary history of partnerships, which identifies three stages of development, each with policy implications.

Stage 1 covers the period from 1960 to the mid-1980s and is characterized by a slow expansion in arrangements involving a small number in FHE institutions. This is also a period where there is little discussion of such arrangements by those concerned with educational policy and with funding and quality issues.

The second stage – from 1985 to around 1992 – is the period of rapid expansion indicated above. Partnerships come to be normal for FE and HE and to involve, for example, half the FE colleges in England. There is a slow dawning of interest among policy-makers in what is going on, characterized by an increasing concern with issues of quality. HMI begins to make prognostications about what is happening (HMI 1989, 1991) and those funding FE become concerned that FE may be becoming too much like HE.

This culminates in stage 3 in which – as a consequence of quality fears and the reining back of HE expansion – collaboration becomes a central concern of policy-makers, who seek, in various ways, to control it.

The central theme of this history is the slow and steady move from a situation in which policy is being made on the periphery – that is, in effect, in individual FHE institutions that are developing links in their own localities – to a situation in which policy-making moves to the centre.

Policy from the periphery

In a sense, in stages 1 and 2 of development there was no policy, if by that we mean the development of principles and practices which guide the development of a range of collaborative ventures nationally. There were many local initiatives in which institutions agreed to cooperate and, in consequence, developed their own criteria for good quality collaboration.

Typically, a small network of institutions that were already involved in some form of collaboration – for example, access courses – would decide to extend that collaboration to elements of HE provision. The rationales for both forms of collaboration were identical: wider access and local provision responding to local needs. In many instances, criteria for quality control and assurance were modelled on those developed for access courses; these in turn were largely developed within the CNAA framework. These local quality systems emphasized openness and transparency as means to mutual trust; in addition, they stressed the need for clear agreements between institutions, setting out joint responsibilities and the importance of staff development, cross-memberships of committees and regular contact between personnel involved in collaboration. The difference between stages 1 and 2 was largely over the degree of formality required to maintain collaboration. Stage 2 came to approximate more closely to a CNAA/access framework, in which informal networks were seen as, in themselves, inadequate. Formal systems developed, but with a commitment to what was often called 'lightness of touch'; that is, to maximum discretion and flexibility for the local provider.

As such a network developed, institutions that were not involved sought to become involved and networks came to include most, if not all, of the institutions in a locality. Such networks were, of course, not free from dissension: those who were on the outside feared that those within networks had an advantage; those on the inside feared that some members were getting special advantages, such as more funding from the local HEI. As such, local networks were unstable: members would join while other members would leave. An FE partner might, for example, leave if another university offered a better financial deal or allowed the FEI to deliver more than the first year of a degree programme.

What is clear, however, is that – although there were worries about some aspects of collaboration, in particular funding – there was no large-scale concern that things were not working. There was a common awareness that things *were* working, and that collaboration was generally of high quality and was serving to meet the needs of local, often mature, students. This point could be taken even further. There was no reason to assume that things were not working, particularly as collaboration was often on a small scale and involved local institutions working closely together. The small scale and the local nature of arrangements seems to have provided some guarantee that quality issues were addressed, and addressed effectively, even when those arrangements were relatively informal.

This informality is, of course, precisely what becomes problematic when there is a desire to develop some national system of funding and quality assurance for collaboration. The more that local arrangements are informal and rely upon custom and practice, the more likely is it that there will be worries and concerns about the quality and effectiveness of provision. The rule is more or less 'What we do not know and understand is likely to be a problem.'

Policy from the centre

'The danger at the stage we are now at is like many things which begin as a grass roots initiative, [and] are then perceived to be a success; [they are] taken over and bureaucratised and used perhaps for purposes for which they were never intended' (Bird *et al.* 1993: 15). This quotation is a view from the periphery, from within a local network which is working and is faced with the prospect of increasing formalization and – from the point of view of this person – with the subversion of collaboration. As it is with the history of access courses and debates over their national validation, so it is with other forms of FHE partnership. Those who had developed and operated successful collaborative arrangements often saw no reasons to formalize them and saw them, if they thought in these terms at all, as examples of value for money and serving the consumers of education.

The view from the centre was very different. This view might be put in the following terms: 'We don't know the extent of what is going on and we don't know its quality.' This lack of knowledge and fear for quality seems to be an example of a general anxiety that policy and practice were out of control, a view that is summed up in an HMI report of 1989:

> There is a lack of statistical information so the extent of franchising cannot yet be accurately assessed. However, most schemes have developed only within the last five years . . . There is little hard information on the numbers of students involved . . . information on students by mode, gender, age, ethnicity and employment status is required.
>
> (HMI 1989: 1, 6)

In addition, there developed a feeling that there may be problems with such collaborative ventures. For example, we find the following in a later HMI document:

> Libraries are inadequate for higher education work . . . Implementation of systems both for validation and for monitoring and review of franchised courses is erratic . . . some teachers have no previous experience of higher education teaching . . . there are few examples of effective liaison between institutions.
>
> (HMI 1991: 6)

While it is difficult to assess how far these worries were real, the policy from the centre developed around two issues: funding and quality assurance and control. In essence, the funding issue related not only to issues of fairness and value for money, but increasingly to driving down the unit of resource across FHE and to reining back on expansion of numbers in HE. The quality issues focused particularly on reproducing the HE student experience in those institutions – usually FEIs – that were involved in HE delivery. As a sub-issue, there was increasing concern over the quality of international collaboration. Although these issues are taken up in later chapters, most explicitly by John Hilborne, John Selby, John Lines and Kate Clarke, and Sofija Opacic, it is worth saying something about funding and the quality of the student experience here.

Funding

As will be indicated below, the vagaries in the funding of collaboration (see Chapter 3) are many and complex. For our purposes, however, issues of funding can be reduced to two axioms: deliver collaboration cheaply and control expansion at the FHE interface.

Although many FEI senior managers have complained in the past about their financial arrangement with HEIs – in particular about whether they are getting a fair deal (Bird *et al.* 1993) – the funding councils have become increasingly open about funding. Large numbers of students are to be taught in FE and HE for less and less money. They have also made it clear (a) that as expansion in HE students numbers is to be controlled, HE provision in FE must take its share of retrenchment, and (b) that quality is to be maintained. Putting the issue of funding differently, FE can always be available as one area in which future expansion of student numbers can be located. This indicates one of the advantages of HE expansion in FE: students will be even more able to study locally and thus to live in their homes, thereby decreasing the burden of student support.

The quality of the student experience

Question: So who's getting the better quality?
Answer: The people at the outside college definitely.

In some instances they [FE] are better than us . . . revolutionary stuff – quality isn't uniform.

(Bird *et al.* 1993: 43 and 17)

Although issues of quality are far wider than the student experience, the HMI view was always that this experience is central and, where FE is delivering HE work, the student experience in FE should reproduce that in HE. While this is, in itself, a not entirely utopian view – after all, if the student experience in FE was radically inferior to that of similar students in HE then there would be occasion for concern – it seems to be founded on an unwillingness to consider the more dystopian side of HE provision.

Students studying HE in FE regularly see the benefits lying with them and not with their counterparts in HE (Bird and Crawley 1994). Whereas the HE experience is characterized by reference to large classes, overcrowded libraries and unavailable teachers, the view of FE stresses accessible staff, small classes and a generally supportive environment. This is a view put forward by FE students who have visited their linked HEI and have talked to HE students; as such, it cannot be rejected as a parody. There is, therefore, a strong feeling among students studying HE in FE that they are willing to trade off some of the benefits of HE (research culture, large libraries) against what happens in FE.

It is over the issue of the student experience, therefore, that there is an immense divergence of opinion. On the one hand, HMI and, subsequently, HEQC stress the nature and operations of systems of quality assurance and control, and the extent to which these make FE like HE; on the other hand, students regularly point out the benefits and disbenefits of FE and HE respectively and are, in effect, arguing that despite the rigours of quality assurance and control, life is often better in FE. This in turn leads students to argue that they want to be able to study beyond the first year of degrees and diplomas in FE.

Retrospect

There are a number of elements to a retrospect. First, to recapitulate the history outlined above, we have moved from simplicity to diversity, and from expansion to retrenchment. There is now a wide variety of partnerships, of which franchising is just one; this variety now operates within a climate in which HE expansion is less and less on the agenda, and in which minimizing the unit of resource is a categorical imperative.

Second, we have seen the end of an era in which local networks developed collaborative arrangements, and are now seeing the policing of partnerships through centralized systems of quality assurance and control. This aspect of the history recapitulates the history of access courses, and includes the fear of the periphery that the centre is going to subvert the whole exercise. While there may be genuine quality fears associated with collaboration there also seem to be *excessive* quality fears and *mythologies of failure*. In particular, these have focused on the more extensive national collaborative networks – 'I worry a lot about the inter-continental ballistic franchise' (Bird *et al.* 1993: 17) – and upon international partnerships. Any real fears raised by HEQC audits have been exacerbated by reports in the educational media (*Times Higher Educational Supplement* 1995). Put another way, there is little dialogue between those at the centre who want assurances that public money is being spent wisely and those on the ground who generally appear to be convinced that it *is* being spent wisely.

Third, the quiet revolution referred to above has, in fact, been very noisy in its implications, producing major changes in the design and delivery of programmes in FE and HE, and stimulating significant developments in central policy-making.

Finally, partnerships are, in part, working against the grain of policy-making in that they are concerned with local autonomy. However, in another sense, they are working with that grain; for example, in favouring local study, with the consequences that has for student maintenance and support.

Prospect

As indicated above, the prospects for collaboration are, at present, not good. There seems little likelihood that, in the short term, there will be an expansion in HE, which could then see expansion of HE provision in FE. This short-term picture is also unlikely to change significantly if, after the next general election, there is a Labour Government. In addition to the problem of retrenchment, there is no clear picture as far as cooperation between institutions is concerned. Indeed, the national picture is a very varied one: in some areas, there is local and regional cooperation through a variety of consortia, while in others there is considerable competition between institutions for students. While it is clear that cooperation is more effective in delivering quality provision to diverse groups of students, it is unclear whether such cooperation will become general and normal (Bird and Yee 1994). Part of the future agenda will include further research to identify those features that make for quality partnerships and, in so doing, to allay some of the more excessive quality fears.

In terms of policy, there is no chance of a return to the period of local autonomy where policy was made away from, and without the knowledge of, the centre. Indeed, there is every likelihood that the centre will try to control funding and student numbers ever more precisely. In addition, there is every likelihood of a single quality and funding body, which could, at least in theory if not in practice, increase the hold that the centre has over partnerships and their workings. Of course, this should not lead us to conclude that the periphery – those on the ground, delivering provision involving FE, HE and schools – are powerless to resist. Perhaps the message for the future is that the centre will try to control but will never entirely wrest power from those in FEIs, HEIs and schools who are responding to the needs of actual and potential students. And perhaps the lesson contained in that message is that most – if not all – innovation in educational provision starts at the local level.

These are, of course, speculations. It is unlikely that someone writing in the early 1980s would have given a reliable prospect for the next ten years. The prospects for the next ten years are no more or less certain.

References

AfC (1985) *The Higher Education Role of Colleges of Further Education.* London, AfC.

Bird, J. and Crawley, G. (1994) The student experience. In S. Haselgrove (ed.) *The Student Experience.* Buckingham, Open University Press.

Bird, J., Crawley, G. and Sheibani, A. (1993) *Franchising and Access to Higher Education: a Study of HE/FE Collaboration.* Bristol, University of the West of England/Department of Employment.

Bird, J. and Yee, W.C. (1994) *From Compacts to Consortia: a Study of Partnerships Involving Schools, Colleges and HEIs.* Bristol, University of the West of England/Department of Employment.

HEQC (1995) *Learning from Collaborative Audit.* London, HEQC.

HMI (1989) *Franchising of Higher Education Courses.* London, HMI.

HMI (1991) *Higher Education in Further Education Colleges.* London, HMI.

Times Higher Education Supplement (1995) Second class degree risk, *THES,* 28 April.

Woodrow, M. (1993) Franchising: the quiet revolution, *Higher Education Quarterly,* 47(3), 207–20.

3

Finance: The Bedrock of Good Partnerships

John Selby

Introduction

Collaboration between separate organizations in education is complex; the financial arrangements seem to add an additional, murky complexity. Many readers of this book may have looked at the title of this chapter and been tempted to skip to those chapters which deal with educational issues; financial management is arcane, many educators are untrained in its complexities and, for many of them, the philosophical, educational and pedagogical issues take precedence. This chapter argues that this is a very foolish attitude; if the financial arrangements are not clear and well managed, partnerships founded on the soundest educational principles will founder. Finance is one of those important background issues that, if well managed, can be taken for granted; if it is mismanaged, the whole partnership can come to grief.

There is a vast range of ways in which HEIs collaborate with FEIs and this chapter cannot consider them all. This chapter is concerned with collaborative higher education in which course provision is shared in some way between an HEI and an FEI. Such sharing may involve accreditation, validation, franchising or credit rating and other similar arrangements, as defined in the HEQC's *Notes for Guidance on Auditing Collaborative Provision* (HEQC 1994a). These different terms will not be defined again here, since they are discussed further in the Introduction and Chapter 2 in this volume. What they have in common is that higher education is being delivered in an FEI, which is collaborating with an HEI in the delivery. The course may lead to an award of the HEI, it may have been designed in the HEI or it may secure credit towards an award of the HEI. In practice, accreditation is rare in this sector, if it occurs at all, since accreditation involves the delegation of power to approve and review courses, and is normally extended to HEIs which do not have their own awarding powers. This chapter will not consider accreditation as such, but will instead focus on the other forms of collaboration.

In all such cases, the HEI has a direct concern with the quality of the provision within the FEI, and the two institutions will need to enter into an institutional relationship. Generally, such a relationship will entail a financial agreement between the institutions and the transfer of funds between them. It is with these financial relationships that this chapter is concerned.

Before we consider them, it is necessary first to consider the general framework for the funding of higher education within the United Kingdom. This is a complex issue and the chapter will provide only a broad overview. The chapter will then consider the question of the different types of collaborative arrangement and their funding. It will consider a range of models for the financing of collaboration, their strengths and weaknesses, and will outline the key factors to be taken into account for HEIs and FEIs in choosing a mode of finance for a particular arrangement. It will not advocate one particular model against others, but it will suggest general financial principles to be followed in collaborative relationships. It will conclude with a retrospect on existing relationships and a prospect on the future development of the financing of collaboration.

The funding of higher education in the United Kingdom

Preamble

The financial structure for HE in the United Kingdom is highly complex and the detail is not relevant to most readers of this volume. It is important, however, in trying to understand how collaboration has been, and may be, financed, that readers have a general grasp of the basic financial framework within which such collaboration takes place. The author would argue that all staff involved in establishing and maintaining educational partnerships need a broad general understanding of the underlying financial structures if they are to avoid making decisions that are financially unviable. This section aims to provide that broad general understanding.

The United Kingdom context

The funding structure for further and higher education was reformed by the Further and Higher Education Act of 1992. This changed the previous structure and established separate higher education funding councils for England, Wales and Scotland, with higher education in Northern Ireland remaining the responsibility of the Department of Education of the Northern Ireland Office (DENI). Further education colleges were incorporated under the Act, again with distinctive arrangements for the funding of further education in England, Wales, Scotland and Northern Ireland.

While the details of the funding methodologies employed for higher education vary between the different countries of the United Kingdom, the Higher Education Funding Council for Wales (HEFCW) and the DENI follow the methodology developed by the HEFCE. The Scottish Higher Education Funding Council (SHEFC) follows somewhat different procedures from the other countries, but there are similar approaches which apply across the four countries and it is these that will be the focus of this discussion. More details can be found in the various circulars and publications of the funding councils, of which key examples are Davies (1994), DENI (1994), HEFCE (1994, 1995), HEFCW (1994) and SHEFC (1994).

Those features which are particularly relevant to collaborative provision are as follows.

- In all countries of the United Kingdom, the bulk of higher education is funded by a mixture of core funding, which is provided through funding councils, and fees, which are paid by local authorities, by individual students or by other sponsoring bodies on their behalf.
- In England, Wales and Northern Ireland the relevant higher education funding council funds the bulk of higher education, whether it occurs in HEIs or FEIs. In Scotland, the SHEFC funds HEIs for all their work, whatever its level.
- In England, Wales and Northern Ireland, there is a clear demarcation line between further education (below degree level or equivalent) and higher education (degree level or equivalent), except that non-prescribed higher education (typically HNCs) in FEIs may be funded either directly by the relevant further education funding council or indirectly by the relevant higher education funding council through an HEI (HEFCE 1995: 15).
- The funding supplied for HE teaching by the higher education funding councils is allocated according to 16 academic subject categories (ASCs) in England, Wales and Northern Ireland and 21 funding subject groups (FSGs) in Scotland.
- The core funding provided for teaching varies according to the level (undergraduate, taught postgraduate or postgraduate research) and the mode of study (full-time, sandwich or part-time) of the course, with different amounts being allocated for each of the four 'cells' in each of the ASCs. In Scotland, the system is slightly different but the principles are the same. HEIs receive different levels of funding for work in the same ASC, partly for historic reasons and partly because their profile of work varies.
- There is some evidence that the cost of delivering higher education in FEIs is lower than the cost of delivering it in HEIs, though this pattern is not uniform.
- The HE funding methodology has been designed to reduce the unit of resource for teaching over time and to cause convergence between institutions in the amount they receive for similar work.
- The further education funding methodology, which may be used by FEIs for their non-prescribed higher education, is based on a system of 'units', which are allocated for different components of a student's participation

in a course. This may be more generous than that which applies for courses funded by the higher education funding councils.

- The fees for full-time higher education courses are set by the Secretary of State in three bands (non-laboratory based subjects, laboratory based subjects and clinical medicine) and may be varied substantially, in order to provide incentives or disincentives for recruitment.
- In 1993–4, the fees were reduced for non-laboratory based subjects (band 1) and in 1994–5 these fees and those for laboratory based subjects (band 2) were reduced. This was designed to reduce the incentive to recruit additional students. Institutions have been compensated for the loss of fee income in proportion to the numbers of students enrolled in the year before the reduction by an increase in the core funding element, but additional students only secure the reduced fees.
- Part-time fees are set by the individual institutions and are normally paid by the student or a sponsor, not usually by a local education authority.
- In 1994–5, maximum aggregate student numbers for full-time students in receipt of LEA awards were set with penalties for over-recruitment. In Scotland, the system for controlling enrolments is different, but the principles are the same.
- The funding councils do not determine how institutions allocate their income internally.
- Most HEIs will have students who are fully funded (core plus fees) and 'fees only' students in any particular ASC or FSG.
- Each of the higher education funding councils distributes some of its funding for specific initiatives, some of which may be appropriate for collaborative initiatives.
- FEIs that receive their funding for higher education directly from the higher education funding councils in England, Wales and Northern Ireland are not eligible for funding for capital projects, for special initiatives or for research funding, other than through an HEI.
- The funding allocation is separate from the process of academic approval or validation. For example, a course delivered in an FEI may be funded by the relevant further education funding council, while it is franchised from an HEI that is primarily funded by the relevant higher education funding council.

As will be clear from the above summary of the key features of the funding methodologies employed in the United Kingdom, the systems are highly complex and there are small but significant differences between the methodologies applied in Scotland and those applied in the rest of the United Kingdom. When we discuss the funding of collaboration below, the significance of the key points outlined above will become apparent.

Readers should be aware that the examples in this chapter will be largely drawn from the author's experience, which is English; it is probable that they can be easily applied to collaboration in Wales and Northern Ireland, which follow similar patterns, but readers in Scotland, while they may draw on the general principles, should be aware of the different financial structures there and consider their implications. For a further discussion of collaborative provision in Scotland, see Chapter 7 in this book.

Types of collaboration

As noted above, there are a variety of ways in which HEIs and FEIs can collaborate with each other. For the purposes of this chapter we will focus on franchising on the one hand and validation and credit rating on the other. The key distinction between these two types of collaboration is an academic distinction but it has important financial implications, which will be considered below.

In a *franchised course*, the fundamental responsibility for the design of the course lies with the HEI that is franchising the course to the FEI. Normally, the course will have been designed by the HEI and will then be franchised for delivery at the FEI. The course will be designed in accordance with the regulations of the HEI and the students will be subject to the HEI's regulations. In practice, the FEI may play a significant part in the course design and the partners may consider the two institutions to have a much more equal relationship than is implied in the term franchising. Nevertheless, the key point is that the students will be bound by the regulations of the HEI and will be *in this sense* students of the HEI.

While the students are academically the responsibility of the HEI, the financial responsibility and responsibility for reporting the student numbers to the funding council may vary. The common pattern, and one which is implied by the academic relationship, is for the students to be the financial and reporting responsibility of the HEI. The HEI will be responsible for securing the income necessary for the delivery of the course, usually from the funding council and from fees, and will pay the FEI a sum for the delivery of the course. Thus, what we might call a 'pure' franchised course is one in which both the academic and the financial responsibility rests with the HEI. The students will 'belong' to the HEI and will be reported to the funding body as part of its student numbers. The financial flow is from the franchiser HEI to the franchisee FEI. This pattern, though typical for HE franchises, is different from the conventional pattern in standard business franchising, in which, generally speaking, the franchisee pays a fee to the franchiser for the right to market a product, such as a particular brand of fast food, designed by the franchiser. The franchisee is responsible for selling the product and securing the income for it (Yorke 1993).

In practice, and for a number of reasons, partners have frequently chosen to separate the academic and financial responsibilities and to create what I have elsewhere called *hybrid franchised courses* (Selby 1994a), which are, in fact, much more akin financially to the standard business franchise. In these courses, academic responsibility remains with the HEI, but the FEI takes on the responsibility for securing the income, either from the relevant higher education funding body and through fees or, in the case of non-prescribed higher education, from the relevant further education funding body. The FEI then pays the HEI a fee for the right to teach the course, which academically 'belongs' to the HEI.

For *validated* and *credit-rated courses*, the academic responsibility lies with the FEI or other body external to the HEI. In a validated course, the course is designed by the FEI and is judged by the HEI to be of a suitable standard to lead to an award of the HEI. In a credit-rated course, the course is judged by the HEI to be appropriate for credit towards an award of the HEI, without necessarily leading to an award itself. Typically, in these cases, the course will have been designed in the FEI or other external body (for example, an employer) and the students will be the academic responsibility of the FEI. Generally, there is a pre-existing course that the FEI or other body brings to the HEI for validation or credit rating. In all cases with which the author is familiar, the financial responsibility for mounting the course rests with the FEI, which pays the HEI a fee for the validation service. It is conceivable that the HEI could take on the responsibility for securing the funding but it would be unusual. We might summarize these relationships as in Table 3.1.

These are the key distinctions between the different models of collaboration in course provision. For a more detailed discussion of these issues, see Selby (1994b). Before we go on to examine the financial issues in detail, it might be helpful for the reader if these types and their academic and financial distinctions are illustrated with examples.

Coventry University has developed a highly successful foundation year in applied science and engineering in partnership with a number of local FEIs. It was developed to help groups generally under-represented in science and engineering courses, particularly women, to enter higher education. It was developed initially by the university and collaboration was sought with local partner colleges in the region. The course has been designed in accordance with the university's regulations and is funded by the university, with core funding from the HEFCE and fee income. The university pays its partners for the teaching they contribute to the course. Although there is a great deal of collaboration between the partners, and staff in the FEIs contributed significantly to its recent redesign, in all formal senses the course belongs to the university and the students are the university's academic and financial responsibility. Although it has some very distinctive features, it is in both formal academic and financial terms a *franchised course*.

It is important to realize that, though this is the typical form of franchising, there are others in which the initiative and much of the expertise lie with partners rather than with the HEI. Coventry University has developed a number of courses in subject areas in which it does not have all the expertise to develop or mount the course. The FEIs with which we collaborate bring their own specific expertise to the course; without it we would be unable to run the course at all. Although the academic expertise and course development are shared, the courses are in other ways like those mentioned

Table 3.1   Models of collaborative provision

Course type	Academic responsibility	Financial responsibility	Financial flow
Franchised course	HEI	HEI	HEI to FEI
Hybrid franchised course	HEI	FEI	FEI to HEI
Validated or credit-rated course	FEI	FEI	FEI to HEI

above. These courses are still formally franchised courses, even though the academic relationship is, in practice, quite different from the archetypal franchised course.

Coventry University also collaborates with a number of local FEIs in the delivery of a number of different HNCs and HNDs in computing and related subjects. These courses share a number of modules and are academically very closely related; they were developed in accordance with the university's regulations and, although the partners make a significant contribution to course development, the academic responsibility for both rests with the university. Financially they are very different, however. The HNCs are run as a franchised course, in exactly the same way as the foundation year in applied science and engineering described above, but the HNDs are run as *hybrid franchised courses*. For the part-time courses, the university secured the funding for the courses and pays the FEIs for their contribution to the delivery but, because the University was unable to secure funding from the funding council to support additional full-time students in this area, the FEIs took on the responsibility of securing the funding for the HNDs and pay the university a proportion of the funds for the right to teach the course. Academically, the HNCs and HNDs are very similar and closely linked; financially they are quite distinct.

As indicated earlier, the financial position of HNCs is ambiguous because they are 'non-prescribed' higher education and may be funded in one of two ways in England, Wales and Northern Ireland. The relevant higher education funding council or the DENI may fund such provision in HEIs or as franchises in FEIs, but may not directly fund FEIs for their delivery (HEFCE 1995: 15). Alternatively, the FEFC may fund these courses in FEIs directly. The ambiguous position of HNCs reflects other anomalies that have arisen at the interface between further and higher education.

The recent HEFCE report, *Higher Education in Further Education Colleges: Funding the Relationship* (HEFCE 1995), discusses the interface between HE and FE and the complexities and anomalies of the funding methodologies. For example, the FEFC is responsible for all capital provision in FEIs but HE providers in the FE sector are not given any additional capital funds to take account of the capital needs of HE work (HEFCE 1995: 19). If they franchise their HE work from an HEI, the HEI will be able to provide potentially more generous funding for capital. Set against this, FEIs may be able to secure more generous revenue funding, at least in the short term, from the FEFC. At Coventry University, we have some HNCs in business and finance that are hybrid franchises, funded through the FEFC, for precisely this reason.

This is only one of the many anomalies in the funding boundary between the funding councils and between HEIs and FEIs (for a detailed account see HEFCE 1995) and, at the time of writing, it is not clear whether or how these will be addressed. These anomalies and the possible approaches to them are addressed in the final section of this chapter. The bulk of the chapter considers the funding position as it exists now and does not consider the direct funding of HE in FEIs where there is no relationship with an HEI.

Coventry University also currently acts as the validating body for a number of certificates and diplomas developed by local FEIs. These courses were designed by the FEIs and operate in accordance with their regulations; the courses are funded by the FEI and the students are registered as students of the FEI. The university's role is to approve the regulations and the courses as of a suitable standard to lead to awards of the university, and to assure itself that the quality of the courses is properly monitored and maintained. The FEIs pay the university a fee for the validation service. These courses are both the financial and the academic responsibility of the FEIs, though the university plays an important role in approving them for university awards. These courses are *validated courses*. In some cases, the courses do not lead to university awards but are *credit rated* against the university's credit accumulation and transfer scheme (CATS). The principles are very similar to those which apply for validated courses, although the relationship is less close and the university is less directly involved.

While these different types of collaboration can be clearly differentiated in terms of the locus of the formal academic and financial responsibility, nothing is implied as to how these responsibilities are exercised. Academic responsibility may lie formally with the HEI but it may, in practice, choose to delegate a considerable part of this to the FEI. Nothing is necessarily implied by the formal financial responsibility about how the money is transferred between the institutions. It may be transferred in the form of per capita revenue payments, capital payments or a mixture of both. It may involve donations in kind, such as library books or computer equipment. This is a matter for agreement between the partners.

The important point about these different models of collaboration is that, while there may be an affinity between a particular formal academic arrangement and an equivalent financial arrangement, there is no necessary connection. Equally, a particular formal academic relationship does not necessarily indicate where the expertise for the course lies. While institutions may wish to standardize on a few types of formal agreement, there is a very wide range of possible forms of partnership that may be entered into within the three broad categories. It is crucial therefore that, when FEIs and HEIs enter into a partnership, both the formal academic and financial relationships are clearly spelled out in a memorandum of co-operation and it is recognized that these may be quite independent of the locus of expertise.

Since this chapter is primarily concerned with the funding of collaboration, we will now move on to consider this in more detail.

The funding of collaboration

General principles

The first general principle that needs to be applied derives from the fact that *collaboration costs money*. There will be travel costs and considerable costs in staff time in order to ensure mutual understanding and maintain quality. While it may be possible to generate additional income for collaborative provision, generally the additional income will not include a component to cover the costs of collaboration itself. The development costs of a collaborative arrangement will be higher than those of an independent development and the running costs will also be higher. It will be difficult to provide a direct incentive for staff to engage in such collaboration: the benefits to staff in the FEI may be relatively tangible in the form of career development, but for the HEI staff there will need to be a real commitment to the aims and objectives of the partnership; there will be little personal incentive. In addition to the relatively measurable costs, there will almost certainly be hidden costs or unexpected costs. There may be some economies if the FEI can deliver the course more cheaply than the HEI because staff or other costs are lower, but these are unlikely to outweigh the costs of collaboration. The overall financial costs may well be higher than the income and, even if surpluses are generated, they are likely to be small. The benefits of collaboration are not financial. They lie elsewhere: in the widening of access, in the development of progression opportunities and in the sharing of expertise. All participants in this process must recognize this and be prepared for it.

The first principle to be applied, therefore, is that *there must be a full and careful costing of the collaborative programme*. This may not be easy, for reasons that will become apparent below, but it is important that the effort is made and all potential costs are considered and set against the benefits.

In consideration of the funding of collaboration, it is important to recognize that nowhere in the United Kingdom is there a neat match between the boundaries of the funding councils' responsibilities, institutional boundaries and academic levels. Equally importantly, the current hazy and unclear boundary is itself currently under review (HEFCE 1995). Further, there can be significant shifts in funding levels for particular courses, as has been seen recently with the reduction in fees for full-time courses. Thus, it is not possible to say of any particular educational initiative involving collaboration whether it will be consistently funded over the lifetime of the link. While there is reasonable stability in overall funding of higher education nationally, albeit with steady reductions in the unit of resource, there has been considerable turbulence in the detail. This can make initiatives that are financially secure in one year financially unviable in the following.

It is important to remember that, within higher education, the way in which institutions choose to allocate the funds from the funding councils and the fee income received is a matter for them and will vary from institution to institution. Equally, collaborative provision is likely to form a minor part of a large HEI's activity and, though proportionately larger, still a relatively small proportion of an FEI's overall activity. Therefore, in the establishment of a collaborative course, it is essential that, as the second general principle, *the collaborating institutions need to give a continuing financial commitment to the programme*, which will not be subject to short-term fluctuations or dependent on insecure income. If course planning and development are to be worthwhile, the institutions need to commit themselves to a definite period of operation of the course, with a continuing commitment to any students recruited. Normally, the minimum commitment should be for three years of recruitment, which may mean that there will be a commitment to six years of operation, though, in practice, the commitment is unlikely to extend this long because most franchising is for less than a full degree programme.

The implication of this is that, for both HEIs and FEIs, *collaborative arrangements have implications for strategic planning*. The partnership may be quite limited in relation to the overall provision of the partners but it involves a commitment and will have strategic implications. Partnerships will tend to grow over time and, although the student numbers may be small, they need to be built into the strategic plans of both institutions. Even where courses are only hybrid franchises, validated or credit-rated, and no student numbers are involved for the HEI directly, students may well progress from the partnership course in the FEI to the HEI and thus have important long-term resource implications for the HEI.

Further, each HEI will receive core funding and fee income for students on courses within ASCs. The number of students enrolled may well exceed the number of students for whom core funding is received, so that there will be a proportion of 'fees-only' students. In developing a franchised course, in which the academic and financial responsibility for the course lies with the HEI, it is important to remember something that is not always understood: it is not possible to identify which students are generating full funding and which particular students are only generating fee income. An HEI may choose to designate certain students on a particular course within an ASC as being 'fees-only' students, but it is quite within its discretion to average the income over all the students. A number of Coventry University's hybrid franchises were established using only fee income to the FEI. It was recognized that fees can be varied substantially at short notice by ministerial decision and fee income is thus inherently unstable; core funding, though it is reducing, is more stable. When the courses were established the partners therefore considered the possibility of income reduction. The fees, though adequate when the courses were established, have, following the cut in fees in 1993 and 1994, become much less adequate. At current fee levels, the courses are under-funded and additional resources have been found to support them. FEIs which operate them have been protected against the impact of cuts in fee levels for existing numbers at the time the cut in fees was imposed. The HEFCE has compensated colleges with which it does not have a direct relationship through the FEFC (HEFCE 1995: 39). Because a number of these arrangements were 'growing in' at the time of the cut in fees, the compensation has not been adequate to sustain the overall planned numbers on the courses and additional funds have had to be found from other sources. This has proved very difficult.

This example demonstrates the application of the third general principle of collaborative provision, which is that *both core and fee income needs to be applied to the collaborative activity*, in order to secure the financial stability that is required under the second general principle. While future expansion of higher education may be possible through fees-only arrangements, if fee levels are again raised, it will always be vulnerable to cuts in fees, and institutions are advised to avoid these arrangements.

All of this implies the fourth general principle, which is that *all parties need to be open and clear about the source of funding for the collaboration and to share the responsibility for dealing with fluctuations in income*. Such responsibilities need to be clearly spelled out in Memoranda of Cooperation.

The fifth general principle is of sufficient importance and complexity that it requires a sub-section of this chapter in its own right. *Collaborating institutions need to be clear about the responsibilities of each partner.*

Definition of responsibilities

As will be clear from the discussion above, the establishment of a partnership between two independent institutions creates obvious problems of boundary definition. Even in the two most clear-cut arrangements, a pure franchised course and a validated course, there is significant sharing of power and responsibility between two independent organizations.

In a franchised course, the HEI retains full academic and financial responsibility for the delivery of the course but the power of delivery is delegated to another organization, the FEI. The course and the students remain the formal responsibility of the HEI but it does not employ the staff delivering the course, and does not directly control the resources available or the day-to-day administration of the course. In a validated course, the FEI retains full responsibility for the course and its students but cedes a degree of autonomy to the HEI in order to secure an award of the HEI. A hybrid franchised course is potentially the most complex: the academic responsibility lies with one organization, the HEI, while the full responsibility for resourcing the course lies with the FEI. In this case, the HEI has responsibility with only very limited formal power.

In each of these models of collaboration, individuals are working 'across the boundaries of organizations' (Matthiesen 1971). This involves persuasion rather than direction, authority rather than power and the exercise of joint cooperative decision-making, rather than independent competitive decision-making. In short, it involves partnership.

In each of these models of collaboration there are key decisions to be made as to which organization has responsibility for providing certain services to students. Students are, in all three models, potentially seen as members of two educational institutions with access to all the services of both. It is critical that the rights of access to services are clearly defined and that they are appropriately funded. Some examples of different approaches to the financial implications of this issue will illustrate the point. Chapter 6 of this volume also discusses it from the point of view of students.

One example of a critical area, which is often discussed in relation to franchising, is library provision. FEI libraries will almost always be smaller, with a narrower range of stock and a more limited range of journals, than HEI libraries. Two views may be taken of an appropriate approach to this. One approach is to provide sufficient resources to the FEI to ensure that it can provide sufficient library materials and other learning resources to meet the needs of the students on the franchised course. The logic of this position is that students on franchised courses, though formally students of the HEI, should not have the right to borrow materials from the HEI library. The same principle can be applied to computing resources, learning support and student union facilities. This is the approach that Coventry University has taken in most of its partnership arrangements after discussion and agreement with its partners.

An alternative view is to argue that, since the students are students of the HEI, they should have the same rights as students based at the HEI. This is the approach taken by a number of HEIs involved in educational partnerships and is probably more common than the first approach. The franchise students thus potentially have access to two libraries, two sets of computing facilities, double quantities of learner support and access to two student unions. They thus have more resources at their disposal than those based at the HEI. If this is the case, the HEI needs to be resourced to take account of the additional use but the FEI also needs to be resourced, because it cannot be assumed that the franchise students will use the HEI resources exclusively. The franchised provision thus requires additional resources compared to those needed for students based at the HEI. In practice, these issues have not always been addressed, and students on franchised courses have been given access to sets of resources without these being properly and fairly funded.

These different approaches were often arrived at in good faith when the scope and scale of partnerships was much smaller than is currently the case.

Each approach has its costs and benefits, though sometimes the costs are not obvious. In the former, students in partner institutions inevitably have more restricted resource provision in the FEI than they would have if they had the right to access the resources at the much larger HEI. In the latter case, there will be significant extra pressure on the resources in the HEI, which may well not be adequately funded to cope with this additional pressure. This may create resentment among the students based at the HEI.

This issue applies to all the services that the students at the franchised institution might use. The key question is where those services are to be provided. The answer to this question is not self-evident and a range of different answers might be given for different services. For example, it might quite reasonably be decided that the FEI will provide all the library and computing services but that student loans, careers guidance and counselling might be provided by the HEI. In principle, a wide range of different solutions might sensibly be adopted, though it is likely that an HEI will wish to develop a limited number of patterns of provision with its partners to avoid administrative complexity.

A difficulty in all these decisions is that many of the services will not be costed in detail and hence will be difficult to price. Even if both the institutions do have a detailed knowledge of the cost of service delivery for their own students, it may be difficult for them to estimate the likely usage of the HEI's services by students based in the FEI. The answer to this question will be much affected by distance and ease of travel, the relative quality of the facilities at the two institutions and whether the students are full-time or part-time.

It is on this kind of issue that many franchise arrangements have foundered. Often the commitments have been made without a full realization of the likely costs, with administrators of the relevant services being left to cope with the additional burdens, often without adequate resources. This can create considerable frustration and resentment for the students based at the FEI, who will have been led to expect a service which the HEI fails to deliver adequately.

These issues apply equally to pure franchised courses and to hybrid franchised courses. The only difference will lie in the direction of the resource flow. The important point is that while, in some ways, it might be simplest for the services all to be resourced and provided at the FEI, this will have important implications for the linkage the students feel with the HEI and may affect progression rates by the students to complete their courses at the HEI. In practice, it is rare for an HEI to insist that all services are provided at the FEI and to exclude the students from using all its services. Normally, a mixed economy operates.

Validated courses and credit-rated courses do not generally generate the same problems of boundary definition and financial confusion. The students of the FEI will not normally be expected to have access to the services of the HEI and the link will be a much more limited one, in which the FEI pays the HEI for the validation or credit rating of its courses and does not expect any other services. If other services are offered, these are normally much easier to specify in a contract or memorandum of cooperation than is the case for franchised courses, in which the prime responsibility is ambiguous.

Retrospect

There has been much confusion in the past because there has been little understanding among academic staff of the funding of higher education and because collaborative arrangements have often been established at short notice without adequate thought for the financial implications. This is understandable given the rapid growth of collaborative arrangements and the lack of clear models for their development. As will be clear, models from commercial franchising that have been examined have often been found to be inappropriate to higher education.

The very rapid growth in educational partnerships between HEIs and FEIs has occurred for complex and mixed motives. Some of the development has been strategic, mission led and carefully planned. Too much has been arbitrary, ill thought out and ill managed. For HEIs, the opportunity to expand student numbers has been seized without adequate thought for the impact of the consolidation which followed the expansion and which was always predictable. When consolidation did occur, some HEIs behaved quite shamefully, and simply withdrew from partnership agreements and 'pulled the numbers back'. This was damaging for students, staff and the reputation of higher education generally. Some FEIs entered into partnerships with HEIs at around the time of their own incorporation without strategic thought, merely because they wished to keep their options open. In some cases, a buccaneering, entrepreneurial spirit prevailed and FEIs sought to play one HEI off against another, switching partners for very short-term financial motives.

There is no definite evidence that this has affected the quality of the educational experience for students (HEFCE 1995: 27) and there is much debate on either side of this particular argument. The cycle of HEQC audits of 'off-campus collaborative provision' and the funding councils' quality assessments have not yet thrown up any firm evidence, though it is clear that, while the educational experience of students on higher education courses in FEIs may be equivalent to that of students in HEIs, it is clearly different. Resolution of the issues in this debate will depend on a much clearer agreement as to definitions of quality than is likely in the foreseeable future.

Whatever else is the case, the net effect of the very rapid growth in educational partnerships has been that we now have a very complex system of educational provision, with incoherent funding methodologies and with very complex patterns of relationships between FEIs and HEIs. FEIs are often in partnership with a number of HEIs, which involves considerable hidden costs, while HEIs may be operating large and far-flung networks, which entail significant administrative costs.

Prospect

The rapid expansion of higher education has led to a rapid expansion of franchising and other forms of collaborative provision, largely because FEIs had spare capacity and HEIs could not expand quickly enough to meet their growth targets. It was encouraged by the financial independence awarded to the former polytechnics under the 1988 Education Reform Act and by the independence granted to FEIs under the Further and Higher Education Act of 1992. It was consistent with the local and regional mission of many of the polytechnics and was a way of widening access (Yorke 1993). It was also facilitated by the growing development of credit-based systems of education. In many cases, franchising has been entered into without the planning and forethought necessary and, most importantly, without a clearly thought through financial model. The costs have often been considerable and under-estimated (Yorke 1993: 180). Much of the collaboration has been developed as a result of commitment and goodwill by staff in FEIs and HEIs but, at a time of great change in other areas, tensions have been generated and there have been concerns about quality (Yorke 1993).

While the recent history of collaborative provision in higher education has been one of rapid growth and rapid change, with the inevitable difficulties associated, it is likely that this period of rapid growth is past. Yorke (1993: 181) predicted further rapid growth, but a number of factors have changed since then. First, the 1993 budget, which imposed limits on full-time numbers in higher education, will restrict new developments at least in the short to medium term. These limits were confirmed in the 1994 budget. Second, while there is room for growth in part-time numbers, part-time recruitment is proving difficult in many areas. Third, FEIs have been set very ambitious growth targets and any spare capacity may well be taken up. Even if spare capacity remains, the main attention of FEIs may be focused on meeting their growth targets in further education rather than in expanding their higher education offerings. Fourth, there is some anecdotal evidence that in both HEIs and FEIs there is a review of some of the collaborative provision. HEIs have been finding other ways of meeting their missions, recognizing the costs of collaboration, while some FEIs, having entered into collaborative provision of higher education without much strategic planning, have taken the decision to reduce their involvement in this work and to concentrate on their main area of competence, further education.

The consequence of these various forces is likely to be a period of consolidation and stabilization. While this might reduce opportunities for students, particularly from non-traditional backgrounds, it is likely to ensure that some of the issues that were not adequately addressed in the period of rapid expansion will now be addressed. Clear administrative procedures and secure financial regimes may be established where previously a series of *ad hoc* arrangements were developed. This can only be to the benefit of students and the institutions themselves.

Given the evidence that partnerships cost money and that good communication between the partners is crucial for their success, it is likely that two developments in partnership will take place. We are likely to see the growth of formal associate college arrangements between HEIs and their main FEI partners where these do not already exist. The consequence may well be that, if these require exclusivity, the HEIs' networks will get smaller and the FEIs will drop some of their minority partners. These arrangements will encourage investment in good communication, with direct linkage of the FEI into the HEI's computer systems for academic and management exchange. The reducing costs of the Joint Academic Network (JANET) and the growth of internet connectivity will assist in this.

A further important change could well occur as a result of the pressures for rationalization within the further education sector. There is initial evidence of mergers of FEIs and there are even proposals for mergers between HEIs and FEIs. If this should happen on a significant scale, we may see the growth of large regional universities with associated community colleges, like those existing in the United States. This will have important implications for the funding of further and higher education, implications which are not considered in the recent HEFCE discussion paper (HEFCE 1995). Ultimately, the increasing complexity of arrangements across the further–higher education divide may well lead to a questioning of the sharp distinction between them and their funding arrangements that was drawn in the 1992 Further and Higher Education Act. We might then see the emergence of a comprehensive tertiary education system, administered through a single funding body. On the other hand, the emergence among some universities of a commitment to developing a strong international research reputation at the expense of a commitment to widening access may lead to a new division between research-dominated, largely postgraduate, institutions on the one hand and open, accessible, regional networks of HEIs linked to FEIs on the other.

At the moment, it seems unlikely that the discussion around the HEFCE (1995) report will produce clear recommendations. There are too many conflicting interests and it is hard to see how they can be balanced. Single funding bodies in each of the four countries of the United Kingdom might resolve some of the problems but the tertiary sector thus created would be very large and diverse. If the Robertson Report (HEQC 1994b) begins to be implemented, there will be further questions about the boundaries between further and higher education and their articulation. In the short to medium term, however, it seems unlikely that there will be a radical change in the funding methodology. It is likely that, apart from some minor tidying up of the grosser anomalies, the current rather messy structure will persist. If a Labour Government is elected at the next general election and begins to remodel the constitution, the possibility of single funding bodies with a much more regional structure may come on to the political agenda, though this will be but a small part of a much wider constitutional debate and will not be implemented for some time, if at all.

In the meantime, the financial issues for partnerships are clear. While it seems unlikely that any single model of financial organization will become dominant, it is likely that, at least within partnerships, much clearer and more uniform relationships will emerge. In developing these relationships, it would do no harm for those involved to bear in mind the financial principles enunciated below.

- There must be a full and careful costing of the collaborative programme.
- The collaborating institutions need to give a continuing financial commitment to the programme.
- Both core and fee income needs to be applied to the collaborative activity, in order to secure financial stability.
- All parties need to be open and clear about the source of funding for the collaboration and to share the responsibility for dealing with fluctuations in income.
- Collaborating institutions need to be clear about the responsibilities of each partner.

Collaboration between HEIs and FEIs has been highly successful in widening and deepening access, in increasing the numbers of students entering higher education and in attracting students from non-traditional backgrounds. (Abramson *et al.* 1993; Bird *et al.* 1993; Further Education Unit 1994; Selby 1994c). The consolidation in student numbers and the restrictions in growth in higher education will enable FEIs and HEIs to consolidate their links, strengthen their administrative frameworks and provide a secure base from which to develop new forms of collaboration. The financial principles enunciated above, which have emerged from good practice around the United Kingdom, will ensure that the sound administrative frameworks and the deep academic and educational commitment will be built on a strong financial base. This will enable partnerships between further education institutions and higher education institutions to survive well into the next century.

References

Abramson, M., Ellwood, S. and Thompson, L. (1993) *Five Years of Franchising.* Preston, University of Central Lancashire.

Bird, J., Crawley G. and Sheibani, A. (1993) *Franchising and Access to Higher Education: a Study of HE/FE Collaboration.* Bristol, University of the West of England/Department of Employment.

Davies, G. (1994) *Overview of Recent Developments in Higher Education.* Bristol, HEFCE.

Department of Education for Northern Ireland (1994) Personal communications to the author.

Further Education Unit (1994) *Approaches to Partnerships: Who Shares Wins.* London, FEU.

Higher Education Funding Council for England (1994) *Funding for 1994–5: Council Decisions,* Circular 2/94. Bristol, HEFCE.

Higher Education Funding Council for England (1995) *Higher Education in Further Education Colleges: Funding the Relationship.* Bristol, HEFCE.

Higher Education Funding Council for Wales (1994) *Recurrent Grant 1994/95,* reference W94/13HE. Cardiff, HEFCW.

Higher Education Quality Council (1994a) *Notes for Guidance on Auditing Collaborative Provision.* London, HEQC.

Higher Education Quality Council (1994b) *Choosing to Change: the Report of the HEQC CAT Development Project* (The Robertson Report). London, HEQC.

Matthiesen, T. (1971) *Across the Boundaries of Organizations.* Berkeley, CA, Glendessary Press.

Scottish Higher Education Funding Council (1994) *Recurrent Grants for Teaching and Research for 1994–5,* Circular 13/94. Edinburgh, SHEFC. Education Funding Council.

Selby, J. (1994a) *Partner Colleges: Types of Courses,* Academic Board paper B26/8R. Coventry, Coventry University.

Selby, J. (1994b) *Quality Assurance Documentation and Arrangements for Updating and Review of Off-campus Collaborative Provision,* Quality Assurance Committee paper BQA 9/4. Coventry, Coventry University.

Selby, J. (1994c) *A Review of Educational Partnerships at Coventry University.* Coventry, Coventry University.

Yorke, M. (1993) Quality assurance for higher education franchising, *Higher Education,* 26, 167–82.

4

Resourcing the Learning Experience

Peter Brophy

Introduction

Both providers and validation bodies have taken it as axiomatic that students undertaking a higher education course under partnership arrangements between universities and colleges should receive an equivalent, though not necessarily identical, learning experience to that offered to their on-campus counterparts. It follows that learning resources must be adequate to enable students to undergo a university level learning experience, regardless of the location at which the course is delivered. Clearly, the off-campus experience cannot be, and indeed should not be, exactly the same as that received on-campus, for the different strengths of further education can be exploited to provide distinct and intellectually stimulating approaches. The provision of information, information technology and other resources will, following this pattern, draw on the strengths the partner institution has to offer, while ensuring that the level of provision meets the requirements of higher education.

One of the characteristics of HE–FE partnership in Britain is that there is a very wide spectrum of provision. In the same way, arrangements between universities and colleges for the provision of access to learning resources, whether formal or informal, differ widely. Colleges vary greatly both in size and in the range of learning resources they are able to provide. While even the smaller universities have libraries with a quarter of a million books and upwards of two and a half thousand periodical titles, all at higher education level, the typical further education college will have a tenth of those resources in numerical terms, with the majority of material pitched at courses below the level required for higher education. Geography plays a part as well. Within an urban setting there may well be almost an embarrassment of library provision, and the key question becomes whether students from relatively small colleges can be guaranteed access to such resources. Colleges in relatively remote rural settings face entirely different problems: they attract their local students on to HE partnership courses, at least in part, because such students are not mobile and are unable, for whatever reason, to travel a distance to a traditional higher education provider. The students cannot be expected to travel to distant libraries, and the key issue is thus how such resources can be made available to them in the local situation.

The formal agreements between universities and colleges might be expected to address some of these issues, although in practice it appears that resource issues are left to validation events, and thus concentrate on subject-specific issues rather than the wider perspective. A research study at the University of Central Lancashire during 1993–5 included a survey of both university and college librarians and demonstrated that learning resources rarely featured in formal agreements (Goodall 1995). Fewer than half the respondents indicated that the provision of library and information services gained a mention in such documents, and those that did appeared to pay lip service or grant only a passing mention to the issue. It may be that the format of validation, which is usually dominated by the course team and subject experts, militates against deeper consideration of broad support service issues, although a review process at institutional level should enable them to be identified and addressed.

Course development, validation and review

It is clear that the most successful FE–HE partnerships, in terms of learning resource provision, are those where there has been a high level of involvement of appropriate learning resources staff in the development of the course from the beginning. No one would claim that this is easy to achieve. Liaison between college and university will concentrate, at a senior level, on staff at both institutions who have a concern with the management of partnership and, at an operational level, on those in both institutions with the subject knowledge and curriculum responsibilities to bring forward a successful course proposal. It is all too easy in these circumstances to allow the provision of learning resources to be left on one side until a firm proposal is ready for consideration. Indeed, it is not unknown for learning resources staff to find themselves faced without warning with a fully documented course facing imminent validation. Moreover, Goodall (1994b) reports that in more than one case the librarian's professional judgement was clearly ignored. Such situations hardly encourage detailed planning of learning resource provision, although the fault may lie on both sides. Librarians do not always have a well developed understanding of the broader issues, especially the political dimension of discussions, while university and college management has become inured to claims that libraries are under-resourced. There is a classic paper by Munn (1989) entitled 'The bottomless pit', which describes the university administrator's view of library resourcing! However, a more positive view would see the development of long-term relationships and strategic understandings between management, course teams and those responsible for learning resources as the crucial issue. It could then be argued that the extent to which the learning resources staff have been involved prior to validation is perhaps among the strongest indicators of the college's maturity and likely ability to deliver a successful course on a partnership basis. At the end of the day, courses must rest within the college's managerial frameworks, and it is reassuring when that framework is shown to be effective from the outset. Furthermore, colleges which aspire to associateship status will need to demonstrate this maturity of self-regulation and self-criticism in order to achieve that further level of autonomy and control over their affairs.

Beyond the planning stage, there remains a need for an involvement of the learning resources service in the validation itself. The model of the CNAA validations in the former polytechnics is thankfully giving way to a more mature approach, but there can all too often be a 'hit and run' approach to learning resources by validation panels. Breaking off from discussions on curriculum, delivery, staff development and the like, to wander round the library – sometimes unannounced – for half an hour is no way to assess the adequacy of the learning resources that will be provided once the course is established. The most useful books will almost certainly be out on loan (not a bad measure of usefulness!), while the way in which staff plan to integrate and develop the provision of resources for the partnership course with existing provision for the whole portfolio of courses offered by the college will not be apparent.

One approach to the validation event that has been developed at the University of Central Lancashire and its partner colleges is, having first ensured that the college librarian is involved from the planning stage, to encourage discussion of proposed courses between the university librarian and the college librarian, leading to a report to the validation panel from the former. This provides an invariably welcome professional perspective from outside the college itself, and also an opportunity to ensure that the issues likely to affect the successful operation of the course are addressed in advance. The validation panel itself is thus able to concentrate on the specific issues of learning resource provision likely to create the most problems for the course in question.

It is common for the outcome of validations to include recommendations and/or conditions to be observed before a course can run. Among the conditions there is not infrequently a proviso that a particular sum of money should be spent on library books and, for some courses, periodicals before the course recruits. Superficially, this is a positive move, for in theory it ensures that there will be specific stock improvement targeted at the course itself. It does, however, raise some problems. First, it is very difficult to ensure that it happens: how is the university to know that *additional* sums have been spent, rather than the bookfund having been 'rearranged' to provide the necessary picture? Second, and much more seriously, if the intention to spend did not come from the college itself, what does this say about the college's management of its partnership course provision? Surely the validation panel should be primarily concerned to ensure that the college has procedures and plans in place that will enable it to deliver the course, including the provision of adequate library resources, on an ongoing basis. Specific demands for money for a course at validation smack of 'sticking plaster' approaches designed to ensure that the college can negotiate the validation hoop. While this mechanism may correct the initial problem, and even alert the college to its responsibilities in this area, it does not augur well for the future. Much more impressive is the college that has a documented strategy for building up resources to support its HE work and, where possible, a demonstrable track record of provision – even if all accept that there is more to be achieved.

Much of what is said above will also apply to the process of course review. Previously expressed concerns of the validation panel will form part of the agenda for this process, but there will also need to be a focus on the actual experience of students who have taken the course. More is said on this in Chapter 6, but it is worth noting here that the review process does need to include the experience of students in accessing and making effective use of learning resources. The responsiveness of the learning resource service to student demands, not all of which can be predicted in advance, will be important.

Standards and guidelines

At a national level, and following work by both university and college librarians, the Library Association (1992) has published guidelines for franchised courses. The guidelines cover some of the issues referred to above and recognize that the needs of franchised courses will differ widely within their overall framework. The US Association of College and Research Libraries (1986) has published an equivalent set of guidelines for 'extended library services'. It must be noted, however, that universities and colleges are independent bodies, and guidelines are exactly that: they do not offer prescriptive minima for provision. Neither do the published guidelines cover areas outside the traditional library, or other aspects of learning resource provision (see below, for example, on information technology). However, discussions have taken place in the Standing Conference of National and University Librarians (SCONUL) on a possible set of performance indicators of library quality for use in HEFCE subject assessments, and the HEQC has learning resources provision on its agenda during institutional visits. Both have application to partnership arrangements.

Individual universities have developed their own guidelines covering the issues of particular importance to their franchising and other partnership activities. Those produced by Liverpool John Moores University library have been published elsewhere (Revill 1991).

The provision of books and periodicals

The library, including its traditional collections of printed literature, remains central to learning and teaching in higher education, and virtually every course will expect its students to make extensive use of the literature of the subject. Of course, the intensiveness of this usage will be very dependent on the subject matter and level of the course. In the humanities and social sciences courses tend to be very literature based; in science and engineering they are less so. However, such distinctions can be misleading. In science and engineering it is essential to have access to very expensive periodical literature, and with student-centred methods of learning such a requirement impacts on the undergraduate to an increasing extent. Level is clearly important, for many first-year degree courses remain highly structured in their demands on libraries. A reading list may be followed closely and there may be one or more textbooks, which, depending on local policy, students may be expected to purchase for their own use. By the time the final year is reached, the picture will be very different. Nearly all such courses contain an extended dissertation or equivalent, demanding the use of the literature in a sophisticated and certainly not predetermined manner.

For college libraries these issues are central. Coping with the demands of non-literature based first-year courses may be relatively straightforward, but higher level courses and other subjects pose greater problems. In general, the approach seems to be that the college library will stock copies of all 'core' books (though the meaning of 'core' is open to interpretation) together with a small selection of periodicals, where that is felt to be appropriate; for example, for higher level courses, or where an independent learning style is being encouraged. Generally, any periodicals will be from the general rather than scholarly end of the spectrum. For more extensive access to the literature, other arrangements may be needed.

A particular issue for college libraries is the provision of access to the secondary literature, abstracts and indexes of various kinds. At further education level there is rarely much call for such resources to be made available. However, in higher education there is increasing emphasis on the student becoming 'information literate', skilled at navigating his or her way through the guides to the literature available in whatever subjects are of interest, and pinpointing books and periodical articles according to need. Unfortunately, abstracting and indexing services tend to be expensive and it can be difficult for a college to justify purchase for what may be a very small cohort of students. Electronic database versions have proved a godsend to many college librarians faced with this difficulty (see below).

One useful way for the college to augment its stock, especially where access to expensive periodicals is required, is for photocopies of selected papers to be added to stock. The University of Central Lancashire operates with its partner college network in this way, supplying photocopies for the use of students on its off-campus courses from its much more extensive stock of periodicals, under the terms of its Copyright Licensing Agency (CLA) licence.

The provision of non-traditional learning resources

One of the striking features of the modern university library is its dependence on non-traditional information sources, most of which are made available in electronic form. While few would yet claim to have implemented the fully integrated 'scholar's workstation', recent years have seen a revolution in the delivery of such resources to library users.

Perhaps the most significant development has been the widespread acceptance of compact disk-read only memory (CD-ROM) for both full-text and index or abstracts services. Before CD-ROMs became available, libraries had to limit the availability of computer-based information services on cost grounds. Nearly all online services were charged on a usage basis and telecommunications costs had then to be added in. The potential for an unsupervised student (or other library user) to run up an enormous bill was clear and no library manager could risk such a scenario. The result was that online searches were severely restricted and often students' only view of them would be from the back of a crowded demonstration. With CD-ROM all this changed. The library pays an annual subscription and unlimited use is then available. The CD-ROM disks can be networked (sometimes an additional fee is payable) to provide even wider access. Suddenly it has become possible for students to become active users of online, state-of-the-art information systems. The popularity of such services has rapidly placed them high among academic librarians' priorities.

A second development for universities has been the introduction of massive datasets made available via JANET. The initial development was of the Institute for Scientific Information datasets (*Science Citation Index, Social Science Citation Index,* etc.) made available to each UK university for an annual fee via Bath Information and Data Services. In addition, various services such as National Information Services and Systems and Bulletin Board for Libraries provide access to a vast range of database and other electronic information services. Once again, unlimited use is possible, and because the communications medium is a private network, there are no telecommunications costs accruing to the library or individual user.

For FE colleges these developments have, in general, been positive. CD-ROM technology has been enthusiastically received and some colleges offer more titles than neighbouring universities. Blackburn College, for example, has had a choice of over 40 titles networked across its campus on its broadband system for some years. While the range of titles held may not accord precisely with the requirements of higher education, there is a surprising amount of overlap of user demand. For example, the major newspapers (*The Times, The Guardian, The Independent, The Daily Telegraph,* etc.) are all available on CD-ROM and can be used at FE level, yet just as effectively as a resource for higher education. Equally, internet access is now routinely available from many college libraries.

Because the numbers involved in off-campus courses are generally small and the courses are predominantly at the lower levels, the lack of easy access to JANET-mounted datasets has not yet been found to be a major problem. Access may be available to individuals via the university library, or there will usually be facilities for using the online equivalents. It is also now possible for colleges to have a secondary connection to JANET via a university.

The 'electronic library' itself is a developing concept, much heralded yet now probably close to fruition. Experiments at the Milton Keynes campus of de Montfort University and at Wirral Metropolitan College, to take two examples not specifically related to off-campus activity, have moved further and higher education closer to the electronic library model. The University of Central Lancashire's Centre for Research in Library and Information Management is coordinating a European Commission funded project, which is specifically designed to develop information technology (IT) based library services for delivery to franchise course, and other off-campus, students (Brophy 1993). North American experience is instructive in this regard (Brophy 1992a).

Library and computing services

Most FE colleges offer the standard range of library services that would be expected for higher education, so that, for example, there should be no difficulty in obtaining inter-library loans, photocopies of items in stock and similar services. Increasingly, college libraries are becoming equipped with integrated computer systems, providing acquisitions, cataloguing, circulation and other functions; and these are helpful in enabling the available stock to be controlled much more closely than would otherwise be the case. Again, this can be important for the student on an HE partnership course who needs rapid access to materials in short supply, and for whom reservation and recall facilities are essential.

While it is not necessarily a library service issue it is worth noting that the provision of photocopying services is subject to both British law (specifically the 1988 Copyright, Designs and Patents Act, which includes a 'fair dealing' provision) and the CLA licence scheme. The latter offers licences both to universities and to further education colleges, although the terms of the licences differ significantly. In general, students undertaking franchised courses should be covered by the university licence (because their numbers are channelled through the university's return to the HEFCs), but staff (who are on the college payroll) will be covered by the college licence. This could, at least in theory, lead to staff being denied resources that are available to their students! However, both staff and students in associate colleges will probably be covered by the college, not the university, licence.

Experience has shown that library and computing centre opening hours can present a problem for partnership course students, especially where part-time courses are being run during the evenings. Care is needed, and early discussion with the course team, to ensure that the students will have adequate opportunities to use the library and other resources. For example, there is little point in making special arrangements to open the library late in the evening when the students are being taught, if all their time on that evening is going to be taken up with class contact of one kind or another. Similarly, thought needs to be given to whether the students will use the library as a study environment or simply as a resource. Again, for the part-time evening course student, there may be little point in arguing for specialist study space. However, circumstances vary, and we need to be aware that some of the disadvantaged people attracted to partnership courses will have nowhere else with a conducive study environment if the college does not provide one.

Colleges often have very good provision of non-traditional learning resource support through open learning centres and similar initiatives. One of the benefits to university libraries of franchising and other partnership activities could lie in the opportunity to learn how such facilities can be used to enable and enhance student learning. Certainly, to take the University of Central Lancashire as an example, contacts with partner colleges, such as those in Preston and Blackburn, have been a source of ideas for enhancing university library provision in these areas.

Information technology

In general there appear to have been few problems with access to IT, as a general resource, for off-campus students. Although generalizations are dangerous, at present it seems that most college students will have personal computer access equivalent to that of their university counterparts. However, this overall picture masks some key issues.

First, there will almost certainly be differences in the software made available for standard tasks such as word processing. Students who progress on to higher level courses at the university may therefore have some re-learning to do. Second, there is as yet little evidence as to whether there are problems with offering specialist courses in IT (or in subjects which make use of highly specialist IT products, such as industrial design) on a partnership basis. Third, the rate of innovation is such that while the basic workstations may be not too dissimilar, the university-based student is starting to gain access to a range of networked IT-based resources which are simply not available outside the sector. The problem for colleges wanting to gain access to the Institute for Scientific Information (ISI) datasets across JANET was noted above, and this could be seen as the forerunner of a more serious issue.

Information skills

Reference has already been made to the development of more student-centred approaches to higher education. To be successful, the student will increasingly need to master a range of learning skills which will provide a basis for life-long learning and development. Among these, the ability to handle information will be prominent. Today's information-intensive world requires knowledge of information structures, together with skills in creating and exploiting information. It is within educational systems, including higher education, that such knowledge and skills can be honed.

Within universities we have seen a resurgence of interest in these issues in recent years, and some programmes now include explicit information skills elements as core skills across the curriculum. It needs to be recognized, too, that much of further education has led the way in the development of skills-based approaches. Again, the challenge of partnership is to marry the experience of further education at its own level with the needs of higher education.

One of the difficulties for further education librarians is that they have to be generalists, skilled in the information resources of a wide range of disciplines and, with higher education partnerships, at a variety of levels. The same subject may be taught from the equivalent of primary school level through to undergraduate or even postgraduate level. By contrast, the university library will almost certainly have subject specialists whose role is to understand and communicate the latest knowledge of the information systems, structures and content of a particular discipline. In the context of the development of information skills, the potential problem for the off-campus student is obvious. Good working relationships between the college librarian and the university's subject librarians provide a partial answer.

Staffing and staff development

The generalist subject approach of the typical further education college librarian has been outlined above. However, this is but one reflection of the problem of isolation for the specialist staff, such as librarians and IT specialists, in smaller colleges. Opportunities for teamwork are inevitably limited, and the resources specialists may well be the only professionals in their discipline on the staff – or even for miles around. Moreover, they may be unable to concentrate on professional duties if very low staff numbers force them to spend time covering clerical duties, such as the staffing of circulation desks.

Staff development for learning resources staff presents a particular issue. Although many colleges are as generous as they are able to be in funding attendance at professional meetings and at courses, these opportunities are inevitably limited and it is difficult to create and sustain a systematic approach to staff development in these circumstances. At the University of Central

Lancashire, the development of a 'partner colleges library network' was, in part, motivated by a desire to give staff development opportunities to partner college library staff, although the difficulties of releasing such staff from everyday duties and bringing them together have limited its effectiveness in this regard.

Cooperation

There can be little doubt that cooperation between learning resource services is vital to the success of partnership arrangements. Nor need such cooperation be limited to the relationship between the university and the college: in some subject areas public libraries may have much to offer, in terms of stock, systems and, possibly, their own professional staff. Cooperation between colleges which are reasonably close to one another can also be helpful. To give one example, a number of colleges in Cumbria have chosen to introduce IT through membership of the county library's network, rather than through separate college systems, and are thus able to access each other's catalogues.

One of the major issues of partnership course provision for librarians is the demand placed on the university library by students based at a partner college; an issue on which there has been considerable debate. Should students studying at a college have access, including borrowing rights, at the university library? The problem for the university library is that if the college and university are physically close, and the university library is the better resourced, students will naturally tend to use it in preference to college facilities. Yet rarely will the university library receive funding to cover the costs of such usage. On the other hand, the university may regard it as part of its commitment to partnership to provide access to its facilities, library included.

The University of Central Lancashire has taken the view that partner college students should be given full access to the university library and university computing facilities. It is noticeable that the only problems experienced with this policy have arisen from the number of students from an adjacent college approximately two miles away who wish to take up these rights, and the difficulty of identifying higher education students and staff with sufficient precision, yet without inordinate bureaucracy. Undoubtedly, geography plays a key role and it is perhaps not surprising that universities which have developed partnership arrangements within their own metropolitan areas are less likely to look favourably on requests for access.

Customers

Higher education, in general, is focusing to a greater and greater extent on the student as a customer, and libraries and computer centres as service departments are well advanced on this front. It is interesting, therefore, to examine in detail the ways in which students actually gain access to, and use, learning resources. The research project at the University of Central Lancashire that was mentioned above is pursuing this line of enquiry by persuading sample groups of students to complete diaries that record such activity (Goodall 1994a), and analysis of these returns has shown that library use is a much more complex activity than many have supposed. At the time of writing this work is ongoing.

Retrospect

The provision of learning resources for partnership course students has been the mixture of triumph and failure that might perhaps have been expected. The negative side has seen students, and college staff, struggling to cope with the demands of higher education without any realistic library or other learning resource provision, while the 'partner' university maintains a lofty indifference. The positive side has seen colleges play to their strengths: both colleges and universities working together to forge a true partnership, and both addressing the issues in a realistic yet innovatory manner. Students who would otherwise have been lost to higher education have been supported and have progressed to later stages and higher level courses at universities with skills and knowledge well developed. Much has been achieved; far more remains to be done.

Prospect

To argue that much remains to be done is easy; to put flesh on that argument by listing specifics is more difficult. Yet the prospects are bright. The distributed higher education library is becoming a reality both on and off campus and the twenty-first century will see very different models of learning resource provision (see, for example, Brophy 1992b). The physical book will remain important but may no longer be as central as in the past, especially for undergraduate work. If higher education shifts its focus more to continuing development – learning though life – the distributed model, which delivers learning resources to people where they are, will become even more central. Partnerships between 'teacher', 'student' and 'learning resource provider' could become much more fluid and productive. Partnerships between college and university that bring in appropriate external agencies – the public library is an obvious example – will enhance this provision by making available expertise as well as materials. The opportunities are there to be grasped, but to succeed we need a determined effort to harness human resources through cooperation and partnership alongside the systematic exploitation of technological innovation. Success could find partnership developing as the model for higher education in the future.

References

Association of College and Research Libraries (1986) Guidelines for extended library services, *College and Research Libraries News*, 47, 189–200.

Brophy, P. (1992a) Distant libraries: the support of higher education students who study off-campus, *Library Management*, 13(6), 4–7.

Brophy, P. (1992b) Distributed higher education – distributed libraries? *New Library World*, 93(1099), 22–3.

Brophy, P. (1993) Franchising higher education: the library's role. In B. Lessin (ed.) *Proceedings of the Off-Campus Library Services Conference*, Kansas City, Missouri, October 1993. Mount Pleasance, MI, Central Michigan University.

Goodall, D. (1994a) Use of diaries in library and information research, *Library and Information Research News*, 18(59), 17–21.

Goodall, D. (1994b) Franchised courses in higher education: implications for the library manager, *Library Management*, 15(2), 27–33.

Goodall, D. (1994) Franchised courses: the university library perspective, *Education Libraries Journal*, 37(3), 5–20.

Library Association (1992) *Library Provision for Franchised Courses*. London, The Library Association.

Munn, R.F. (1989) The bottomless pit, or the academic library viewed from the administration building, *College and Research Libraries*, 50(6), 635–7 (reprinted from *College and Research Libraries*, January 1968).

Revill, D. (1991) Franchising courses: library resources, *COPOL Newsletter*, 56, 62–5.

5

Ensuring Quality in Further and Higher Education Partnerships

John Hilborne

Overview

This chapter builds on the published findings of three HEQC reports on quality issues in relation to higher education provision in further education colleges leading to university awards (HEQC 1993, 1995a, b). Two of these reports (1993, 1995b) are based on field studies conducted in England and Scotland in 1993–4. The third report (1995a) is an analysis of the first 14 separate HEQC academic audits of collaborative provision for the same period. The reports highlight the implications of the findings of this work for practice.

The two field studies were undertaken to inform the development of the HEQC's policy and work in quality assurance and quality enhancement in relation to higher education in further education. They involved visits to 11 universities and 13 FE colleges. Discussions were held with government departments, accrediting bodies, Scottish HMI and those who have been prominent in developing or commenting on HE provision in FE settings. In order to encourage an open discussion of practice, participants were given an assurance that neither they nor their institutions would be identified.

There is a tremendous diversity in the pattern of FE and HE working in the United Kingdom. There are differences in educational tradition, culture, funding, quality assurance and the accreditation of awards between each of the four countries. There is also diversity of practice and provision within each sector. FE and HE colleges have different missions, different academic and pedagogic cultures, different staff contracts and expectations, different approaches to vocational qualifications and different expectations of students. For example, a useful comparison between England and Scotland can be found in HEQC (1995a, b); other aspects of this diversity are found elsewhere within this volume. This chapter, however, focuses on the general findings and conclusions that can be drawn from quality assurance in HE provision taught in FE colleges, and leading to university awards. There are five sections. The first deals with some issues in contemporary quality assurance in higher education and is followed by an examination of the context of current collaborative arrangements. The third section examines approaches to quality assurance in FHE working and draws together current feelings about what constitutes good practice. A discussion of the characteristics that might underpin quality assurance in collaborative arrangements as a whole leads to an exploration of some of ways in which quality assurance in FHE might develop in the future.

Introduction

There may be some useful analogies to be drawn between current popular views on marriage and those on FHE partnerships. As the Book of Common Prayer might well have it, neither 'should be entered into lightly or wantonly, but in due consideration of the purposes for which it was ordained'. There is a strong belief, current in some quarters, that the quality of marriage and of higher education has become adulterated – the standards of both have been lowered. In the case of marriage this view refers to some notion of Victorian excellence or a media picture of the nuclear family, with 'two-point-something children' and both partners living together. For higher education it is probably based on some idealized conception of what undergraduate life was like in a collegiate university for well heeled 18-year-olds, some time around the publication of the Robbins Report in 1962.

It is, of course, entirely proper for society, politicians and quality assurance entrepreneurs to be concerned about the maintenance and enhancement of the quality and standards of education. It may come as a surprise to some of those who have recently developed an interest and expertise in these areas that teachers in FE and HE institutions are equally concerned about them. It is important that those who are concerned about the present standards of higher education and higher education in further education should ground their anxieties in evidence and not tabloid anecdote.

The debate about the quality of HE in FE in this country should not be confounded with anxieties concerning a few arrangements reached between UK universities and a minority of overseas institutions. The evidence we have concerning the quality of HE in FE, from HMI reports in the 1990s through to the latest clutch of funding council assessments, is that the quality of teaching and learning experienced by HE students in FE colleges is similar to that of comparable students reading similar courses in universities. On the other hand, there is considerable variability in the ways in which FE–HE partnerships are planned, implemented and evaluated, in resourcing and in staff development and the rights and privileges of staff who teach and students who study in FE colleges. We need to distinguish between what little we know about the quality of HE courses in FE and what we know about the quality of the assurance processes associated with them.

There is considerable evidence that all may not be well with the quality assurance systems that universities use to assure themselves and others that the standards of university awards and the courses which lead to them, offered in collaboration with other institutions, are satisfactory. The recent HEQC interim report, *Learning from Collaborative Audit,* underlines this. In particular, it commented on the failure to provide adequate monitoring and review systems for collaborative partnerships. Despite the headline which appeared in the *Times Higher Education Supplement* (1995) on the date of the report's publication, it has little directly to say about the quality and standards of the courses or the level of achievement of students in the universities that were audited.

Students, teachers, politicians, employers and parents need to be warned that there is no necessary or sufficient relationship between a good quality assurance system and good quality provision, or vice versa.

The context of FHE collaborative working

The growth of FHE partnerships in the early part of the decade took place during a period of considerable turbulence within the UK further and higher education systems. The 1992 Further and Higher Education Acts for England, Scotland and Wales introduced radical changes in both funding and quality assurance for both sectors. Greater emphasis was placed on accountability and funding was linked to assessments of quality. Within a broad framework, colleges and universities were encouraged to develop their own mission statements, build on their own strengths, address their own markets and cater for local and regional needs. Both FEIs and HEIs were therefore confronted with the need to develop quality assurance mechanisms that would allow them to demonstrate the quality of their provision and the effectiveness, incisiveness and coherence of the quality assurance systems which underpinned it.

In higher education, an uneasy compromise was reached between the government and the universities (Wagner 1992). The HEFCs are responsible for funding HE, which previously fell within the remit of the Universities' Funding Council and the Polytechnics' and Colleges' Funding Council (PCFC). Funding was to be set against some assessment of the quality of provision. The HEQC was to be responsible for auditing the quality assurance processes that universities use to assure themselves that the quality objectives stated in their mission statement and strategic plans were being achieved. The situation became both more and less complicated for further education. Broadly, funding councils were set up for further education in England and Wales, which incorporated both assessment and audit, and the same principle of accountability, linked, in intention at least, with some attempt to assess quality, became central to arrangements made in Scotland and Northern Ireland.

It is, however, possible to exaggerate the importance of 1992 in the history of quality assurance. The public sector of HE (the ex-polytechnics, colleges of higher education and Scottish central institutions) had developed internal quality assurance systems to meet the CNAA requirements for course approval, review and institutional visits. These were further developed in response to the development of the PCFC's system of funding, which rested in part on HMI assessments of the quality of provision. The established universities were exposed to the requirements of the professional and statutory bodies. Their staff advised on the mechanisms for development by the CNAA and were members of CNAA council, committees and boards.

Similar moves towards the development of quality assurance strategies and mechanisms were apparent in the FE sector prior to the 1992 Act, if not on the same scale as in HE. The Manpower Services Commission and its various successors funded against quality specifications which FEIs had to meet. Increasingly, FEIs were developing their own courses as well as gaining greater freedom and autonomy in the design and interpretation of national syllabuses, such as those of the City and Guilds of London Institute (CGLI) and the Business and Technical Education Council (BTEC). They faced competition from private providers of vocational education and training and responded with marketing strategies, including the development of quality assurance structures and processes and demonstrable measures of quality.

Neither was collaboration between universities and other colleges new. For example, a wave of universities was created in 1948 from former colleges which had collaborative links with the University of London. Universities have long-established relationships with theological colleges, teacher training colleges and specialist colleges in, for example, agriculture and, more recently, colleges of health.

What differentiates the present decade from its predecessors as far as collaborative working is concerned is the growth in the scale and range of the enterprise and the requirement for public and transparent accountability, not only in educational provision but also in management and funding. Universities have always been responsible for the quality and standards of the provision offered in their name. They have always had arrangements with other organizations and colleges for the teaching of courses leading to their awards. One of the major changes introduced by the legislation in 1992 was the requirement to *demonstrate* stewardship and quality rather than to *assert* it.

Similarly, within further education there was a long history of collaborative working between FEIs and HEIs, particularly in Scotland (see Chapter 7 in this volume). The further education requirements for developed, transparent and effective systems of quality assurance occurred at a time when FEIs were taking over responsibility for the management of their own affairs from local authorities. They were also rapidly claiming, and being granted, a measure of autonomy from national bodies such as BTEC, SCOTVEC and the CGLI. As junior partners with these bodies and as agents of the local authorities, few FE colleges had the opportunity to develop extensive systems of internal management and academic quality assurance. They were, however, moving towards these in the latter part of the 1980s and early 1990s.

From the standpoint of quality assurance in FHE partnerships, perhaps the major achievement of the 1992 legislation and its implementation will be a move towards the synergy of structures, procedures and processes that results from FEIs and HEIs having to meet similar demands from outside agencies for quality data. To return to the form of marriage in the Book of Common Prayer this should increase 'the satisfaction that each should have of the other's quality assurance mechanisms'. A similarity of approach should also allow the development of more transparent systems of quality assurance, which allow students and other non-educational specialists to acquire an informed view of what is on offer.

Aspects of good practice in quality assurance

The UK educational systems encourages diversity in post-16 education. Both FEIs and HEIs are encouraged to develop their own mission statements, building on their own traditions, their strengths, local requirements and an estimate of the demand for their services. All the funding councils and the HEQC assess or audit institutions against their own mission statements. Almost without exception, all areas of collaborative working in which universities are now involved have developed as pragmatic and local responses to locally defined needs (Bird *et al.* 1993). They have developed outside the national framework, and then recently have either been a focus of government policy or initiative, or attracted the attention of bodies such as the Committee of Vice-Chancellors and Principals (CVCP). Collaborative working in recent years has largely been about access; about taking higher education to communities and individuals who would otherwise not have benefited from it. In the initial phases of the recent expansion it owed much to the enthusiasm and commitment of individual members of staff and was frequently marginal to both types of institution. It is hardly surprising, therefore, that there is a tremendous diversity in the ways in which various partnerships have approached collaborative working. Among these are differences in the approach to quality assurance and differences in the relationships that have been established with partners.

FHE partnerships are inescapably unequal. This is because the HEI is responsible, and will be held responsible, for maintaining the standards and quality of its awards. It cannot, under current legislation, delegate its responsibility to institutions that have not been granted degree-awarding powers. Universities have chosen to approach the task of satisfying themselves that the quality of what is on offer in their name is what it should be in a variety of different ways.

Approaches to quality assurance

The approach to quality assurance that characterizes a particular partnership is largely determined by the university concerned. Approaches differ between universities and between partnerships. Thus, the same university with multiple partnerships might have multiple approaches. Sometimes this will arise because of the different characteristics of the partnerships themselves, and at other times it will occur as a result of the fact that over a period of time the university has worked with a number of other organizations and has not yet had the opportunity to consolidate or reflect on its practice.

Some HEIs see themselves as largely facilitating quality assurance and blending their experience with their FE partners in shared responsibility for the process. Others, particularly those involved in large partnerships, see themselves not only as facilitating development and implementation of quality management systems but also as acting as brokers, with the assent of their partners, to ensure a unified system. In a small number of cases there are universities that see themselves as sole arbiters of quality serviced by their own staff. For these universities, other than supplying the relevant data and access to materials, their partners play no important role in the quality assurance process itself. This type of approach has been more common in the past and is currently found where one or other of the partners is a newcomer to HE provision in FE or where the university maintains that there is a qualitative or perhaps unbridgeable gap between itself and its partners. HEQC auditors would seem to favour a facilitative approach in which the responsibility for quality assurance is acknowledged and shared between partners and accommodates the need of the university to assure itself that the level of its awards is being maintained.

As associate college and affiliate college arrangements increase, HEIs are involved in both the assessment of provision and the auditing of quality assurance systems that they and their partners use to ensure that the provision meets specification. Some carry out rigorous and detailed audits and assessments; others have moved away from detailed assessments towards audit as confidence in the partnership develops; yet others have started with relatively informal systems and have been persuaded to support the more formal structures and more elaborate procedures. There is, however, a move to a more organic partnership based on a closer mutual understanding of aims, ethos and *modus operandi.*

Analysis of audit reports and other material shows considerable variation in the documentary basis of quality assurance used within and between universities. This can vary from rather loose guidelines and understandings and a fairly diffused memorandum of association, on the one hand, through to the publication of criteria and codes of practice, and the promulgation of standards that provision has to meet, on the other. Many universities and colleges are currently refining their documentation. More informal partnerships are underpinning the networks of relationships that have so far supported their work with documentation describing the aims, objectives and structure of the arrangement and the procedures and criteria it uses. Others have concluded that an over-cautious and duplicative approach to quality documentation can be stultifying and, in a rapidly changing situation, frequently does not match with practice as it has emerged. They have tended to move away from detailed rigid specifications.

Given the Secretary of State's interest in threshold standards and comparability, a movement towards more formal documentation may be unavoidable. In some instances, where the processes that lead to course approval and validation, monitoring and review are not sufficiently explicit, this may be a welcomed development despite cries of 'over-bureaucratization'.

The role of staff in quality assurance between partners is perhaps the issue on which practice differs most widely. Some partnerships take the view that there is a necessary common culture which must exist or be developed to support teaching at degree level. Teachers in FE colleges are, therefore, part of the academic community. They are peers who can, and must, be expected to play a central role in quality assurance alongside their university colleagues. On the other hand, there are partnerships in which staff in partner institutions are seen as qualitatively different. Their input is restricted much more to the delivery and execution of specific programmes. They are not normally expected to participate in curriculum development and review, and in some instances their role and judgements in assessment are secondary or non-existent. Staff are affected by, but do not influence, the quality assurance or the underlying strategic academic development of the scheme.

Between these two positions, there are situations in which the partnership has developed a maturity that is not yet reflected in its formal documentation. As a result, staff in partner institutions are actively encouraged to take an interest in the wider aspects of the provision or arrangement, and exercise considerable informal influence in programme validation and monitoring, implementation and review. The development of such informal intermediate positions may be productive in the short term, but need to be formally negotiated by partners and included in an agreed formal scheme of quality assurance.

In general, Scottish universities have tended to take a Presbyterian model in their approach to quality assurance. For them there is a priesthood of all believers, with the university and its staff on occasions acting as elders. In contrast, a more Anglican model has been evident in England, although there are exceptions. The university priesthood licenses the equivalent of lay readers and teachers to teach on its franchised and validated courses. The difference between the two countries may be owing to the greater prominence of articulation, as opposed to franchising, north of the border, and the existence within Scotland of an established body of FE teachers accustomed to teaching, assessing and evaluating HND provision. In England there is a strong move away from university exclusivity in quality assurance arrangements towards inclusivity as partnerships acquire greater experience and greater confidence. In both countries a more 'exclusive' approach may be indicated, where partners in a collaborative arrangement have little experience of HE in FE or where the HE provision in an FEI is so small that it is more convenient to place the major burden for quality assurance on the university.

Good practice

There is, and can be, no definite and unambiguous statement of good practice in quality assurance in FHE collaborative working leading to university awards. The differences between and within UK countries and between and within the sectors preclude this. There is no 'right way' of doing it. There is, however, clear consensus emerging on some general features of quality assurance systems which underpin, or at least are thought to underpin, good practice.

It is perhaps worth repeating here that a good institutional quality assurance system is no necessary guarantor of good provision or vice versa. As the Book of Common Prayer might have it, quality systems and procedures have been 'ordained for the greater rewarding of academic virtue and the punishment of academic wickedness and vice'. They do not guarantee either.

There is universal assent to the proposition that the primary focus of any quality assurance system must be that the programme or arrangement concerned is of a satisfactory quality or standard for the award being offered and that the main judgement should be on the students' learning experience and achievements. However, a summative assessment only passing judgement is not enough. An adequate quality assurance system needs to be integrated into the partnership programme. At the heart of such a system lies critical, reflective practice used formatively to help partners achieve their objectives. Ideally, the summative judgement of formal validation and review events should be a public recognition of this critical and reflective practice.

Quality assurance should be a routine and expectable part of both the programme and its implementation which facilitates the arrangement of all partners. Some partnerships take the view that if there is a cycle of quality assurance activities, which reflect the management of academic tasks that have to be done throughout the year, then the compiling of annual reports and indeed more formal periodic reviews merely records and celebrates what has happened. Such formal accounting largely endorses what has been planned and what has been identified as needing further attention, rather than requiring large investigative exercises in their own right.

Successful and effective partnerships are those that are carefully and jointly planned. They seem to work best where partners share and agree to develop a common understanding of the nature and requirements of successful higher education teaching, where there is in the relevant areas an affinity between academic management systems and approaches to quality assurance.

Some of the features which recur as characteristic of good quality management are as follows.

- Each partner has a clearly articulated rationale and a set of objectives for entering into FHE partnerships, against which the value of a specific programme or proposal to their overall objectives can be assessed and reviewed.
- There are clear definitions of possible types of arrangement which are used consistently throughout the institution and are made accessible to partner institutions. This is particularly important whenever an FEI or HEI has multiple relationships with a number of partners.
- The information and documentation required, the criteria that will be involved and the processes that will be utilized in reaching quality judgements are understood and shared with partner institutions and with internal and external staff.
- The provision is integrated within the academic, financial and support structures of the partner institution, i.e. it is not marginalized.
- Wherever possible, the existing quality systems of partner institutions are adapted and adopted. This involves partners being clear about their requirements and flexible about the ways in which these can be met.
- There is a clear, well developed executive framework for initiating, developing, implementing and evaluating programmes and arrangements.
- Documentation and guidance is sufficiently well developed, clear and accessible to permit all those who have an interest in the scheme to understand its *modus operandi* and their role within it.
- There are advantages to be gained from calling on the advice of external examiners and practitioners with experience of the field at all stages in the development, validation, implementation and monitoring of programmes and arrangements.
- There are mechanisms to ensure that all those associated with the programme are aware of the criteria and processes which will be applied to it and the purposes it serves for each of the partners.
- An adequate database is established which is accessible to all those who want to use it in the development, implementation and evaluation of the course.
- Publicity and guidance given to students before admission and during the course of their studies is accurate, helpful and accessible.
- Robust communication and feedback mechanisms are established which ensure that, for example, external examiners' reports and comments are circulated throughout course teams.
- Mechanisms exist which ensure that students in partner institutions have appropriate access to the quality assurance machinery and that their views are taken into account.
- Partners collectively and individually have arrangements which allow them to discuss and share good practice.
- Sufficient staff development opportunities are provided to enable staff from

all partners to acquire an appropriate knowledge of the scheme and their place in it.

All these points and others are elaborated in HEQC (1995a) and other reports. The major lesson to be learnt is that good partnerships require active and inclusive management from the very beginning. In particular, there must be an agreement between all those involved about the aims and objectives of the partnership. This should include a careful consideration of the reasons for involvement in the first place, the circumstances under which the partnership can be terminated and arrangements for providing for students in the case of termination to ensure that they are not disadvantaged. This in turn requires an openness and accessibility to the structures, procedures and criteria that will be applied in the approval, validation, implementation and in monitoring and evaluation.

HEQC work suggests that the weakest aspect of current collaborative working concerns the monitoring and evaluation of provision and the quality assurance process associated with the partnership itself. To return to the analogy with marriage, FE–HE partnerships have to be worked at to be successful.

There are two frequently unstated assumptions about the quality of higher education and its quality assurance. The first of these is that the primary guarantee of acceptable quality and standards lies in the sharing and acceptance of a set of values concerning higher education, what is needed to teach at this level and what can and should be concluded and expected of a specific programme or programmes in general. An adequate system of quality assurance underpins and underwrites the exercise of judgement based on this culture and this understanding. It cannot replace it; it is a servant of the programme, not its master.

The second assumption refers to a belief, most evident at present in Scotland, in the need for degree teaching to be underpinned by an academic community and lively academic network. FE teachers at degree level need to share in that network and be an accepted and respected part of it. This involves the acceptance and recognition that HE itself has much to learn from the practices, and particularly the pedagogic skill, of the FE sector. It follows that the criteria and standards which derive from that sector may need to be incorporated, along with others, in the assessment of HE provision and in HE and FE partnerships.

Retrospect: towards a framework of collaborative working

FHE links are only one of a number of types of collaborative arrangement leading to university awards developed by UK HEIs. Others, as we have seen, include links with colleges of health, industry and commerce, the professional bodies, voluntary bodies and overseas organizations. Most, if not all, of the work on FHE partnerships and other forms of collaboration has focused on the situation as it existed at the time data collection was undertaken. Several writers (Bird and Yee 1994; Bocock and Scott 1994) have noted that forms of provision and partnership have undergone rapid change in the past few years. It is also possible to stand back from what we know about FHE partnerships in particular, and collaborative working in general, and suggest a set of criteria which any adequate quality assurance system for collaborative working might satisfy. The logic of such an approach is that it offers underlying principles that are not time- or context-specific, and some guidelines for meeting changing needs and circumstances. What follows is based on work currently being undertaken between the National Health Service Executive and HEQC, which is designed to stream-line current quality assurance arrangements for non-medical health care education.

From a quality assurance standpoint collaborative arrangements can be seen as consisting of two components: a quality specification; and a working agreement. The quality specification consists of a set of principles covering the design and delivery of an education programme or arrangement. Once agreed, this is the standard against which the subsequent arrangement or provision will be assessed and its quality measured. It will include guidelines about credit accumulation and transfer schemes (CATS) and accreditation of prior learning (APL) and would underpin the partnership's approach in developing its arrangements. A working agreement focuses on operational issues. It identifies the respective roles and responsibilities of partners and the interface between them. Such an agreement might embody agreed purposes, principles and definitions and the evidence that needs to be gathered to inform judgements about quality. It would include the processes whereby that evidence can be best gathered and subsequently shared and exchanged between stakeholders.

A quality assurance system that includes better quality specification in the working agreement would need to meet a number of criteria. It would need to be sufficiently comprehensive to cover the development, validation and review of courses and programmes in the context of the partners' broad quality procedures, academic and management culture and objectives. The extent to which there is a synergy between the partnership or provision and the context in which it operates is a central question for all collaborative quality assurance systems. The second set of characteristics concerns the legitimacy and openness of the system. A quality assurance system needs to be recognized by all stakeholders as providing objective, transparent and accessible measures of quality. It requires the sharing of data and criteria and demands an inclusive rather than an exclusive approach. It requires the ownership of the quality assurance system by the partnership rather than by an individual partner. In this way the distinctive and differing roles and responsibilities of partners can be recognized and the blending and sharing of duplicated roles facilitated. It should be possible for all partners to incorporate elements of a quality assurance system into their own procedures, modifying these minimally as necessary. It also should provide support for any particular judgements that any of the partners might need to exercise.

Many of the early partnership agreements were cast predominantly in terms of the requirements of the university. Other partners have legitimate quality assurance expectations and requirements of HEIs with which they work. Students and employers have requirements of both.

If collaborative partnerships are to work effectively they need clear specifications of roles and means of identifying, assessing and incorporating any role drift that may develop. Responsibilities must be clearly and publicly stated. In particular, there should be support for the collection and collation of evidence in support of necessary judgements. Given all this, an adequate quality assurance system should be judged by the extent to which it results in judgements which are meaningful to all stakeholders and to informed decision-making. Its output should inform change and improvement and it should be efficient and cost-effective. This means that it should be open to review.

Prospect: the future of quality assessment in FHE partnerships

Nationally, the compromise reached over quality assurance in HE in 1992 can only be transitory. There is a need for a unitary system that satisfies the legitimate needs of all stakeholders effectively and efficiently. There are two views at the moment as to how this is best achieved. Both take it as given that the basis of any quality assurance system lies in the ability and willingness of those involved in higher education to review their activities critically and regularly. Both agree that quality assurance is best conducted by peers, perhaps spiced with a few lay persons who can represent industry, commerce and the man on the Clapham omnibus. On the one hand, there are those who argue that the system should be largely self-regulating and that individual HEIs and their partners should carry out quality control activities. The focus of quality assurance according to this approach should be on proofing and verifying the quality assurance systems used. On the other hand, there are those who see external assessment – inspection by any other name – as the key to ensuring standards.

The 1992 FHE Act brought quality issues to the fore. More recently the Secretary of State has raised the question of threshold standards and comparability of awards in higher education. At the time of writing, the HEQC is seeking to ascertain through a variety of projects the extent to which HE considers an approach to quality assurance which is based on the articulation of threshold standards as desirable and feasible.

At the national level, the future of quality assurance arrangements and the extent to which they are linked to funding remains unclear. There are, however, clear trends in the way in which FEIs and HEIs are tackling quality assurance issues at a local level. Associate and affiliate college agreements are becoming more common and provide a framework within which individual programmes can be validated and evaluated. Partnerships, once established, are likely to become much more equal. FEIs have to justify their operations to a wider number of stakeholders and preserve a balance between their activities. As FE staff acquire more experience of HE work they will increasingly have a place in universities and in their quality assurance systems.

There is now a clutch of partnerships which potentially have a life of their own. Two such partnerships are the Local Integrated Colleges Scheme (LINCS) associated with the University of Central Lancashire and the FHE partnership associated with the University of Sheffield. They may well develop to a stage at which, in practice if not in principle, it may shortly no longer be feasible to hold the associated university responsible for the awards offered in its name. Some of the larger partnerships may become autonomous and acquire degree-awarding powers in their own right.

Any increase in participation in HE will probably involve the extension of degree work in FE colleges. Over the past twenty or so years an increasing number of FE staff have become graduates. The balance of postgraduate and graduate staff in the larger FEI providers of higher education courses is not much different from the balance which existed in the former colleges of advanced technology before they formed part of the 1964 wave of new universities. This will inevitably lead to a further interpenetration of the academic systems of FE and HE institutions. It may also involve the extension of the boundaries of the HE academic community to include some FEIs and many FE teachers. As FEIs and their staff develop confidence in HE through scholarly and research activities, their claim to be treated as academic peers in all forms with their university counterparts will be increasingly difficult to resist for those that have a mind to do so.

Amid all this uncertainty it is unlikely that the demands for external accountability will lessen. Indeed, the students and their significant others have increasingly to bear the pecuniary and social costs of higher education. They will become powerful stakeholder groups that need to be satisfied.

References

Bird, J., Crawley, G. and Sheibani, A. (1993) *Franchising and Access to Higher Education: a Study of HE/FE Collaboration.* Bristol, University of the West of England/Department of Employment.

Bird, J. and Yee, W.C. (1994) *From Compacts to Consortia: a Study of Partnerships Involving Schools, Colleges and HEIs.* Bristol, University of the West of England/Department of Employment.

Bocock, J. and Scott, P. (1995) *Re-drawing the Boundaries: Further and Higher Education Partnerships.* Leeds, Centre for Policy Studies in Education, University of Leeds.

Higher Education Quality Council (1993) *Some Aspects of Higher Education Provision in Further Education Institutions.* London, HEQC.

Higher Education Quality Council (1995a) *Learning from Collaborative Audit.* London, HEQC.

Higher Education Quality Council (1995b) *Aspects of FE/HE Collaborative Links in Scotland.* London, HEQC.

Times Higher Education Supplement (1995) Second class degree risk, *THES,* 2 April.

Wagner, L. (1992) The teaching quality debate, *Higher Education Quarterly,* 47(3), 274–85.

6

The Students' Experiences
of Franchising

Sofija Opacic

Introduction

This chapter delves into one of the National Union of Students' (NUS) recent research concerns, namely identifying students' experiences of franchised courses (see NUS 1994a) and draws on four principal sources: NUS casework from individual students and student unions; two franchising surveys conducted in East Anglia and the West Midlands in early 1994, involving over 140 franchised students; an NUS franchising seminar held in March 1994, attended by 55 student union officers; an extensive trawl through the ever-increasing reports, commentaries and suggestions on FHE collaborations.

In the early 1990s education franchising was one of the most rapidly expanding areas of FHE collaboration. Between 1991–2 and 1992–3, for instance, the number of franchised students grew from 10,000 to 34,919 in England (Bird *et al.* 1993; HEFCE 1993). The NUS supported the development because it was seen to extend student choice, widen access and enhance flexibility.

However, the first part of this chapter will concentrate, almost exclusively, on the main problems faced by franchised students. It then moves away from what some may call the negative of students' complaints about franchised courses to discuss some of the NUS's ideas on how to improve the franchised students' experiences of HE in an FE context.

What is a franchised course?

Each summer the NUS trains about 120 new student union education officers. At 1994's event, we included a franchising negotiating exercise. Inevitably, one of the first questions asked was: What is a franchised course? Many were painfully aware – from personal negotiation and lobbying experience within their own institution – that definitions of franchised courses differ not just between individual institutions, but among external agencies.

At the NUS we use the CVCP definition of a franchised course:

A whole course, or a stage of a course, designed in one institution [the franchiser, e.g. an HEI] and delivered in, and by the staff of, another institution [the franchisee, e.g. an FE college]; overall responsibility for the quality of the course and the assessment of the students resides with the franchising institution.

(CVCP 1993a: 1)

We also use the HEFCE's (1993) definition of a franchised student:

One who is taught under a franchising arrangement by one institution whilst being registered at another. In general, a student can only be registered for any individual course at one institution. The institution which receives funding from a funding council and/or receives the tuition fee from the student or from a local authority or other body on behalf of that student is to be regarded as the institution which registers the student.

Within the next five minutes student union education officers are also informed of the following.

- That franchising is just one form of partnership arrangement between FEIs and HEIs.
- That franchising is not another name for accreditation, validation, joint or access courses (see HEQC 1994b, 1995).
- That franchising is now perceived as a relatively unsophisticated concept as compared with other partnership arrangements, such as associate colleges, where the FEI has an exclusive agreement with just one HEI and the FEI is rewarded with preferential funding and higher levels of strategic planning.
- That franchising is now less lucrative to the FEI than taught A level courses, given recent changes in the FEFC funding. The brakes have therefore been put on further franchising expansion in the short term.
- That franchised courses vary in academic level from access courses to postgraduate (full-time or part-time).
- That franchising is most popular in the non-charter, new university sector.

These findings are clearly detailed in a raft of recent national reports (HMI 1991; Grindlay *et al.* 1992; Abramson *et al.* 1993; Bird *et al.* 1993; Woodrow 1993; AfC 1994; HEQC 1994a; HEQC 1995).

Why franchise?

'So why franchise?', student union officers ask. 'What is in it for the student?' Preliminary findings from Bocock and Scott's (1995) two-year FHE partnerships research project at the University of Leeds provide some answers to the question: Franchised students – who are they? Their research shows that partnership courses are aimed at students who tend to be (very) local, to be mature, to need to study part-time (or flexibly), to be (so far) under-achievers, to have caring responsibilities and to face financial difficulties.

NUS research suggests that these students therefore appreciate franchised courses for four main reasons: accessibility, cost-effectiveness, an intimate atmosphere and flexible modes of attendance.

Accessibility

Franchised students say they appreciate the relatively easy access to local FE colleges. As mentioned, many are mature, adult returners, with family and employment commitments. The other main group of franchised students are those who gained access through the clearing system.

Franchising also provides HE in parts of the country where it was formerly unavailable. For example, the East Anglia Rural Access Programme is delivering franchised HE courses to rural areas in Suffolk and Norfolk; while LINCS has enabled learners to take up HE courses in remote areas of Cumbria.

Cost-effectiveness

Franchised students see undertaking a franchised course as a means of reducing financial hardship, because it enables them to study locally and for longer.

An intimate atmosphere

Franchised students feel that they can build up their confidence more easily in the less threatening FE environment. They also often mention the importance of the one-to-one personal support available to them, which they see as their first and most vital point of contact when making a query or complaint. Students in FE colleges also have the opportunity to work in smaller groups. This means that students' needs can be met more readily: lecturers can vary their approach, and provide appropriate individual support where necessary. This suggests that – up to now (and leaving funding and changing lecturer contractual arrangements aside) – students' experiences of teaching and learning in FE are different from those in HE, although there is no research to suggest that the quality of their teaching and learning is enhanced by these differences.

As franchised students explained in the NUS surveys: 'I am a mature student and I expected qualified and experienced lecturers, who could draw out my potential – so that all my abilities were fully utilized – and that happened.' 'I expected the college staff to help as much as possible, to be sympathetic to my needs, and they were.' 'I expected a pleasant supportive atmosphere – and I got it.'

Flexible modes of attendance

Finally, franchised students appreciate the freedom of selecting the type of attendance that best meets their needs, whether it be part-time, full-time or evening.

The main problems

Identification of the problems faced by franchised students was at the centre of two NUS research projects set up in East Anglia and the West Midlands in early 1994. Preliminary findings suggest that problems exist at each of the three key stages: pre-entry, on course and exit.

Pre-entry

Erroneous marketing material and unprofessional recruitment practices at both the HEI and the FEI were identified as the two main problems experienced by franchised students at the pre-entry stage. Consequently, some students felt that they had been misled and complained that their needs had been ignored. NUS casework shows that irresponsible marketing material by HEIs can sometimes fail to make clear which courses have been franchised out. One student, for example, was told by a university that he had been accepted on to its degree course. In fact, he had been accepted on to an HND course at an FE college. Another case involves a mature student who sold his house in the north to move south to what he believed from the university prospectus to be a university-based course. He bought a house in the university town, then discovered at the beginning of the academic year that his course was at an FE college 50 miles away.

Admissions tutors at HEIs can also provide misleading advice. One NUS case involves an HEI admissions tutor who failed to inform the student that her course was franchised out to an FE college 30 miles away.

NUS research shows that it was these involuntarily franchised students who perceived their HE experience at the FEI most negatively. They complained of being over-spill students, and being denied access to a variety of services and resources that their equivalents in the HEI received. In contrast, voluntarily franchised students – those who chose to stay on at FE or applied directly to the FEI – had more realistic expectations. For instance, they did not expect to have the same experience of HE in their FEI as their HEI equivalents. It is important to point out here that the experiences of students studying on HE programmes in FEIs and in HEIs are different; and that each has its own strengths.

To place these problems in some sort of context, only eight of the 79 respondents in the West Midlands survey said that they were not getting what they expected – although they then moved on to criticize the courses in some detail. All eight dissatisfied respondents belonged to an HND business course, where the facilities available were generally inadequate.

On course

Many issues were identified by students in the NUS's franchising surveys, but this section will concentrate on the four most frequently mentioned academic or course-related problems:

- Limited or non-transparent written information on the aims, objectives, outcomes and assessment modes of the course.
- Ineffective student feedback and representation mechanisms.
- Inadequate or non-transparent complaints procedures.
- Limited learning support resources.

Limited information
As mentioned above, some franchised students complained that their course was not what they expected. Part of the problem, they argued, was that they had only been given non-transparent, verbal information on their course. In the NUS's West Midlands survey, for example, only 19 of the 79 students said they had received any information about the nature of their course at induction. Eleven received a brief chat from their tutor, five were given leaflets and three were provided with college brochures containing franchised course details.

Ineffective student feedback and representation
Both sets of students in the NUS's franchising surveys highlighted the inadequacy of available FE student feedback and representation systems. Student feedback systems were criticized for being unimaginative, tired, repetitive, end-of-year questionnaires, which failed to reassure them that: their ideas and complaints were being listened to; the process was being taken seriously by the institutions; they were being actively involved as equal partners in the process; something would be done quickly to remedy problem areas.

Inadequate complaints procedures
Both surveys reconfirm NUS casework findings that complaints procedures often fail to define the services franchised students can complain about at

the institutional level, and who has responsibility for the complaint (the FEI or the HEI).

This can have serious repercussions for the student. For example, there are cases where neither the HEI nor the FEI wants to accept responsibility over franchised students' complaints. For instance, one of the NUS's recent cases involves a student, with children, who complained about limited library opening hours. While dealing with the complaint, she said she felt bounced from pillar to post as the FEI's learning support facilitator advised her to talk to the HEI's quality assurance manager, and vice versa. This is a troubling scenario when you consider that research shows that about one in four franchised students would have to travel over 50 miles to reach his or her franchiser institution (i.e. HEI) and about one in ten over 100 miles (Grindlay *et al.* 1992).

In cases where complaints procedures are inadequately detailed, the franchised students may be placed in the invidious position of having to approach the principal (FE) or vice chancellor (HE), who suggests *ad hoc*, temporary arrangements to deal with the complaint. NUS casework shows that this can lead to disciplinary procedures being invoked against the student for supposedly making a complaint with malicious intent (i.e. one that is inappropriate or irresponsible).

This situation may be exacerbated in certain franchising arrangements, because neither the HE nor the FE student union (if there is one) feels able to take on the responsibility for the franchised student's problem. This is often because of funding difficulties, compounded by the absence of the student union's responsibilities being clearly laid out in the memorandum of cooperation.

Interestingly enough, one of the questions on the NUS's recent West Midland's franchising questionnaire was: 'When you enrolled on to your course, what did you expect to get from your student union?' Those who responded to this question wanted a representative body to voice their concerns. In reality, however, FE student unions are under-funded and under-resourced compared with their HE equivalents, so that FE student representation systems tend to be under-developed. This limits the franchised student's voice, and limits the likelihood of complaints being effectively taken up.

Limited learning support resources
Limited learning support resources have been highlighted as a major cause of concern for franchised students in previous research reports (see Brady and Metcalfe 1994). The NUS's casework confirms that franchised students are frustrated by the limited equipment, computer and library facilities. Franchised students feel especially aggrieved that they should have to experience problems in accessing inter-library loans, and are sometimes only allowed to borrow two or three books from the HEI as compared with the average of six.

Exit: course progression from FE to HE

NUS research tends to bear out the general conclusion reached by Abramson (1994: 110) that:

> Where complete courses are franchised, such as Higher National Certificates (HNCs)/Higher National Diplomas (HNDs), academic and geographical progression to the [HEI] is not an issue. For degree franchises, however, the norm has been to franchise only part or lower levels, and even though academic progression is usually guaranteed exploiting such a guarantee may be a geographical impossibility.

A number of NUS cases go one step further, though, in showing that certain franchised students are required to receive higher grades than their HEI student equivalents to progress to the second or third year at the HEI. The NUS research department has cases on file where both part-time and full-time franchised students were falsely promised HE places, which at the crucial stage failed to materialize, even though they could access the HEI relatively easily.

A way forward

The NUS believes that NUS-style learner agreements, institutional student charters, course representative systems and transparent complaints procedures are four important ways of eliminating many of the problems identified in the previous section.

Learner agreements

Learner agreements are one idea, highlighted in the NUS's Student Charter (1992), that can be used to help to clarify the student's needs and expectations and the FEI's and HEI's obligations. The ideal learner agreement, currently being fought for by a number of HEI student unions, is divided into three parts: institutional, departmental and individual (see NUS 1993).

With a franchised learner agreement, part 1 would be negotiated between the FE and HE student unions, and both the FEI and HEI, and then agreed and signed by the respective vice chancellors(or equivalent) and HE and FE student union executive members. It would include responsibilities for levels of welfare, academic and learning support, as well as student feedback mechanisms. It should answer questions of concern to franchised students, such as: 'Who is responsible for academic appeals: the HEI or the FEI?' 'How can I get a complaint through to the Academic Board of the HEI?' (i.e. 'Who is available to represent me at the FEI and the HEI?') 'What HE progression routes are available?'

Part 2 is negotiated at the faculty or department level, by the FE head of the faculty or department and franchised course representatives, and includes information on modes of attendance available, progression routes and grades required, access to learning support facilities etc. Again this section should ensure that the student has specific information on crucial areas, such as what grades she or he needs to progress to university. Where NUS-style learner agreements exist, the first two parts should be published in the institution's prospectus to ensure that accurate information reaches franchised students.

Finally, part 3 is negotiated between the individual student and lecturers. It includes induction processes, individual course plans for students, aims and objectives of courses, assessment procedures, progression routes, teaching–learning schemes, student representation and feedback mechanisms and appeals and complaints procedures at the course level.

The NUS believes that it is both the HEI's and the FEI's responsibility to resource this initiative. Managerial responsibilities should reside with the institution, the faculty or department and the lecturer for parts 1, 2 and 3 respectively.

Institutional student charters

At the NUS's Charters Seminar in May 1994, HE student union officers were asked whether their institutions were preparing their own charters, given that it was not obligatory to do so (only FE charters are mandatory); 80 per cent said yes. An opportunity therefore exists to use institutional charters to detail franchised students' rights and responsibilities in both franchisers' (HE) and franchisees' (FE) charters. Some might argue that franchised students are HEFCE-funded, so the FE college has no obligation to include details of franchise arrangements, and should remain a non-participant in any HE charter consultation and review process. Others, however, rightly argue that working together is in the true spirit of FHE collaboration and that all HE charter consultative and review committees should at all times include the FE college, franchised students – possibly elected course representatives – and the FE student union (if it has one). Only then will the HE charter be representative of franchised students' experiences while enrolled on that particular HEFCE-funded course.

Student feedback and course representatives

The NUS believes that student feedback is a key element in an institution's quality assurance system. In fact, student feedback conforms to all four of the NUS's quality measures, by enhancing openness, extending student representation, promoting partnership and being responsive to the needs of individual students.

Since the 1992 Further and Higher Education Act, and the setting up of the HEFCE assessment exercise and the HEQC's audit process, HEIs have become increasingly concerned about their own quality assurance procedures, and the place of student feedback within it. As the CVCP's (1993b: 1) report points out:

> Feedback to universities and colleges on their work and their performance is now a statutory obligation. Students are key consumers and stake holders of Higher Education. This makes gathering feedback from them no longer an optional extra for a few enthusiastic academics; rather it means that their critical commentary on the learning experiences provided is central to quality assurance procedures and processes at all levels of the institution and the HE system as a whole.

In contrast, FEFCE quality assessment procedures exclude student feedback processes, so the FEI is under no obligation to maintain or enhance student feedback mechanisms. Consequently student feedback systems in FEIs suffer from being even less well developed than those in HEIs, which are criticized as being top-down, management-style models that overly rely on questionnaires (refer to HEQC 1994b).

Some may argue that this hardly matters, given that franchised courses will be visited by HEFCE assessors and HEQC auditors respectively. This is not strictly true. The HEFCE assessment process requires that 'Responsibility for quality in franchised provision rests with the institution, which receives the [HEFCE] Council grant' (i.e. the HEI) (paragraph 60, HEFCE Circular 3/93). So the HEFCE expects the HEI to cover franchised courses in its self-assessment.

However, paragraph 60 goes on to explain that 'The Council will need to agree with institutions individually, in the preparatory meeting [before the assessment visit], the best way in which account can be taken of education franchised out to other institutions.' So the HEFCE negotiates with the HEI as to whether a visit will be made to the franchised course. This remains true despite the new assessment methodology contained in HEFCE Circular 39/95.

The HEQC will propose a separate audit visit to a franchised course, 9–12 months after the initial HEI audit visit, if it feels that the HEI's collaborative arrangements are extensive. However, this separate collaborative (what was called validation) audit will not review the standards of franchised provision, but will focus on the HEI's responsibilities and how it discharges those.

Collaborative audit reports have a narrower focus than the main audit and concentrate on four main areas: first, how effectively institutional responsibilities are defined; second, the means by which collaborative/partnership arrangements are monitored and reviewed; third, identifying how feedback from programme providers and students is secured; fourth, how information from feedback is reported and acted upon in that particular collaborative partnership.

So how can franchised students effectively voice their concerns, express their grievances and suggest improvements? One way forward is to set up an effective course representative system. Like any quality drive, the setting up of a course representative system has to be seen as a partnership, with shared ownership, between the seven main franchising stakeholders: the institutions (FE and HE), the student unions (FE and HE), the course representatives, the staff and the students.

Moreover, as with any quality drive, feedback has to be encouraged from the very top: with the vice chancellor or equivalent and senior academics endorsing their support; with students being treated as full and valid members of committees (by other committee members including the chair); with feedback sessions being scheduled when students can attend; with administrative support on hand to disseminate information collected; and finally with newly elected course representatives being given an induction by the relevant head of department or chair of the course committee, and trained by the student union to collect student feedback.

The recruitment and retention of course representatives is often given by quality assurance managers (or their equivalents) as a reason not to get involved in course representative development work. However, these are relatively simple to resolve if the institution is truly committed. Prospective course representatives need detailed information on their role, so that they know what to expect, and – possibly – academic recognition for their course representative training and skills learned.

Many universities, including Loughborough University, have developed the novel approach of using opportunity profiles to help students to understand the course representative role. Loughborough University's course representative opportunity profile covers two sides of A4, and generally includes: an introduction to the student union; the responsibilities of course representatives; experience required; a time commitment estimate; how to become a representative (i.e. the selection procedure); support, training and supervision available; likely rewards (skills developed etc.); plus further opportunities (in the student's union, for instance).

Academic recognition of course representative training and skills learned has also become a powerful incentive in the *recruitment* and *retention* of course representatives. Coventry University, for example, will have a pilot student representative module in place for 1995–6 which includes seminar, workshop and individual project work. To meet the requirements of the module the participant will be expected to have successfully completed the module (150 hours at level 2, 100 per cent coursework). The module includes 25 hours of workshops, 20 hours of seminars (two hours per week), 40 hours of guided study and supervision and 65 hours of self-directed learning (e.g. student representative work).

Workshop (skills-based) topics – led by tutors and practitioners in the field – include listening skills and confidentiality, presentations and committee skills, project management (goals/target setting) and negotiating and assertiveness. Seminar (academic-based) topics include university organization and committees, HE today, student charters, quality etc. student diversity, equal opportunities, student union organization and support services. A variety of external and internal speakers will be brought in to run the seminars, including the registrar, the pro-vice chancellor, the university's officers and NUS staff. The individual project is chosen by the student, and could include computer support, curriculum critique or a survey of students' opinions of a course or school. So the module is experience-based, where the student reflects and analyses her or his own activities as an elected student representative.

The development of systems of course representation, therefore, offers an effective solution to one of the most pressing problems for the franchised student: getting her or his voice heard. Course representatives have a vital role to play in student–staff liaison and course committees and, through contact with the student union, have a voice on numerous committees at the faculty and institutional level (refer to NUS 1994b).

Course representatives – with the help of student union franchising introductory days – can also promote learner teams for part-time franchised students, initiate theme meetings for the aforementioned students – if need be – and provide information in the course representative newsletter on burning issues of relevance to franchised students.

Complaints procedures

This final sub-section concentrates on what the NUS considers would be an ideal institutional model for dealing with franchised students' complaints. It covers three main areas: rights and grounds of complaints, procedure and notification.

Rights and grounds of complaint
It should be the responsibility of both the FEI and the HEI to collaborate and specify minimum service levels in, for example, learning support facilities (e.g. libraries and IT), lecturer competence (e.g. prompt marking, punctuality) and progression routes. These minimum service provision levels should be negotiated with the student union and incorporated into the student's learner agreement.

Procedure
It has been a long-held view within the NUS that an independent ombudsperson needs to be appointed (either within or outside the institution) to have overall responsibility to deal with complaints. She or he should be independent, and have the power to make institutions change their practices.

Notification
The NUS maintains that franchised students should be given simple and easily accessible information, which answers certain fundamental questions.

Retrospect

The NUS continues to support the development of FHE partnership. As discussed in the first part of this chapter, research evidence now confirms that collaborative arrangements have served to extend student choice and enhance flexibility. However, recent research on whether franchised courses have actually widened access remains equivocal. For instance, research from the LINCS suggests that the programme was unsuccessful in attracting older and retired students, the unskilled and black people (Abramson *et al.* 1993). While other research suggests that where students feel that the franchised provision is of more direct relevance – for instance, black students doing HNC/D business courses – higher recruitment can be achieved (Bird *et al.* 1993).

Catching up with the rapidly changing mode of educational provision within FEIs and HEIs has been a major challenge for student unions and their officers. Although both sets of institutions claim to welcome student input into the way this is shaped, many student representatives feel as if they have been asked about the pattern of the wallpaper after the decorators have packed up. The 'problem' of franchising seems to be an extreme example of this.

Student union membership and servicing of franchised students' academic (as well as social) needs are a forgotten component of many memoranda of cooperation. As many student unions are not invited to be part of the team that draws up the memorandum between the two institutions, this may not seem surprising. However, it may expose the underlying oversight that has led to some of the quality assurance problems identified earlier.

Another issue that cannot be overlooked is that many HEI student unions have decided not to service their franchised students, because the HEI has failed to provide additional funding for them in the student union's block grant. The block grant rarely makes distinctions between type of student. The NUS maintains that one of the HEI student union's responsibilities is to argue for an enhanced block grant from the HEI to serve the extra needs of another diverse group of students. The Education Act 1994 may well push student unions that have decided not to service franchised students' needs to reconsider their positions, because it is now possible for franchised students to complain about the quality of service they have received from the HEI student union via the new code of practice for student unions. In the future it will therefore become increasingly difficult for HEI student unions to ignore the membership clause in their constitutions, which states that all registered students at the HEI (except those who have chosen to opt out) are members of their student union.

The NUS's immediate response to the emerging pattern of common student problems in the early 1990s at the national level was to draw up a *joint protocol* to act as an agreement on the role of the two student unions in the franchise situation. Put simply, the franchiser (HEI) student union's role was seen as: lobbying for an enhanced level of grant funding from the institution to cover franchised students; pursuing the academic interests of students via its student union representative on the HEI's academic board and/or sub-committee of the academic board; supporting academic appeals on behalf of the franchised students; enabling franchised students to participate in all the student union activities of the franchiser institution; and, finally, communicating with the franchisee college (student union and course representatives etc.). The role of the franchisee student union (FEI) was seen as: lobbying for an appropriate enhanced level of grant funding from the franchiser institution; dealing with immediate welfare and academic issues; and, finally, communicating problems to the franchiser student union.

Prospect

What future is there for franchising, given that FHE collaborations in general are undoubtedly going to continue growing, thanks to the government's immediate expansionist plans for FE? Questions like this are difficult – if not impossible – to answer, especially since so much seems to depend on the whim of government financial and political decision-making.

Some economic pragmatists argue that franchising will die out because it is more lucrative now for FE to teach A level type courses. In contrast, some social idealists predict the continuing expansion of franchising, while at the same time criticizing it as a relatively unsophisticated model of FHE collaboration as compared with exclusive associate college arrangements, for instance.

Therefore, a more fruitful question might be: what can student unions do to enhance partnership arrangements, and ensure that franchised students' interests are safeguarded? Perhaps a first step – which many FEIs and HEIs have accepted – is to work together via a dual student union membership arrangement, as discussed earlier. This means that franchised students have access to both the FEI's and the HEI's student union facilities and services.

The NUS's six-point checklist on dealing with franchising arrangements, detailed in NUS (1994c), provides further practical advice on how student unions can effectively integrate franchised students into both student unions. This chapter closes with the five-point checklist.

1. Ensure that there is a student support element in the memorandum of cooperation, which includes funding for both the FE and the HE student union.
2. Liaise and communicate effectively; discuss the NUS protocol or a version of it; identify a franchised student as a contact, if no FE student union exists; arrange regular meetings between the two student union representatives and franchised student representatives; provide the franchised student representatives with training, including in the role of being a course representative and how to input into the quality assurance mechanisms – both internal and external – with or without the

student union's help. In the past, many FEI and HEI student unions have failed to set up effective communication channels for joint organizational issues. Franchising offers FE and HE student unions a chance to increase their understanding of each other's sector.
3. Monitor information received from franchised students on the reliability of information used in marketing the course, the standard of learning and support facilities, availability and access to tutors and other quality assurance areas. Perhaps even help to set up a course representative theme meeting in the FE college to discuss these issues. Ensure that franchising and any issues associated with it are raised in meetings with auditors and assessors of the HEQC and the HEFCE respectively (e.g. liaise with the HEI so that the HEFCE receives student union information gathered at the course representative theme meeting and main issues raised from franchised courses casework).
4. Establish the idea of joint HE and FE student union induction workshops for franchised students (especially important for part-time, mature students, who may feel isolated). Promote awareness of various student support schemes that help learners to help themselves (e.g. learning teams for franchised courses or part-time mature franchised students; peer tutoring and mentoring schemes).
5. HE student unions should fine-tune a postal vote system for franchised students' returns.

References

Abramson, M. (1994) Franchising, access, quality and exclusivity: some observations from recent research into further and higher education partnerships, *Journal of Access Studies*, 9, 109–14.

Abramson, M., Ellwood, S. and Thompson, L. (1993) *Five Years of Franchising: an Analysis of the Profile, Performance, and Progression of LINCS Students, 1985–90.* Preston, University of Central Lancashire.

Association for Colleges (1994) *Nature and Extent of Higher Education Provision Offered by Colleges of Further Education.* London, AfC.

Bird, J., Crawley, G. and Sheibani, A. (1993) *Franchising and Access to Higher Education: a Study of HE/FE Collaboration.* Bristol, University of the West of England/ Department of Employment.

Bocock, J. and Scott, P. (1995) *Redrawing the Boundaries: Further and Higher Education Partnerships.* Leeds, Centre for Policy Studies in Education, University of Leeds.

Brady, D. and Metcalfe, A. (1994) Staff and student perceptions of franchising, *Journal of Access Studies*, 9, 271–7.

CVCP (1993a) *Draft Revision: CVCP Code of Practice 1987 – Validation by Universities of Higher Education Programmes in External Institutions.* Lancaster, Council of Validating Universities, University of Lancaster.

CVCP (1993b) *Student Feedback – Context, Ideas and Practices.* Sheffield, CVCP/USDU.

Grindlay, G., Mendick, H., Sims, L. and Woodrow, M. (1992) *Report of the Access News Franchising Survey.* London, Access and Community Education Services (ACES), University of North London.

HEFCE (1993) *Higher Education Students Early Statistics Survey* (HESES 93), Circular 38/93. Bristol, HEFCE.

HEQC (1994a) *Notes for Guidance on Auditing Collaborative Provision*. London, HEQC.

HEQC (1994b) *Learning from Audit*. London, HEQC.

HEQC (1995) *Learning from Collaborative Audit: an Interim Report*. London, HEQC.

HMI (1991) *Higher Education in Further Education Colleges: Franchising and Other Forms of Collaboration with Polytechnics* (Report 228/91/NS). London, Department of Education and Science.

NUS (1992) *NUS Student Charter*. London, NUS.

NUS (1993) *The Right to Learner Agreements Briefing*. London, NUS.

NUS (1994a) *NUS Draft Franchising Briefing*. London, NUS.

NUS (1994b) *Developing a Student Feedback System Handout*. London, NUS.

NUS (1994c) *Education Officers' Handbook*. London, NUS.

Woodrow, M. (1993) 'Franchising: the quiet revolution', *Higher Education Quarterly*, 47(3), 207–20.

7

Working Together: Further Education–Higher Education Links in Scotland

Norman Sharp and Jim Gallacher

Introduction

While relationships between HEIs and FECs are now well established throughout the United Kingdom, the particular focus and balance of these relationships in Scotland is significantly different from elsewhere (HEQC 1995). In Scotland the majority of links between further and higher education at both access level and higher education level have been based on FE college led provision rather than on franchising or other forms of partnership based on courses developed primarily by the HEIs. At both levels links have been established, mainly on the basis of SCOTVEC courses that have been developed and taught within the FECs. At the higher education level, articulation arrangements which facilitate the progress of students from SCOTVEC HNCs and HNDs into degree programmes have been particularly common. This has reflected the context within which these links have developed, and in particular the operation of a number of national organizations and initiatives such as SCOTVEC, the Scottish Wider Access Programme (SWAP) and the Scottish Credit Accumulation and Transfer Scheme (SCOTCATS), which have created national frameworks within which these developments have been shaped. This chapter will outline the national context within which these links have emerged, discuss the types of arrangements that have been established and consider some of the issues that these raise for the future development of further and higher education provision in Scotland. The focus will be on links that have been established at the higher education, rather than access, level, reflecting the major developments which have taken place in recent years.

The context of links between FECs and HEIs in Scotland

The development of the distinctive pattern of FE–HE links in Scotland has been shaped by a number of factors. In this section these factors will be outlined and their impact examined.

The FHE framework in Scotland

There have been major changes in the organization, funding and priorities of the FECs during the 1980s and 1990s, and in the national context within which they have operated. These changes have helped to shape the nature of the FE–HE links that have emerged.

Prior to the Further and Higher Education (Scotland) Act 1992, the FECs were part of the local authority educational provision. However, in the White Paper on Scottish further education (Scottish Office 1991) the government outlined proposals for change. Since then they have become incorporated institutions, responsible for their own management and receiving funding directly from the Scottish Office Education Department (SOED). There are now 43 of these colleges throughout Scotland. They vary considerably in size, with 19 having over 1,500 full-time equivalent students (FTEs), while the three smallest colleges have less than 500 FTEs. The role of these colleges has also been changing, associated with wider changes in the economy and society. In particular, changes in the occupational structure, the decline in the apprenticeship system and the growth of unemployment have led to a move away from craft-based courses, which were an important area of work for many colleges. This, and the increasing emphasis on lifelong learning, has resulted in a greater emphasis on developing a range of educational provision to meet the needs of new student markets within local communities. One important outcome of this has been that many of these colleges have placed a new emphasis on provision for adult returners to education. This was initially seen in the development of access and similar types of courses designed to encourage adult students to re-enter education, a development which was supported by the SWAP initiative. However, more recently, it has also led to significant growth of full-time higher education courses within the SCOTVEC HNC/D framework, many of which have also attracted large numbers of adult students. These developments have been associated with growing differentiation between colleges in the range of courses they provide, with some having a clear emphasis on the provision of higher education courses, while others have more clearly identified themselves as community colleges with a responsibility to provide a wide range of courses.

More recently, changes associated with the incorporation of the FECs on 1 April 1993 have contributed to further changes in provision in the colleges and to significant growth of full-time higher education. Prior to incorporation, the SOED removed the requirement for colleges to seek approval

Table 7.1 Students registered in FE colleges in Scotland by qualification and mode of attendance 1980–1993

	1980–1	1985–6*	1990–1	1993–4	Percentage change 1980–93
Full-time					
Higher education	4,167	6,996	9,431	20,342	+388.2
SCE H and O grades	8,762	7,300	3,155	2,054	−76.6
National Certificate	0	18,986	27,661	26,500	n.a.
ONC/D, C&G, other	10,528	2,840	1,655	5,347	−49.2
No recognized qualification	2,241	1,248	930	1,211	−46.0
Total	25,698	37,370	42,832	55,454	+115.8
HE as percentage of total	16.2	18.7	22.0	36.7	
Part-time					
Higher education	24,836	23,029	23,722	26,879	+8.2
SCE H and O grades	38,681	31,799	26,865	15,761	−59.3
National Certificate	0	43,759	66,969	45,209	n.a.
ONC/D, C&G, other	42,460	18,310	6,329	15,844	−62.7
No recognized qualification	24,951	20,949	43,840	40,911	+64.0
Total	130,928	137,846	167,725	144,604	+10.4
HE as percentage of total	19.0	16.7	14.1	18.6	

*Before 1985 Napier Polytechnic and Glasgow College of Technology were local authority colleges and are included in the FE college statistics, but are excluded from the FE college statistics from 1985 onwards.

for the establishment of new HNC/D courses, and many of the newly independent colleges took the opportunity to develop new courses in their desire to meet the needs of new student markets. There was also, initially, a financial advantage to the colleges in establishing these courses, in that the fee income for higher education courses was considerably higher than that for non-advanced provision. This fee differential has not, however, been maintained, and there is now no clear financial advantage to colleges in developing higher level provision.

The impact of these changes on the profiles of the colleges can be seen in Table 7.1, which provides data on the changing nature of the student population in the Scottish FECs. The extent to which these colleges have been seeking, and have established, a new role for themselves during the 1980s and 1990s can be seen in the growth of full-time provision, which increased by over 115 per cent between 1980 and 1993. Within this the growth of full-time higher education has been even more rapid and significant, at an increase of 388 per cent. Full-time higher education provision is therefore now well established as a major feature of provision within the

FECs. Part-time higher education, by comparison, has seen very limited growth, and while the total number of students is still higher than the numbers on full-time courses, in terms of FTEs full-time students now greatly exceed part-time students.

Another important aspect of this change has been the growing importance of SCOTVEC provision, both at National Certificate (non-advanced) level and at higher education level (Table 7.2). The role of SCOTVEC in shaping developments within FECs, and their links with the HEIs, has been increasingly important.

It is in the context of this growth in FE led full-time HE, based on HNC/D courses, that the links between FECs and HEIs must be considered. This has been a major feature contributing to the growth of articulation agreements, which allow students with HNC/Ds to progress into degree courses in the HEIs, rather than other forms of relationship.

This contribution of SCOTVEC, and that of other national frameworks, in shaping this growth of HE provision and the FE–HE links associated with it will now be considered.

Table 7.2   Students registered in FE colleges by HE qualification studied and mode of attendance

	1990–1	*1991- 2*	*1992–3*	*1993–4*	*Percentage change 1990–3*
Full-time					
Postgraduate	99	121	102	121	+22.2
Degree	59	514	173	222	+276.3
HND	5,655	7,039	8,624	11,053	+95.5
HNC	2,651	4,091	5,417	8,123	+306.4
Other	967	609	876	823	−14.9
Total	9,431	12,374	15,192	20,342	+115.7
Part-time					
Postgraduate	113	159	174	265	+134.5
Degree	489	909	1,246	1,239	+153.4
HND	513	457	1,013	862	+68.0
HNC	10,782	11,955	14,554	18,283	+69.6
Other	11,825	11,548	10,683	8,230	−30.4
Total	23,722	25,028	27,670	26,879	+13.3

Source: SOED (1995a).

National frameworks supporting the development of higher education in Scottish FECs

A distinctive feature of the Scottish educational system has been the establishment of national organizations and initiatives. These have helped to create the frameworks within which provision is developed and delivered. In this respect Scotland can be seen to be different from a number of other societies, in particular England, where there has been less success in developing such national frameworks, and where local or regional initiatives are more prevalent and important. The importance of these national frameworks can partly be explained by the relatively small scale of Scottish society and the cohesive nature of the Scottish educational elite, which have facilitated the reaching of agreements between national government, local government and the educational institutions over issues of educational policy and provision. A number of national organizations have been of particular importance in shaping further education and the links with HEIs during the period of change referred to above.

Scottish Vocational Education Council (SCOTVEC)

SCOTVEC was established in 1985 to replace the two previous vocational educational councils (SCOTEC, which covered science and technology, and SCOTBEC, which covered business). SCOTVEC has established a framework for the development of courses at both non-advanced and advanced level. At non-advanced level this is provided through the modular, competency based, National Certificate programme, within which over 3,500 modules have now been developed. While this was initially established for the 16–18 age group, it has increasingly been used to develop flexible modular provision for adult students across a wide range of discipline areas. It can be seen from Table 7.1 that National Certificate modules have now been established as a major aspect of provision in the FECs. They are used both to provide clearly vocational courses across a wide range of occupational areas and to provide more academically oriented courses, particularly for adult returners. In this respect they have replaced the traditional Scottish Certificate of Education Higher and O Grade courses in many cases. When SWAP was established by the SOED it was also made clear that where possible these National Certificate modules should provide the framework for the access courses that were developed. In this way SCOTVEC's non-advanced provision has helped to establish a national framework for the developing role of FECs in Scotland in providing routes back into education for adult returners and links between FECs and HEIs at this level.

SCOTVEC has also established a framework for the development of Higher National units and for HNCs and HNDs, based on these units. These awards are vocationally oriented, and based on the assessment of competence. While HNC/D provision existed prior to the creation of SCOTVEC, the latter has created a framework that has encouraged the involvement of staff within the FECs in the development of the Higher National units and the HNC/D courses. It is responsible for providing support for staff in the development of Higher National units and awards, validating these awards, approving centres to offer its awards and supervising and supporting the system of assessment for students who are studying for its awards. It has, therefore, provided a quality assurance framework within which higher education has developed in the FECs, which has been independent of the universities and distinctively different in approach. In this respect the situation in Scotland has been considerably different from that in England, in that BTEC has been prepared to devolve the power of validation to the universities. This has encouraged links and course development between the universities and FECs based on franchising, while in Scotland the FECs have been encouraged to develop within the SCOTVEC framework.

The Scottish Wider Access Programme (SWAP)

SWAP was established in 1988 as a result of a major national initiative by the Scottish Education Department to promote access to vocationally relevant education. A central aspect of SWAP was encouragement to establish consortia of HEIs and regional councils, which were then responsible for FE. This was part of a strategy to encourage the establishment of permanent arrangements to make easier, more effective progression from further to higher education (Scottish Education Department 1988). Three large consortia emerged, covering the west, east and north of Scotland. The major activity within SWAP was the establishment of full-time access courses within the FE colleges, based on programmes of SCOTVEC National Certificate modules. Successful completion of these courses guaranteed students a place on an appropriate higher education course. These were to be targeted towards adult students, over the age of 21, and to focus on vocationally relevant subjects, particularly science and technology. There was also a recognition of the need to target traditionally under-represented groups.

Some indication of the impact of this initiative is given by the fact that by 1992–3 a total of 2,103 students were enrolled on these courses (SOED 1993). The impact of this national initiative may, however, have been more significant than would be indicated only by the numbers of students involved, in that it has contributed to the wider process of change in the missions of FECs and HEIs. It has helped to emphasize the importance of FECs in providing routes into and through higher education for adult students. It also helped to establish a model of relationship between FECs and HEIs which was based on consortia of HEIs and FECs and on the national currency of SCOTVEC qualifications, rather than bilateral agreements between institutions. It is perhaps this last point that is of particular importance in the context of this chapter. SWAP marked an early stage in the development of links between FECs and HEIs, and it was clearly established at national level that exclusive relationships based on an HEI's recognition of an access course were to be discouraged, on the grounds that relationships of this kind limited student choice. Instead it was made clear that all institutions were expected to work within the frameworks of national qualifications and regional consortia.

The Scottish Credit Accumulation and Transfer Scheme (SCOTCATS)

The SCOTCATS agreement, to which all HEIs are signatories, was established in 1991 to create a common credit framework for higher education in Scotland, within which credit may be accumulated for learning from a variety of sources towards academic awards. Following the Further and Higher Education (Scotland) Act 1992, the Committee of Scottish Higher Education Principals (COSHEP) and HEQC jointly constituted the Scottish Advisory Committee on Credit and Access (SACCA) to manage the SCOTCATS framework. Within this national framework for credit accumulation and transfer there is a general agreement with SCOTVEC that HNC awards will equate with up to 120 credit points at level Scottish Degree 1 (SD1) and HND awards up to 240 credit points at level SD2. An additional 120 points at level SD3 level would be required to complete a degree, and a further 120 points at level SD4 for an honours degree (HEQC/COSHEP 1995). This credit framework has been an important factor in helping to create a unified trans-binary system of credit accumulation and transfer and a framework which has assisted the recognition of HNC/Ds as potentially having a significant contribution to make towards degree programmes. However, it is important to note that this agreement provides general guidelines regarding the maximum credit that students may receive for these awards. Within this context, the extent to which students will be able to realize this potential credit will depend on the closeness of fit or articulation between the HNC/D and the degree programme applied for and also the policy and judgement of the academic staff in the HEI to which application is made. There is a wide variety of practice across the sector in this context. In many cases HNC/D programmes are now being designed with articulation arrangements in mind. In other cases HEIs are designing level SD3 programmes specifically for articulation with existing HNDs. In some cases institutional CATS arrangements within the HEI are being used to design individual degree programmes within which maximum credit for an HNC/D may be awarded. In some cases these arrangements are being facilitated by wider institutional arrangements for credit-based learning, including links between the HEI and FECs.

The establishment of SCOTCATS as a national framework has been important in contributing to the development of a culture within tertiary education which encourages the development of degree programmes drawing on a range of provision, including that of both the FECs and HEIs. This is likely to be increased further given the current work taking place in relation to SCOTCATS and the emerging vocational qualifications structure in Scotland.

Funding for further and higher education in Scotland

The funding system in Scotland is different from that which exists in England, and this has helped to shape the distinctive pattern of developments in Scotland. Core funding for all work, including higher education, in FECs in Scotland comes from the SOED, while the HEIs are funded through the Scottish Higher Education Funding Council (SHEFC). This contrasts with England, where the HEFC funds all higher education work in both HEIs and FECs. The full impact of these different funding systems on the development of links is difficult to assess without systematic investigation, which has not yet taken place. To date it seems to have contributed to a situation in Scotland where there are relatively few links between FECs and HEIs that involve substantial transfer of resources. It should, however, be noted that SHEFC has stated that funding mechanisms should not act as a barrier to fruitful collaboration (SHEFC 1993). The direct funding of HE in the FECs by the SOED has also permitted them to carry on with a very rapid expansion of this level of work in recent years, when the universities were already working within a climate of 'consolidation', although FECs are now also being required to work within a similar policy of consolidation (Tables 7.1 and 7.2).

The role of the HEIs in developing FE–HE links

One important element in shaping the development of links between FECs and HEIs has been the policy and role of the HEIs. Whereas in England a number of universities seem to have been fairly proactive in developing franchising links with the FECs, this pattern has been less common in Scotland. The majority of links have been developed in the context of staff in FECs seeking to establish articulation agreements that will allow their students to progress into a degree course in an HEI after completion of an HNC/D. However, a number of the universities have actively sought to establish strong collaborative relationships at a course or institutional level. While this represents only a small proportion of the links that currently exist, the examples of strong relationships which have been established, and the implications of these for future developments, are of considerable interest and will be discussed below.

Possible explanations for the fact that the Scottish universities have generally been less proactive in pursuing franchising, or similar links, may reflect their recognition of the encouragement that FECs were receiving, through SOED and SCOTVEC, to develop their own HE provision, and that links should be based on these nationally recognized qualifications. The separate funding arrangements also provided little incentive for close collaboration. The higher proportions of school pupils achieving university entrance level qualifications, and progressing to higher education, may be a further factor that has resulted in HEIs in Scotland being less active in seeking to establish new markets of this kind. However, given the need for further research, these explanations can only be seen as tentative at this point.

FEC and HEI links in Scotland

Having considered the contextual factors which have helped to shape the FE–HE links, the nature and extent of these links will now be considered in detail. It is helpful initially to perceive the links between the HEIs and FECs in relation to course-related links and institutional links.

Course links

The majority of links between HEIs and FECs in Scotland have been established at the level of individual courses and take a variety of forms, including articulation, joint provision, validation, franchising and subcontracting (SHEFC 1993; HEQC 1995). In most cases these links are based on SCOTVEC HNC/D provision, and the dominance of articulation as the principal foundation of course relationships in Scotland has already been emphasized. However, a number of institutions with extensive collaborative arrangements are involved in more than one type of course relationship. There is also a considerable blurring at the edges between the different types of relationship, and there is frequently a development over time from one category to another. The main types of relationships and their characteristics are outlined below (HEQC 1995).

Articulation
Articulation is the most common form of link between FECs and HEIs in Scotland. In a recent survey of FE–HE links in Scotland, 80 per cent of responding FECs reported some form of articulation relationship, and in a number of cases multiple links had been established (Gallacher *et al.* 1995). These arrangements have been made most commonly between HNC/Ds and degree/honours degree programmes. While FECs have been keen to establish these links as a means of providing opportunities for progression for their students, SCOTVEC's requirement, that evidence should be provided of the opportunities for students to progress to employment or further study on completion of an HNC/D, has created additional pressure to establish these agreements. The nature of these relationships varies considerably both within and between institutions.

In a number of cases formal agreements have been established, and these may specify a number of guaranteed places that will be available for students who successfully complete the HNC/D. In some cases it may be agreed that students should undertake some additional enhancement material, or additional assessments, if they are to progress into the next year of the degree programme. This will depend on judgements which are made about the closeness of fit between the content of the HNC/D and the degree programme. In other cases the agreements are more informal, and have emerged out of a history of cooperation between the staff within the FEC and HEI over a number of years. The formal relationships seem more likely to emerge in discipline areas where there is a high demand for student places and it is necessary to establish clear ground-rules for progression. There is also considerable variation in whether students progress into the next year of the degree programme, or lose a year in the process of transfer. This may again be associated with the closeness of fit between the content of the programmes, although there also appears to be variation among students progressing as part of the same agreement.

In addition to specific course-based articulation agreements there are individual articulation arrangements negotiated through the CATS and combined studies frameworks of some HEIs, as discussed above.

Joint provision
Agreements to develop joint provision are still relatively rare in Scotland. It appears that about 10 per cent of FECs have established relationships of this kind (Gallacher *et al.* 1995). As with articulation, these arrangements take a number of different forms, even within the one institution, depending upon the history of the relationships at course level. In almost all cases they will involve a formal agreement between the institutions. In some cases they will involve joint development and delivery of degree programmes, while in others third-year degree programmes are built on existing HNDs. In some of these arrangements students move between institutions at different stages of their study, while in others the students are able to complete their studies within the FEC. Responsibility in relation to assessment will be shared on an agreed basis. The HEI is responsible for validation and ultimately, therefore, for quality assurance, although this will be related to the internal quality assurance processes of the FEC.

Validation
There are also a few cases where the collaboration may best be seen as a validation arrangement, rather than joint provision, because there has been little active involvement of the HEI in the curriculum development or arrangements for teaching. It does, however, remain responsible for the validation process and revalidation on a periodic basis. In a small number of cases this approach has been used to build a third-year degree programme on an HND. Relationships of this kind are relatively rare outside the joint provision discussed above.

Franchising
Franchising of programmes developed by an HEI to an FEC is undertaken on a relatively limited basis. While 45 per cent of FECs reported links of this kind, few of these are strong links involving significant numbers of students (Gallacher *et al.* 1995). In five of the FECs the franchise reported was the same HNC in applied sciences that has been developed by one of the universities. In this case the university does not itself run the HNC, but

is using it as an access route into the second level of various science degree programmes. In a number of other cases, while a formal franchise relationship has been established, the numbers of students who have actually been enrolled on courses have remained small. This figure of 45 per cent therefore gives an impression of more activity than has actually taken place, and the franchising of degree programmes remains a very limited aspect of the links between FECs and HEIs in Scotland. Included in this figure are recent limited developments associated with the franchising of degrees from English HEIs. Given the differences between degree structures in England and Scotland, this gives rise to a number of interesting issues, which will require further investigation if these developments become established as a feature of the Scottish scene.

Subcontracting
In these cases one institution subcontracts the teaching of a minor part of a course component to another institution. An example of this would be where a skills element within an engineering degree is taught within a neighbouring FEC. This type of relationship is also relatively uncommon.

Institutional links

Associated with the links at course level, institutional links have begun to emerge. These vary considerably in their strength and significance. While, in general, course-based links have been more important in shaping developments, there are now a number of cases in which institutional frameworks have become increasingly important in creating the context within which course level links are emerging. However, there are difficulties in describing and classifying these links because of the problems in identifying clearly defined categories of the kind associated with course level links. Furthermore, the same term may be used differently in different institutions. Given these qualifications, the following types of relationship can be identified.

Affiliate colleges
Affiliate colleges represent the strongest level of link to have emerged so far. This category of relationship has been clearly identified by one of the universities, and there are indications that others are moving towards a similar type of relationship, although they may not currently use this terminology. This involves an agreement at institutional level to work together in the joint development of a broad range of provision. This has included: articulation agreements; guaranteed places; joint course planning, development and delivery; and agreements on access for staff and students to facilities and services. It involves an element of exclusivity, in that the FECs are not expected to establish similar relationships with other HEIs. One university that has established a strong policy of affiliate college links has

initially formed this relationship with three FECs. These colleges are ones with a relatively high degree of specialization in higher education work in areas complementary to the university, and with a history of cooperation between the two institutions. The links have already formed the basis for a considerable level of cooperation across a range of issues, and it is expected that there will be a continuing process of development between these institutions.

Community college consortium

An alternative form of link that has emerged is a city consortium involving five community colleges and two universities. This has involved an agreement to work together in developing linked educational opportunities. However, there is no principle of exclusivity involved in these relationships. Progress towards joint developments appears to have been somewhat slower than with the affiliate colleges, and this may reflect the range of institutions and interests involved.

Associate colleges

Associate colleges have been designated by some universities. These also involve the agreement to work collaboratively to establish further opportunities for students. There is again no agreement regarding exclusivity. The obligations and responsibilities of the partners in these relationships seem to be relatively loosely defined, and it is difficult, at the moment, to identify major developments associated with these links.

Others

In addition to these categories of institutional relationships, a number of other formal links have begun to emerge at an institutional level, which underpin and support the course-based links.

One of the most interesting examples of these links has been the institutional agreements between universities and FECs to collaborate in the provision of third-year unclassified degree programmes. It would appear that these agreements are based upon existing HNDs, and will be delivered in the FEC. This type of development is clearly of considerable significance, both because of the opportunities it creates for FECs to offer degree level courses in their own right, under the auspices of the university, and because of the increased opportunities it can provide for students, particularly in areas which are relatively remote from the universities, and where travel would be a problem for some student groups, particularly adults.

In a number of other cases institutions have entered into formal agreements as part of articulation agreements. These will specify formally guaranteed numbers and conditions that must be met by students who wish to progress.

Institutional links are therefore becoming an increasingly important dimension of the relationships between FECs and HEIs, and the significance of these links for future developments will be discussed further below.

Retrospect

Implications for Students of FE–HE links

As indicated above, there has been a very rapid growth in higher education provision in the FECs in recent years. There is now a significant number of students who have already completed their HNC/Ds in FECs; however, at present, few systematic data are available regarding their experience within the FECs and since leaving. Initial investigation of this growth has indicated that a significant number of these students are undertaking these courses with a view to obtaining qualifications that will allow them to progress to degree level study. The experiences of these students are now being investigated as part of a national study of FE–HE links in Scotland. In the meantime, however, a number of issues associated with these developments can be identified.

First, there is the question of how satisfactory the links are as mechanisms which allow students to progress to degree level study. Given that most links between FECs and HEIs are based on articulation agreements, some of which are relatively loose and informal, there are often no guarantees that students will find suitable places in HEIs. While it is clear that a significant number of students have now progressed from the FECs to the HEIs, there are no systematic data regarding the scale of the transfers and the extent to which the arrangements that have been established are satisfactory in meeting the needs of the students involved. There is some evidence that in a number of cases HNCs are providing entry to the first year of degree programmes, rather than progress to year 2. In some cases this may be appropriate, if the content of the HNC does not fit closely with the first year of the student's chosen degree programme. It may also be that in some cases the students chose to enter year 1 within the HEI because of expected difficulties associated with transition to degree level study. Further investigation of these issues is required.

Second, there are issues associated with the transition of students from the learning experience associated with FECs and SCOTVEC HNC/D programmes, with an emphasis on competence in the achievement of specified learning outcomes through a criterion-referenced system, to the more traditional norm-referenced systems that operate in HEIs. In some cases additional bridging material and assessment has been built into the FEC courses, but it is not clear at present how extensive this practice has been, or how necessary it is for the success of the students who make the transition. In this respect a crucial question concerns the success of the FECs and HEIs in helping the students to develop study skills and the characteristics of independent learners. Related to these issues is the need to examine the question of the success of these students within the HEIs, and, if possible, their further careers after graduation. The limited evidence so far available would indicate that these students are reasonably successful, but again systematic data are required.

Third, there are issues associated with the social characteristics of the students involved. It is clear that a significant number of higher education students in FECs are adult returners. In 1993, 64.9 per cent of all entrants to higher education courses in FECs were aged 21 or over (SOED 1995a), and while the age profiles for those transferring to HEIs are not available, it seems likely that a large number will be adult returners. Beyond this there is little systematic data at present regarding the social and educational characteristics of these students, and the extent to which these courses are being successful, not only in increasing access, but also in widening access to higher education.

In addition to these issues associated with students and their experiences, there is perhaps some merit in making brief reference to issues associated with quality assurance. The earlier discussion in this chapter highlighted the role of SCOTVEC in quality assurance arrangements for higher education within the FECs. Increasingly in the post-1992 era, FECs have been developing their own internal quality assurance arrangements, which will support and facilitate the granting of devolved authority to a varying extent under SCOTVEC's quality framework. For those FECs with substantial elements of higher education and links to HEIs this is providing valuable opportunities for the integration of quality assurance systems to support their overall missions. This may facilitate an increasing level of FEC–HEI interaction as appropriate systems can be designed for this purpose. The quality assurance arrangements within the FECs are subject to SCOTVEC's quality audit processes, while the collaborative provision in the FECs, for which the HEIs are responsible, is subject to the quality audit arrangements for collaborative provision of the HEQC.

Prospect

A number of important issues can be identified at national, institutional and course level that will be of importance in shaping the future development of these links.

The impact of 'consolidation' of full-time higher education in FECs

The SOED introduced, in December 1994, a policy of 'consolidation' with regard to full-time higher education courses in the FECs (SOED 1994a). In the letter announcing this policy the SOED also referred to the importance of developing more part-time provision. These announcements mirror similar policies already established within the HEI sector. It has been shown above that the FECs have used the development of full-time higher education courses as an important means of developing new student markets in recent years and that rapid expansion of full-time HNC/D provision has resulted. The rapid growth in this independent higher education provision has clearly been an important priority for FECs and has helped to shape the FE–HE links that have emerged. However, further developments of this kind will not be possible while this policy of 'consolidation' is in force. This can therefore be expected to create new pressures for change in the relationships with HEIs. In some cases this may result in the building of closer relationships with the HEIs; in other cases it may lead to the exploration of new opportunities in part-time education.

New partnerships between FECs and HEIs

It was indicated above that the majority of links between FECs and HEIs have been established through articulation agreements. In many of these links it is doubtful whether the concept of partnership is the appropriate one to describe what has been established. Some other concept, such as collaboration or cooperation, may be more appropriate. However, reference has also been made to a number of different and closer forms of relationship that have been established. At an institutional level the affiliate college links which have been established are the most striking example and it appears that other universities may be seeking similar types of relationships. There has also been the establishment of the community college consortium. Reference has been made to the establishment of the agreements between universities and FECs to validate the third level of several degree programmes that will be delivered in the FECs. With respect to franchising an important development has been the establishment by one of the universities of an HNC programme in applied sciences, which it has franchised to five FECs. In all these cases the concept of partnership is probably a more appropriate one, because of the much closer working relationships that have been established between the institutions involved. Looking to the future, it seems likely that there will be further development of these partnership relationships, which will be shaped by a number of factors.

First, one effect of 'consolidation' in both the FEC and HEI sectors will be to encourage institutions to find new opportunities for development, and partnerships of this kind can potentially be advantageous to institutions in both sectors.

Second, this is still a period of rapid change and development for many FECs, in which they are establishing their identities post-incorporation. Some of these colleges are increasingly seeing their future in the development of higher education, and a 'polytechnic group' of colleges has now been established. A number of these colleges are likely to welcome increasingly close links with the HEIs as a means of developing and strengthening their higher education provision. Indeed, in some cases the possibility of some form of merger with an HEI seems possible, particularly since there is at present a relatively large number of separate FECs in Scotland. However, most of the colleges see themselves as continuing to provide a range of educational opportunities for the communities they serve, and some have consciously adopted the term 'community college' in describing themselves. For colleges in this group an important factor will be to open as wide a range of opportunities as possible to their student groups, and to provide routes into and through the system of qualifications, beginning at the return to study or pre-access level, and continuing through to degree level. Closer links with the HEIs can clearly be of advantage to them in developing the full range of opportunities. However, it seems likely that in developing these links colleges will wish to build on their existing HNC/D provision, rather than develop extensive franchising. Many colleges see this as a way of maintaining their independence and keeping open the widest range of opportunities for both themselves and their students. Within this group of colleges, future mergers also seem a possibility, and this could shape the development of these colleges and their FE–HE links.

Third, there are questions relating to the future shape of higher education provision, which is currently a specific dimension of the review of higher education that is being undertaken by the Secretary of State for Education. Not only is this an area where the answers are uncertain; it is also one where the right questions are still being identified. However, a number of interesting trends have already emerged: there are many initiatives in work-based learning currently under way; the professional bodies, employers and HEIs are identifying new ways of jointly providing programmes of continuing professional development; financial pressures and consolidation may increase significantly the importance of part-time provision; the development of the SCOTCATS framework and the expansion of modular structures are increasingly providing a context where coherent customized programmes are being developed within the context of a wide range of learning opportunities. One response to these developments is that award frameworks are becoming superimposed on different types of learning opportunities. Within this context the development of Scottish Vocational Qualifications (SVQs) and General Scottish Vocational Qualifications (GSVQs) may provide parallel and linking credit routes within higher education, although currently their impact is uncertain. To some significant extent these developments can be seen to be reflected in developments associated with *Higher Still*, the new proposals for a post-compulsory award structure of Highers and Advanced Highers in Scotland (SOED 1994b).

Within this broad context there are interesting prospects for different forms of working between the FECs and HEIs, which build upon their existing partnerships and strengths. The close relationships between FECs and local employers, and their experience in relation to SVQ and GSVQ development may provide experience that will be valuable as these initiatives begin to impact more on higher levels. If the changing shape of higher education is related to supporting individuals who are engaged in a process of lifelong learning following some initial period of full-time study, then the future relationships between FECs and HEIs are likely to become more complex as each focuses on different but interrelated aspects of the emerging comprehensive credit framework.

Fourth, it seems likely that the role of the SOED will be of importance in shaping these developments. While in the period leading up to and since incorporation it adopted a relatively *laissez-faire* approach, in which market forces were allowed to shape development and growth in the sector, there are signs that it is increasingly interested in intervening and helping to shape the processes of development and change. The introduction of the policy of 'consolidation' and its impact have already been discussed. During 1994 the SOED also began a consultation exercise, in which it sought views on the development of FE–HE links. This resulted in the publication of a circular in April 1995, which provides a framework for the development of links between FECs and HEIs (SOED 1995b). While this recognizes that formal links can be of benefit to students by assisting progress, it also specifies criteria to be considered in forming these links, and requires colleges to provide evidence that these criteria have been considered. The circular also stipulates that written approval will be required from the SOED for new degree courses, and for links with HEIs which are 'intended to effect any material change in the character of a college, for example a change involving joint planning of all higher education provision between a college and an HEI'. It also states that a proposal to merge an FEC with an HEI will require formal approval. The SOED can also influence developments through its funding policies, and at the time of writing a new formula for funding is being introduced within the FE sector. The long-term impact of this new system on college budgets is still not clear, but it seems likely that it will influence decisions about the balance of provision within FEIs, and indirectly may help to shape FE–HE links.

In summary, it is clear that while FE–HE links are currently an important feature of educational provision in Scotland, and that they have emerged in a form which is significantly different from that in England, the next few years may see further interesting lines of development, in which new forms of partnerships between HEIs and FECs may become increasingly central. However, it also seems likely that these will continue to be shaped by the distinctive features of the Scottish educational landscape.

References

Gallacher, J., Alexander, H., Leahy, J. and Yule, W. (1995) *Links between Further and Higher Education in Scotland: an Analysis of Recent Developments.* Glasgow, Centre for Continuing Education, Glasgow Caledonian University.

Higher Education Quality Council (1995) *Aspects of FE/HE Collaborative Links in Scotland.* London, HEQC.

Higher Education Quality Council/Committee of Scottish Higher Education Principals (1995) *The SCOTCAT Quality Assurance Handbook 1995.* Glasgow, HEQC.

Scottish Education Department (1988) *Scottish Wider Access Programme.* Edinburgh, Scottish Education Department.

Scottish Higher Education Funding Council (1993) *The Future Funding of Collaborative Courses Involving Higher Education Institutions and Further Education Colleges*, Circular letter no. 46/93 and attachment, August. Edinburgh, SHEFC.

Scottish Office (1991) *Access and Opportunity*, Cm 1530. Edinburgh, HMSO.

Scottish Office Education Department (1993) *Review of the Scottish Wider Access Programme*. Edinburgh, Scottish Office Education Department.

Scottish Office Education Department (1994a) *Letter to Principals of All Scottish Further Education Colleges*, December. Edinburgh, Scottish Office Education Department.

Scottish Office Education Department (1994b) *Higher Still – Opportunity for All*. Edinburgh, HMSO.

Scottish Office Education Department (1995a) Statistics on students in further education colleges, unpublished data, Scottish Office Education Department, Edinburgh.

Scottish Office Education Department (1995b) *The Provision of Higher Education by Further Education Colleges*, Circular (FE) 9/95. Edinburgh, Scottish Office Education Department.

8

The International Dimension

Peter Lines and Kate Clarke

Introduction

This chapter will examine in some detail the issues relating to academic quality in collaborative provision of programmes of study between United Kingdom universities and international partner institutions. The terms 'accreditation', 'validation' and 'franchising' are used to describe the nature of the collaborative provision and follow broadly the definitions used by the Higher Education Quality Council (1995).

The rapidly growing involvement of United Kingdom universities in such international collaborative provision has not been without controversy. Indeed, it has been claimed that the international reputation of British university degrees is being undermined amid allegations of widespread malpractice (*The Observer* 12 June 1994). While it is no doubt true that a small number of partnerships have presented problems, there are many others that have proved highly successful. It is paradoxical that instances of actions taken by UK universities to preserve quality and standards (in the extreme by withdrawing from a particular partnership) are often precisely those cited as evidence for malpractice! There are also clear and continuing tensions between highly restricted systems of higher education and those which are more widely accessible. These tensions are found not only within the UK but also across international boundaries, which can contribute to further misunderstandings. Nevertheless, there is now sufficient experience and expertise in international collaborations to enable us to highlight some of the concerns and the pitfalls, and to share good practice.

The HEQC offers guidelines for good practice. Part of its remit is to undertake quality audits of institutions engaged in collaborative arrangements and a recent report (HEQC 1994) reviews the lessons to be learned from the first wave of such audits. In addition, a longstanding and growing influence in the sector is the Council of Validating Universities (CVU). Originally constituted from the universities that had used their powers as awarding bodies to validate programmes at other institutions, the CVU has grown dramatically since 1992, and now has 78 member institutions, representing the full range and diversity of UK higher education and a number of professional and statutory bodies. In 1994 it published a code of practice on validation (CVU 1994), which is endorsed by the CVCP and HEQC and is currently being revised to include guidance on overseas collaboration. In short, the sector is well aware of the special challenges for quality assurance posed by overseas collaboration and is actively and vigorously seeking to identify and disseminate good practice. This debate and the emerging principles which have been identified through the work of the HEQC and CVU therefore informs much of what follows, though it is also based on the authors' experiences of working through a growing range of collaborative contexts.

Whatever the nature of the collaboration, there are two fundamental principles which must be observed and encapsulated within formal memoranda of agreement. The first is the preservation of academic quality and standards, as evidenced through, for example, the curriculum, staffing and resource support, teaching and learning methods and assessment. Such issues will be familiar to UK academic staff who will be setting up the partnership, but nevertheless are set in a different context and need considerable care and attention. The second principle is that of responsibility for the care of students who will be studying a considerable distance from the awarding university, and often within a very different educational and social culture. This can present issues that may be much less obvious, and it is important that every effort is made to identify them at an early stage.

Should a partnership collapse – for example, for financial, political or legal reasons – the implication for the university will be substantial, not least in its responsibility to find ways of allowing students (perhaps in substantial numbers) to complete their studies.

Growth in international collaboration

The past few years have seen substantial growth in collaborative provision of programmes of study between UK universities and overseas institutions, predominantly in Europe and in South East Asia. The provision covers a wide range of subject areas (perhaps with particular emphasis on business and engineering) and all academic levels from foundation years to postgraduate. A recent survey (CVU 1995) indicated over 22,000 students undertaking programmes of study overseas and registered with over 70 UK degree-awarding institutions, but these figures are almost certainly an understatement.

Some UK universities have been active in this field for many years, but the recent growth demonstrates a welcome international dimension to the UK higher education scene. It has been prompted by the large growth in demand for higher education across the world, and by the realization that many UK programmes can be adapted relatively easily to meet the needs

of other countries. Given the diminishing public funding of higher education in the UK, collaborative programmes also represent income generating opportunities; there are, however, considerable dangers in such a
perspective, which we shall return to later in this chapter. Nevertheless,
these activities can lead on to a growth in international student and staff
exchanges, joint development of new programmes, joint research activities
and the internationalization of UK higher education, all of which may
contribute to greater international understanding and cooperation in other
areas.

The present growth also reflects the lack of opportunity for access to
higher education across the world. Many countries still have very restricted
access to state-funded higher education. This often leads to a range of
private institutions which are meeting some of the demand for degree level
education but are not entitled to award degrees. Such providers look to
other countries – typically Australia, Canada, the UK or the United States
of America – to validate their provision, to offer progression to other awards
or to operate franchised provision.

Clearly, UK institutions must remain sensitive to the potential for accu-
sations of a new kind of cultural imperialism. Respect for the educational
culture of the partner institution is an important prerequisite for any
successful partnership. This is a sensitive area: it is, after all, UK qualifications
which are sought and which are to be awarded, and the quality and standards
of which must be maintained. It will be essential, therefore, that the partner
institution understands from an early stage of discussion that it will necessarily
be subject to some distinctively British educational or quality assurance
requirements, which may be unfamiliar. The honours classification system
and the use of external examiners are just two examples. There are, however,
benefits for the UK system; in seeking to articulate such features to overseas
partners, we are being forced to re-examine them ourselves.

Assessing prospective partners

All collaborative programmes will require a thorough assessment of the
prospective partner institution, and this can be a difficult task. Initial assessments made at an early stage are often crucial; they should involve at
least one visit from senior academic staff in the discipline concerned, and
should be informed by all available information about the institution and
the culture and context in which it operates. A mistaken judgement at this
stage can be very costly in terms of development time and loss of goodwill
if the proposal subsequently has to be abandoned. It is usual for the partner
institution to cover the costs of this initial visit, though this has to be largely
a matter of judgement in individual developments. In establishing a partnership, a university will wish to be assured that the partner institution:

- Is of good reputation and standing.
- Is a well found, financially stable, institution with effective management
  and administrative staffing systems.

- Offers an ethos and culture appropriate to higher education.
- Has effective quality assurance and quality control systems in operation.
- Has the appropriate specialist staff expertise available to support the proposed scheme of study.
- Has the appropriate mechanisms and resources available to identify and implement staff development.
- Has the appropriate general and specialist resources available to support the proposed scheme of study.

The relative attention to be given to each will, of course, vary from proposal to proposal and from institution to institution. Nevertheless, assurance is needed on all these issues, even where the institution is part of government-funded provision.

It is particularly important to establish clearly, at the outset, the place of the institution in the country's system of higher education, and the extent of any legal restrictions on its activities. It is quite normal for degree-awarding powers within particular countries to be restricted to universities, but there may be further legal limitations on other institutions in respect of collaborative activities that lead to an award through franchised or validated programmes, and there may be distinctions between public and private providers in this respect. It is also possible that the institution, or the UK university, may be bound by exclusivity agreements as part of other collaborations.

Even if there are no legal limitations there may well be other pressures, exerted, for example, by government policies or by key personalities, which can cause substantial difficulties. For example, if a government is not well disposed towards franchising or validation operations it might react by removing the UK partner from the list of preferred UK universities for its overseas students! It is also important to ascertain at this stage whether there are any pending or planned changes in relevant government policies, and what effect any change of government might have. It is often not possible to gain definitive answers to such questions, but all information is helpful in assessing the costs and benefits of the collaboration, and in safe-guarding the interests of prospective students.

Many UK universities employ their own staff with professional expertise in international matters, and bodies such as the British Council and the United Kingdom Council for Overseas Student Affairs can be valuable sources of information. There are also professional agents, often retained inde-pendently by several different universities, who can be used to develop contacts with potential partner institutions.

In consideration of prospective partners there is a natural tendency to concentrate heavily on academic judgements. However, it is essential that the academic programme is set in a context which is administratively and financially sound, and for this reason administrative and financial audits should be undertaken. With many institutions these will be very sensitive issues and need to be handled with tact and diplomacy.

Administrative audit

The purposes of administrative audit are: (a) to evaluate the organizational structure and the administrative support provided to staff and students; and (b) to evaluate the integrity and robustness of student administration systems. Such issues are often taken for granted in established universities, but they are areas where there is considerable scope for error, misrepresentation or fraud, unless there are high integrity systems which are effectively managed and controlled. It is not necessary to expect the partner institution to replicate all the many and varied administrative systems of UK universities, but there must be appropriate systems in place to safeguard standards and the interests of students.

For example, there have been a number of cases where overseas institutions have issued substantial, and sometimes misleading, marketing material well in advance of any formal approval for the collaboration. Students have been offered firm places on a course leading to an MBA of the University of Poppleton even though the partner institution was well aware that the franchise was unlikely to be approved. When subsequently told that the course is not available, students naturally become very angry and have been known to threaten legal action; such anger and threats may then be used by them through the partner institution to pressurize the university. A similar response may be prompted by misrepresentation of rights of progression to study in the UK.

Such misrepresentations may result from over-enthusiasm on the part of the partner institution, misunderstanding of what has been said by UK staff, or a deliberate attempt to pressurize the UK university. Whatever the cause, the effects can all too easily be to mislead prospective students, to damage the reputations of both partners and to prejudice the development of an effective partnership.

The student admissions, registration and records processes must be such as to assure the university that there are, for example, mechanisms for verifying the entry qualifications of students, for monitoring attendance and for keeping accurate and secure records of assessment, progression and award.

UK universities have very well established systems and procedures for the conduct of examinations and the setting and marking of examination papers. Many overseas institutions will have similar systems and procedures, but some may be less accustomed to the requirements for absolute integrity and security. It is a *sine qua non* that any university entering into partnership with an overseas institution ensures that all procedures associated with examinations and assessment are acceptable to the university and comparable with its own principles and practices.

Administrative audit does not necessarily need to be a single concentrated activity at a particular point in time. The process by which a collaborative activity is set up will typically extend over several months, and evidence and information can be gathered throughout that process, by academic and/or administrative staff of the UK university. What matters is that there should be a checklist of items which the university will need to investigate and on which it will need to be satisfied before final approval can be given. In cases where the partner institution is part of state-funded provision, the process may be relatively straightforward; for private providers it may be more problematical, and it is often advisable to arrange a separate visit or visits to consider such administrative matters.

Financial audit

Financial audit seeks to ensure that the partner institution has a sound financial base and appropriate financial processes and controls, with integrity of operation, before proceeding to approval. It is important to recognize that students recruited in collaborative programmes will normally be registered students of the UK university, and that the university will have obligations to enable them to complete their studies should the partner institution run into financial or management difficulties.

Financial audit may be unnecessary in the case of partner institutions that are part of state-funded provision. Private providers, however, may vary from the very small and simple to the very large and comprehensive. Bankers' references may be sought, together with copies of annual accounts, to establish financial viability. A local branch of a Western bank or independent accountants may also be used for audit. However, it is not unknown for such requests to be reciprocated and for UK university accounts to be compared unfavourably with those of the prospective partners!

Financial control mechanisms also need examination. Payments to the UK university will normally be based in part on the fee income of the partner institution, and it is therefore essential that the university knows how tuition fees are invoiced and how payments are monitored.

Cultural issues

Many international collaborative programmes operate in cultures that are quite different from those in the UK. Differences will arise in curriculum, in teaching and learning methods, in national law and in student and staff expectations and relationships. The resolution of such differences is seldom simple, and it is often neither possible nor desirable simply to impose UK values and cultures on a collaborative programme. It is for each university to decide what the key issues that must be implemented are, and these should normally be those which directly affect academic standards.

A general question that each UK university entering into overseas collaborations will have to address sooner or later is which of its regulations apply to the collaborating institution, its students and staff, and which do not. Many universities have complex and detailed ordinances, policies and regulations, most of them developed and instituted without reference to collaboration. There may, for example, be policies and regulations related to issues such as equal opportunities or ethics, which may present particular problems of conflict with national policies or religious practices. A certain degree of equity may be necessary; for example, while it may not be possible to implement a policy of equal opportunities for the admission of students because of external constraints, a denial of equality of rights and opportunities in for example, assessment and examination would not be acceptable.

Universities may also have to face difficult moral decisions; for example, on the extent to which they are willing to enter partnerships in countries where there are no formal UK government restrictions on collaboration, but where human rights are known to be an issue of concern. The challenge in such cases is whether to work through partnerships to promote change, or whether to reject partnerships unless, and until, change occurs. Such decisions should be taken consciously by the university as an academic community, and as an integral part of its quality assurance processes.

The teaching curriculum of a collaborative programme may well need modification to reflect the cultural values, traditions and needs of the native students. One might expect that legal aspects would normally be taught in the context of the country's own legal system unless there are particular requirements to cover English law. Similarly, the technologies taught in an engineering course might well be modified to match the specific needs and industries of the country concerned.

In the case of vocational programmes, it is particularly important to ensure that any difficulties likely to arise with national employment law and professional bodies are recognized at an early stage. It cannot be assumed that graduates will qualify for a licence to practise in the UK and/or the country concerned; restrictions on such licences are often very substantial, particularly in areas such as the health professions. Reference has already been made to the potential for misleading students, and it is important for the university to make it clear from the outset that it must approve all promotional material associated with programmes leading to its awards.

Development of collaborative programmes

The most common form of international collaboration is the franchising of programmes which are already well established in the UK university, although they may sometimes be newly designed specifically to meet the needs of the partner institution. This section will focus on the development of franchised programmes as a model, but the issues raised will be applicable across all forms of collaborative provision.

The suggestion for franchising may arise as a market opportunity perceived by staff of the UK university, or as a request from a prospective partner institution. In either case the initial stages are crucial, and represent expectation management. It is essential that both sides have a clear understanding of what is required, of the constraints within which any programme(s) will operate, and a broad outline of the expected financial arrangements and the areas to be covered by the memorandum of agreement. Both institutions need to be clear about the timescale and mechanism of the approval processes; it is not unusual for those (on both sides) with little experience of such processes to assume that they are largely a formality and can be achieved in a very short timescale. Such assumptions are dangerous because they may lead to false expectations, premature marketing and loss of goodwill. It is helpful to involve staff having quality assurance responsibilities at an early stage.

It is good practice to ensure an early visit to the partner institution by senior key staff from the discipline area. Their role is to establish whether in their view there is a *prima facie* case that the partner institution has the required resources and capabilities to offer the proposed programme. This is, in many ways, the most important visit, because it establishes an initial level of trust and confidence for all the subsequent developments. If the situation is seen as marginal, the partner institution must be left in no doubt that this is the case and given some indication of the areas of particular concern. In any case, it must be made clear that the final decision will rest with an approval visiting party when all the development work has been completed.

Where initial discussions have proved fruitful, formal decisions to proceed with negotiations should be taken at senior management levels. This ensures that, from an early stage, both parties are fully aware of the nature of the proposal, can set it in the context of the university's strategic planning (taking account where appropriate of the progression of students to the university) and can properly assess the academic and resource implications well in advance of the preparation of the memorandum of agreement and formal approval.

The development process will normally include a number of visits, meetings and discussions between staff of the university and of the partner institution. These discussions will focus initially on the proposed curriculum and on any changes required to meet the needs of the particular students, potential employers and partner institution. If such changes are significant – or if a substantially new programme is to be designed – validation will be needed under the normal procedures of the UK university, preferably before the final franchise approval visit.

During this development phase, the staffing and other resources available are assessed against curriculum requirements. Where possible, it is useful for some staff of the partner institution to spend time at the UK university department following a planned staff development programme. This enables them to see how the resource support for the programme is organized and to participate in teaching activities. It is particularly helpful in the context of teaching and learning methods. For example, staff may well be accustomed to quite formal and traditional teaching situations and have little experience of groupwork, open-ended laboratory or design work, or the importance attached to the development of personal and interpersonal skills. Similarly, experience of assessment methods, honours classification systems, project supervision and the operation of boards of examiners may be useful features. Where necessary, such staff development programmes may be extended into the early years of operation of the programme.

The assessment of physical resources available to support the programme will obviously include laboratory and workshop facilities and equipment where relevant. The availability of library and computing facilities is also very important, but needs to be assessed in the context and culture of the partner institution. The UK concept of substantial centralized facilities should not necessarily be seen as the only model. For example, some partner institutions may have relatively poor library facilities of their own, but their students might have access to a major university library in the same city. Some private providers may make it a condition of admission that each student purchases a personal computer and/or a particular set of books. Nevertheless, the expectations and provisions must be clearly understood.

Most UK universities would then proceed to a final franchise approval visit. However, such visits should not normally take place unless there is a reasonable expectation of approval, or unless the institution has been clearly warned that there are still outstanding concerns. Partner institutions will inevitably seek to impress by providing good hospitality for visiting parties and firmness can be needed in ensuring that all aspects of the programme are fully covered.

The CVU code of practice offers guidance on the composition of visiting parties for validation. It is good practice for the visiting party to have a measure of independence and, for this reason, many universities require a chairperson who is a senior academic from another discipline within the university. In some cases a similar independent member from the partner institution may also be appropriate. A member external to the university and the partner institution should be involved, preferably one who has a knowledge of the discipline and experience of higher education in both the UK and the country concerned, though it must be acknowledged that such individuals are a rare breed. There may also be a need for language skills if part of the programme is to be taught in the native language.

Where external panel members are nominated by partner institutions, it is essential that the university is satisfied that they have the appropriate expertise and can act impartially. If a fee is to be paid, this should come from the university and not from the partner. The party will also benefit from the inclusion of one or more university staff who have been involved in the development phase, have gained a detailed knowledge of the partner institution and will be involved in ongoing operation of the programme. In due course the university may be able to build a team of staff with experience and expertise in international collaboration, and to network experience across the sector.

The franchise approval visit should be a formal and fully recorded event, informed by prior documentation about the proposed programme and details of the partner institution. Documentation must include a definitive document describing the programme aims, objectives, curriculum and assessment regulations. The volume of documentation required may vary substantially depending on the magnitude of the proposal, the university's knowledge of the partner institution and the university's quality assurance requirements. The franchise approval report should contain a summary of the substantive issues that have arisen during the visit together with clear statements of all conditions attached to the approval. Approval is given for a specified period, normally not more than five years.

It is good practice for the memorandum of agreement to be included in the validation documentation for discussion. It should have been substantially finalized by this time, and can be ratified for formal signature subsequently.

Memoranda of agreement

The memorandum of agreement – other terms may be used – represents the legal contract between the UK university and the partner institution. It must therefore set out clearly and unambiguously the rights and responsibilities of the parties, the financial and administrative arrangements, the means by which academic standards are to be maintained and the rights of students. As with most legal documents it may only be called on *in extremis*, but must then cover every eventuality. In the space available here, it is not possible to cover fully all aspects of the contents of memoranda of agreement; however, it may be helpful to indicate the broad areas that should be considered.

There is a need for a clear statement of the purpose of the agreement and of definitions and interpretations of terms used, some of which may be unfamiliar to partner institutions.

The rights and obligations of both parties must be stated, together with the ownership of the intellectual property. The rights of students and graduates should be identified, including, for example, any rights of access to university facilities and services and any rights of entry to other university programmes of study.

It is essential that financial obligations and indemnities are identified, together with detailed financial agreements and arrangements under which they may be reviewed from time to time. Administrative arrangements will normally include agreement on how student number targets are to be agreed, the arrangements for applications, admissions, registration, student records examinations, conferments, awards and awards ceremonies. The nature of the award certificate and any transcript needs to be very clearly stated.

Academic issues should include details of the language to be used for teaching and assessment, arrangements for monitoring and evaluation, for making any changes to the programme, for university staff visits and involvement in teaching and staff development, for the provision of any teaching and learning materials, for the appointment and briefing of external examiners, for the setting and marking of examination papers, for the operation of boards of examiners and for student appeals. Partner institutions should be left in no doubt that the programme must be provided and assessed as described in the definitive document, and may not be changed without formal approval.

Other matters may cover the provision of library and computer services, teaching and specialist accommodation, student services and any student or staff visits to the UK university. Contractual issues will include matters such as termination arrangements, applicable laws and necessary consents and confidentiality. The memorandum will normally be drawn up and any disputes resolved under UK law.

It is important to recognize that students will not normally have access to the memorandum of agreement, and the university should ensure that appropriate summary information is made available to students on collaborative programmes, particularly in respect of the relative roles and responsibilities of the partner institution and the UK university.

Quality assurance systems

The assessment of quality assurance systems will be highly dependent on the nature of the collaborative activity.

At the level of institutional accreditation, the institution's full range of quality assurance policies, systems and procedures will be a major focus of the accreditation process. In this context there may be little difference between the accreditation of a UK institution and that of an overseas institution, except that there needs to be a willingness on the part of the UK university to work within the culture of the country concerned as far as possible, where this can be done without prejudice to academic standards.

In the case of a validation or a franchise the focus on the institution's quality assurance systems will depend on the extent to which the UK university intends to adopt a 'hands-off' approach. For example, if a programme is to be validated or franchised for a five-year period with minimal oversight this virtually amounts to institutional accreditation and should be treated accordingly.

Many franchises, and some validations, are operated with much tighter oversight by the UK university, at least in the early years. In this case it is the ongoing monitoring and evaluation of the programme that is critical. Over a period of some years this can be used to monitor how the partner institution is developing and operating its own quality systems, with a view perhaps to increased delegation of authority at some stage in the future.

It is necessary during the process leading to validation or franchising to reach agreement on the formal and informal systems to be used for monitoring and evaluation. Detailed arrangements may vary across different forms of collaboration, will depend on the university's own quality assurance systems and may develop and mature over time.

In cases where the university has a number of different collaborative arrangements with the same partner institution – for example, across a range of disciplines – it is highly desirable that a common approach be taken to requirements for monitoring and evaluation and that this be agreed at university level and clearly explained to the partner institution. Many partner institutions are not familiar with the level of formal quality assurance required in UK higher education, and an approach which is – or appears to be – different in each discipline can be confusing and unhelpful.

Similarly, the UK university should seek, where possible, to limit the extent to which different requirements are imposed on different partner institutions in this respect. Some differences in requirements may be justifiable, but a multiplicity of different arrangements can lead to uncertainty among staff at faculty and departmental level about the particular expectations for any given partner.

External examiners and assessment

External examiners should be appointed for all collaborative programmes, and the instrument of accreditation or memorandum of agreement must record how this is to be implemented. All external examiners should be required to submit annual reports in the language normal to the UK university.

In the case of accredited institutions, nominations will normally be made by the institution, but may be subject to approval by the UK university. Appointments, briefing and payment will normally be carried out by the partner institution. Annual reports are made to the partner institution and must be reviewed as part of annual course monitoring and evaluation.

For an institution to be accredited there must be total confidence in its quality assurance and quality control systems and procedures; in these circumstances it should not be necessary for the university to receive copies of external examiner reports as they are received. Instead they will be considered as part of the periodic review of institutional accreditation and/or of individual programmes, at which time the university will wish to assess how the reports have been received and what actions have been taken in respect of comments made by external examiners. The university may wish to retain the right to see any reports as and when they are submitted.

In the case of franchised programmes (and most validated programmes) it is more normal for the external examiner to be appointed and briefed by the UK university and for annual reports to be routinely sent to the university, normally through the partner institution. This facilitates close monitoring, which is particularly important in the early years of collaborative provision.

Finding appropriate high quality external examiners can present great difficulties. The examiner needs knowledge and experience in UK higher education, and at least one examiner within the team should have previous experience of external examining. However, he or she should ideally have some knowledge of higher education in the country concerned and may also need appropriate language skills. The workload and time involved can be substantially greater than a UK external examiner appointment requires. The search to identify a suitable external examiner team should therefore start at an early stage and if at all possible the nomination should be known at the time of the validation or franchise approval visit. It is good practice for at least one of the external examiner team for the university programme to have his or her duties extended to cover the equivalent franchised programme if he or she is willing.

Many overseas partner institutions may be unfamiliar with the roles, responsibilities and rights of external examiners. These must be fully explained and discussed with internal examiners at the outset, or there can be considerable tensions at the stage at which papers are set and/or results are discussed at boards of examiners.

It is not unusual for staff in new partner institutions to have little or no awareness of the UK honours classification system and to have little experience of setting and marking examination papers and other assessments against normal UK honours expectations. Marking cultures in some countries are quite drastically different; for example, staff may be used to setting examinations which routinely produce averages of 70 per cent or more (a first class honours mark in most UK degree programmes) and in which a mark of 60 per cent is considered a poor performance. In some cases marks may be based on a grading system which is commonly used in that country but is difficult to translate into honours classification.

This book is not the place to debate the merits or otherwise of various assessment and marking systems, but it is absolutely crucial that the standards of awards at the partner institutions are equivalent to those within the university's own programmes. This requires ongoing dialogue between staff of the university and those of the partner institution about all aspects of the assessment process. It requires total clarity and understanding about the nature of assessments, marking schemes and marking criteria, matters which are often regarded as intuitive within UK universities. In the early years of a collaboration a relatively high level of moderation may be necessary, both of coursework and of examinations. The language in which assessments are undertaken may well be an issue in this respect.

For all these reasons it is helpful if sample examination papers and assignments are provided for the partner institution, and if draft assessments are discussed in detail prior to submission to the external examiner. This can prove difficult in practice because of timescales, but should be given a high priority. Similarly, there must be ample time to consider and discuss marking standards and overall results prior to meetings of boards of examiners. It is good practice, at least in the early years of franchised programmes, for boards of examiners to be chaired by senior university staff who are the chairpersons of the corresponding university boards. Similarly, boards of examiners for validated programmes should be attended by or chaired by appropriate senior university staff.

Monitoring and evaluation

Formal annual monitoring and evaluation should be required for all collaborative provision. The requirements should be clearly established in the instrument of accreditation or memorandum of agreement. For accredited and many validated programmes this will follow the partner institution's own quality assurance procedures, as agreed at the time of accreditation or validation.

Many franchised and validated programmes, however, represent new experiences for partner institutions which have not previously offered degree programmes, and which may well not be familiar with UK practice in monitoring and evaluation. There is some variation of practice even across UK universities in this respect, but annual monitoring reports are now widely required.

The annual report(s) required of a partner institution should follow closely the requirements of the UK university for its own programmes, and should be owned and discussed by the course team. There is a responsibility on the UK university to ensure that details of the appropriate quality procedures are provided, and it is also helpful to provide examples of monitoring and evaluation reports as prepared within the university.

Annual reports should take account of the report(s) of the external examiner(s) and give details of actions taken to resolve any concerns. They should also contain student progression and award statistics and an account of mechanisms used to gather student feedback, together with a summary of major points raised and actions taken. When received by the UK university, reports should be considered and discussed in the same way as for the equivalent in-house programmes. If possible, a representative of the partner institution should be present for the discussion and a report of the discussion should be fed back to the course team and the management of the partner institution, with recommendations or requirements for actions considered necessary.

It is good practice for external examiners to receive copies of annual monitoring reports together with the minutes of the meeting at which they were considered.

In the early years of collaboration, informal monitoring is particularly important. For this reason there should be provision for one or more visits during the year by staff of the UK university, and perhaps for reciprocal visits by staff of the partner institution. Visits to the partner institution may provide opportunities to contribute to the teaching programme, to meet students and gain feedback from them, to discuss with staff issues relating to the curriculum, to teaching and learning methods and to assessment, and to identify needs for further staff development activities. A nominated member of academic staff at each institution should carry responsibility for operational management of the collaboration and it is helpful to establish clear terms of reference and reporting structures.

The resources required for effective monitoring and evaluation to assure a high quality programme are frequently underestimated, particularly in terms of staff time. The need for travel can be reduced by telephone, electronic mail, video conferencing and other forms of telecommunications, but there is still considerable need for personal contact, particularly in the early stages of the collaboration. University departments need to take conscious decisions to limit the number and scale of partnerships to those which can be effectively managed by academic and administrative staff, so that quality and standards can be maintained.

Retrospect

The growth in UK university involvement in international collaborative programmes through franchising, validation and accreditation has been substantial in recent years. The controversy and concern over the maintenance of standards has certainly been exaggerated but has led to misunderstandings and concerns in government circles, both in the UK and overseas. Nevertheless, a small number of programmes have run into major difficulties, and many UK universities have been on a steep learning curve. The HEQC and CVU are now beginning to facilitate the sharing of good practice and the identification of problem areas.

There has been a natural tendency to concentrate on academic issues in the development phase of collaborative programmes, but it is important to consider a wide range of cultural, administrative, financial and legal matters which should be subject to audit and included within formal memoranda of agreement, together with recognition of the university's responsibility of care to students registered for its awards.

The income earned from collaborative activities may be attractive to the under-resourced UK higher education sector, but it is clear that the maintenance of quality and standards has proved much more costly in terms of time and staff resources than many had anticipated. Nevertheless, there are many benefits which are now becoming apparent in terms of the internationalization of higher education.

Prospect

The demand for international collaboration has partly reflected a lack of opportunity for higher education in many countries with very limited state provision. In this context it may be seen as a helping hand at this particular stage of development. As and when the state higher education system grows, or private providers are licensed by legislation, the need for an external input may well diminish. Thus we might expect some international franchising and validation activities to have a relatively short life-cycle, although of course they may lead to longer-term partnerships of a different nature in areas such as research or student exchange. As this happens, UK universities will seek new opportunities in other countries, so the profile of collaboration will vary substantially over time.

We have seen within Europe a growing variety of cross-institutional programmes of study facilitated by easier travel and electronic communications. These developments will surely be reflected at inter-continental level, with much greater mobility of students and staff and extensive use of multimedia communications for the transmission of learning and assessment materials.

There are enormous benefits, as yet largely untapped, to be gained from international collaboration. Opportunities for student and staff exchanges, for research projects with an international perspective and for greater international understanding are immense. Collaboration can inform international debate about the future shape of higher education in areas such as curriculum development, learning and teaching methodologies, the deployment of learning resources and assessment methods. It will also focus minds within UK higher education, providing external peer review that will force us to reassess our own systems and educational methods. Chief Emeka Anyaoku, speaking at a council meeting of the Association of Commonwealth Universities, has argued that the most successful partnerships are based on the premise that each has something to contribute to the welfare of the other, with resources and knowledge flowing in both directions.

On quality assurance and control, UK institutions will need to continue to develop consistent and rigorous policies and procedures, which at the same time recognize institutional autonomy. Nevertheless, links must be encouraged and not deterred by bureaucracy (Fielden 1994). The HEQC and CVU have important roles to play in establishing national guidelines through debate and consensus.

The key challenges for the future will be to respect and harness the diversity of educational experience which international collaboration will allow us to offer students, and to take maximum advantage of the potential of worldwide electronic communication systems.

References

Council of Validating Universities (1994) *Code of Practice on Validation of Higher Education Programmes Offered in Partner Institutions.* London, CVU.

Council of Validating Universities (1995) *Survey of External Validation by UK Degree Awarding Institutions.* London, CVU.

Fielden, J. (1994) Managing international links, *ABCD*, 115, October.

Higher Education Quality Council (1994) *Guidelines for Good Practice in Quality Assurance.* London, HEQC.

Higher Education Quality Council (1995) *Notes of Guidance for the Audit of Collaborative Provision.* London, HEQC.

Part 2

Case Studies of Partnership

9

Smaller but Beautiful: Bath College of Higher Education and Strode College, Street

Anne Stennett and Stephen Ward

Introduction

This is a case study of an HE–FE partnership between Bath College of Higher Education and Strode College of Further Education in Street, Somerset, and their joint development of a BSc honours degree in social sciences during 1992–3. It is designed to offer practical advice to those in small HEIs who may be interested in forming partnerships with FEIs. The key benefits of such an initiative for small institutions are explored more fully below. Here they may be summarized as:

- Raising the profile of both institutions in the region.
- Offering equality of opportunity to a wider range of students than the traditional entry.
- Exchange of perspectives between academic staff in each institution and improved networking.
- Sharing of staff expertise to widen the academic scope within a course.

In September 1993 a group of 20 full-time students embarked on the first year of the degree at Strode College. At the same time some 50 students started the same course at Bath College of Higher Education (BCHE). The degree course had been jointly planned by members of the two institutions during the preceding 15 months, and validated by BCHE in March 1993. On the basis of understandings reached between the two institutions during the period of course development and on conclusion of formal institutional recognition, associate college status was accorded by BCHE to Strode College in June 1993.

Both colleges are relatively small and, at the time, were new to franchising arrangements. The two colleges were late starters, joining the second generation of franchising, and the time available to develop the course was very restricted. Furthermore, the period was one of contraction in resources for such developments. However, each institution appreciated the significance of securing a stake in franchising as a means of extending its regional provision, and each was equally intent on developing a distinctive role in the FHE world.

The relationship between the colleges was managed in such a way as to produce some distinctive features of course development and quality assurance between HE and FE. The two institutions set out aiming to develop a relationship with the following characteristics.

- An association that would be mutually beneficial to both institutions within a framework of partnership and mutual respect.
- Rejection of the asymmetrical power relationship embodied in the terms franchiser and franchisee, with their commercial connotations.
- A course planning process that actively involved both FE and HE staff as equal partners in the formulation of the proposal.
- Validation arrangements that, while preserving the responsibility of the validating HE institution, allowed participation of FE colleagues in genuine peer review.
- The evolution of a particular form of institutional recognition, associate college status, which assured the validating HE institution of the maintenance of quality, without diminishing the peer status of the FE college.
- Rapid conclusion within a short timescale.
- The achievement of quality provision against a shrinking funding base.

The case demonstrates the ways in which the principles of peer review can be achieved sensitively, to the benefit of both HEI and FEI, quickly and effectively at a time of diminishing resources. It should be of interest to those staff working in small institutions, but also to those in large universities who are concerned to improve upon the traditional franchising model (see Gunn 1994). The account offered here documents the ways in which these aims were realized.

Background and institutional profiles

The Bath and Bristol area is rich in higher education provision, with three universities and BCHE. The historical relationships between the college and the universities is significant. The college was formed initially in 1976 from a merger of two former teacher training institutions. During this period its degree programmes were validated by the University of Bristol and later by the University of Bath, both chartered universities. However, in diversifying from teacher education during the 1980s, it moved to validation by the CNAA and in 1983 the college merged with the Bath Academy of Art, another CNAA-validated institution. As the CNAA ethos grew stronger in the college it looked towards a relationship with Bristol Polytechnic, now the University of the West of England (UWE), and in 1987 a successful joint modular in-service programme for teachers was developed.

During 1990 and 1991 the college engaged in a series of merger talks with the University of Bath. When the talks broke down in December 1991, the college turned to achieving academic independence through accreditation by the CNAA. This was achieved by September 1992, when the college was given the authority not only to award its own taught undergraduate and masters degrees but also to approve any which might be franchised in whole or in part to other institutions. So, after its association with each of the three universities in the region, the college became a fully independent institution with the same potential to develop formal institutional relationships with FEIs as had already been secured by the universities.

In 1992–3, student numbers at BCHE totalled 2,270, with a range of undergraduate and postgraduate courses in art and design, music, human ecology, humanities, social sciences, applied sciences and initial and in-service teacher education. Postgraduate provision included a Postgraduate Certificate in Education for intending teachers; a part-time modular professional development programme (including MA/MEd); and masters degrees in visual culture, creative studies and health promotion. So, although it is a major provider of higher education, with international, national and regional recruitment, BCHE is modest in size in terms of student numbers and their spread across academic subject categories. Its single and independent status made it possible to plan for growth towards university designation. The college's strategic plan (1993) notes: 'it is important to continue to demonstrate that quality of provision is exactly comparable with the "university sector", that business and financial strength are equal to other HE institutions, that BCHE's ability to diversify and develop are on a par with "competitors".'

One means of growth towards university size was seen at the time to be through franchising with FE colleges, using the newly designated degree-awarding powers. Of course, this brought the College face to face with its *competitors*. While the chartered universities of Bath and Bristol had not been particularly active in HE–FE relationships, the University of the West of England had well established and respected franchise arrangements with a number of the FE colleges in the region, and appeared to dominate the field. In particular, the university had strong links with the nearby City of Bath College of Further Education. However, at the time there was a good deal of interest among many of the FE colleges in making HE provision. Although there are four HE institutions in Bath and Bristol in the County of Avon, the adjoining counties of Somerset and Wiltshire have no HE institutions and travel problems limit opportunities for the mature population to take HE courses. So it was evident that there were opportunities to extend the scope for local recruitment within the region. However, this also brought possible competition from the south from the Universities of Plymouth, Bournemouth and Exeter. The college needed to create a distinctive form of franchising that would be attractive to FE institutions in the region and would ensure the strengths of quality assurance that had attracted its degree-awarding powers.

While the task seemed difficult because of the college's size and inexperience in franchising, there were other features which facilitated it. First, the college had been successful in its relationships with other institutions, notably with the University of the West of England in the joint in-service modular programme. Moreover, the college had for nearly ten years developed a wide range of access courses with 12 of the FE colleges in the region. These provided a strong basis of trust and familiarity with the institution's staff, policies and practice. It was in a climate of confidence and optimism that the college turned to the FE colleges with which it already had good relations and a number of them responded to the suggestion of franchising the first year of a social sciences degree.

Street is a small town about 30 miles from Bath. Strode is a tertiary college linked to four 11–16 comprehensive schools, for whose leavers it is the designated provider of post-16 courses. It also provides vocational courses for two other comprehensive schools with sixth forms, and adult education throughout the region it serves, in the towns of Street, Glastonbury, Shepton Mallet and Wells and the surrounding rural areas of central and north Somerset. The college has a strong community role.

Student numbers in 1992–3 totalled 1,325 FTE, of whom some 990 were full-time day students following a full range of A level, BTEC, CGLI, Royal Society of Arts (RSA) and Certificate in Pre-Vocational Education (CPVE) courses in a wide choice of subjects. In September 1992 the college began its first access to higher education course. This had been developed in close collaboration with the access tutor from BCHE and recognized by the Western Counties Access Validating Agency. A significant proportion of mature students who attend Strode live to the north of the college in the direction of Bath. Strode is one of five FE colleges in Somerset: the others are in Bridgwater, Taunton and Yeovil, with the Agricultural College at Cannington near Bridgwater. Each of the other colleges has its own independently arranged provision, and/or plans for collaboration, with one or more of the HE institutions outside Somerset: the Universities of the West of England, of Plymouth and of Bournemouth. Strode's higher education policy, which had been developed by the group head of business studies, was to widen access to HE to non-traditional groups through the development of local provision and progression, and to target particular courses according to perceptions of need, demand and access to expertise. The plan for 1993–6 was to make available some HE in its four curricular groups: arts and communication; business, secretarial and leisure; maths, science and technology; social studies. In line with this plan the college was poised for some collaborative activity when the present principal took up his appointment in January 1992. As former vice-principal of Somerset College of

Arts and Technology (SCAT) in Taunton, he had played a major role in developing franchise arrangements with the then Polytechnic South West in Plymouth. Strode's emergent ambition to develop some HE provision was thus further stimulated by the new principal's enthusiasm for, and experience in, franchising.

The new principal's arrival also coincided with approval of a £1.5 million building programme for the college, with construction beginning in early 1992. The prospect of additional and enhanced accommodation made it possible, for the first time, for Strode College to give active consideration to the introduction of higher education provision. Shortly after the arrival of the new principal in March 1992, the dean of the Faculty of Education and Human Sciences at Bath approached the head of business studies at Strode regarding franchise possibilities. It was this initiative from BCHE, combined with Strode's readiness to collaborate, that led to the launch of Strode College's HE plan.

Accordingly, during 1992–3, BCHE embarked on the validation of a new three-year social sciences degree, jointly planned with Strode College; with the first year to be delivered at BCHE and at Strode. A linked access course had just been developed and it was expected that some access students would progress to the first year of the new joint social sciences degree course at Strode, and then on to BCHE to complete the degree.

Mapping the partnership

There were two strands to the partnership: on the one hand course development and validation; on the other the institutional recognition of the FE college by BCHE. These were seen as interdependent, but separate, categories in the sense that it would have been possible to have validated the course to include a one-year franchise at Strode without affording recognition to the whole institution. These two processes occurred simultaneously, and it is difficult to separate them completely. However, they are described here under two headings in order to facilitate the telling of a fairly complex story.

Course planning and validation

Exploratory discussions between the dean, the group head and subject specialists at each institution produced, by the middle of summer term 1992, an outline degree proposal in social sciences which was to be planned with the following remit.

1. Develop a modular degree with a September 1993 start date, the modular provision to facilitate study in full-time and in part-time modes. Modules to be at two levels: level 1 (year 1, compulsory) and level 2 (years

2 and 3, optional) modules, permitting students to choose a particular pathway according to career intentions or subject preference.

2. Plan the whole new degree in collaboration with appropriate specialist staff at Strode College. In particular develop together the six compulsory level 1 modules since these are to be taught, to some extent, on a team-teaching basis and simultaneously to cohorts at both Strode and Bath.

3. Build on degree level teaching in the social sciences as already undertaken by members of the Faculty of Education and Human Sciences at Bath, incorporating some already validated units – as level 2 modules – from established BCHE programmes of study.

The planning was jointly led by the BCHE course director, a sociologist, and the course manager for the BTEC National Diploma in business and finance at Strode, who had complementary expertise in economics. The course director had prepared for planning during the summer; joint planning began in September 1992 and continued through the autumn and spring terms. The staff at Bath and Strode worked effectively as a team. This involved careful scheduling of meetings, alternating between the two college sites, regular exchange of papers and frequent telephone communication. Tutor librarians were also consulted regarding the learning resource requirements of the course and reciprocity of access to campus libraries. The course proposal was approved, subject to two conditions, in a validation meeting in March. The conditions required the clarification of aspects of the admissions regulations and the collation in a single document of all papers relating to Strode. It was agreed in March that the course could be advertised, permitting recruitment for the 1993 intakes to each institution to begin.

The last paragraph summarizes briefly a period of intense and stressful activity. It is important to stress the features that made it successful. These were the ways in which the team worked collaboratively, avoiding any sense of institutional dominance and with a sense of shared knowledge and expertise. This occurred through the clear designation of responsibilities within the planning team and the genuine distribution of expertise between the two institutions; for example, the Strode team members' expertise in economics and psychology, which complemented the strength in sociology of the Bath members.

Additional pressure was created by the government's autumn financial statement in 1992, reducing the LEA tuition fee from £1,800 to £1,300 and threatening the whole resource base of the proposal (see also below). This proved a challenge to the planning team, who needed to be additionally creative in their deliberations about resources. Two other colleges that had been initially interested in the franchise felt obliged to withdraw from the arrangement under the financial limit proposed. But the bond between Bath and Strode was, if anything, strengthened by the autumn statement 'test', and the drive to make the course provision for the local community was a very strong feature of the team's resolve to overcome these problems.

The institutional dimension and associate college status

While course planning was already under way during the autumn term of 1992, there were discussions between members of the management in each college about the institutional dimension: the readiness of Strode College to undertake HE work, as against the capability of the teaching team to deliver the proposed course. It was then that the notion of *partnership*, rather than *franchising*, was consolidated and the notion of associate college status as means of institutional recognition was adopted. This term is, in some ways, problematic because it has other uses in the HE world, such as for a college of higher education whose courses are validated by a university. Recently it has been used by the University of the West of England to refer to the recognition of an FE college by an HE institution. This gave the term local currency and the college decided to use it, but to develop the formulation originally made by the UWE (Bone *et al.* 1993) as appropriate to the college's proposed relationship with FE colleges. The term is defined by BCHE in the following way:

> Associate College Status constitutes formal acknowledgement that the Associate College's institutional aims and its procedures for the delivery of higher education courses have been scrutinized by means of documents and a visit, and found to be congruent with both the mission of Bath CHE and the commitment of Bath CHE to Quality Assurance in course organization, delivery and review, separately from the validation of a particular course.
>
> Associate College Status is separate from the validation of a particular course, but means that the institutional dimension of a Partnership course proposal can be assumed to be satisfactory at a course validation.
>
> 'Associate College' does not imply an exclusive relationship between the Associate College and Bath College of Higher Education. However, it presupposes an appropriate level of shared strategic planning to permit optimal course development between BCHE and the Associate College to occur.
>
> Associate College status is granted for a period of three years and is renewable, subject to satisfactory review of arrangements.

The intention in this formulation of associate college status was to reflect the joint quality of the course planning. However, it had to be acknowledged that there was an issue of seniority within the partnership, given that the HE institution is the degree-awarding body. This was resolved in terms of the *responsibilities* of each partner. It was understood that the academic board of BCHE would have ultimate responsibility for ensuring that the terms of the validation report were carried out, for admissions and assessment, and for overall quality assurance. All this, it was agreed, was to be enshrined eventually in memoranda of cooperation. It was also understood that while these formalities would, from time to time, point up the responsibilities of one of the partners, a commitment to consultation at each stage would make the partnership authentic.

In a series of meetings between the management of each college, involving visits to both campuses, policy papers were discussed and approved by the BCHE academic quality and standards committee. The single most influential policy statement was that defining *principles for partnership*, and these were important in providing a secure framework. They served both institutions well in three ways: first, in establishing a shared understanding of the key concepts (partnership course, the institutional dimension, associate college); second, in affecting the style of debate and decision-making on funding and on fee distribution; and, not least, in thrashing out formal academic and administrative memoranda of cooperation (academic and administrative). The six guiding principles are as follows.

Principle 1: quality in course proposals. There should be confidence that any course proposal should meet the following criteria.

1. Can meet all quality tests appropriate to the level and type of course.
2. Allows and encourages student progression through stages of the whole course regardless of the location of any part.
3. Can be appropriately resourced; and, in terms of staff time, takes account of conditions of service in the partner institutions.
4. Adds to the complement of regional course provision and seeks positively to facilitate provision for non-traditional students in terms of ethnicity, gender, disability and social class.

Principle 2: the ethos of partnership. Partnership should pervade each part of the process and should characterize course planning. In this way ownership of course content and pedagogy is fostered among all who deliver the course, and underwrites its quality. This is notwithstanding the fact that the locus of responsibility for the course overall (its validation and approval, admission and assessment, quality assurance) rests ultimately with BCHE.

Principle 3: commitment to quality. This is encouraged by the adoption of rigorously tested processes of validation, of monitoring and of periodic review.

Principle 4: resourcing partnership. Special circumstances apply to partnership courses where the total student experience spans more than one institution. To ensure the quality of the total student experience, attention should be paid to the facilities of each provider and to the support service for students across different locations. Cost implications such as staff travel and student academic counselling must be identified. Formal agreement as to how these costs are distributed between the partners is a validation issue and, thereafter, subject to careful monitoring. There should be academic parity of treatment for all students registered for a BCHE award, regardless of the study location.

Principle 5: staff development through collaboration. Attention to staff development (for example, in relation to subject updating, to mode of delivery, to course management) is of paramount importance in the successful operation of the course. Collaboration is a significant means of providing staff development, e.g. through team teaching, through shared experience of monitoring practices, through involvement in assessment at various levels, by informal moderation and through curriculum review. Again there are resource implications of collaboration, which need to be costed.

Principle 6: clarity of management responsibility. The success of partnership courses is dependent on the quality of the professional relationships that are forged between the partner institutions. To ensure this quality there must be clear articulation and shared understanding of the liaison arrangements and the allocation of responsibilities in relation to course development, validation, quality assurance, course operation, resourcing and forward planning. While informal contacts often initiate a partnership and remain important, a formal structure for managing the planning and the delivery of courses is the ultimate safeguard for all parties in guaranteeing course quality. Appropriate memoranda of cooperation will therefore be drawn up and these will incorporate in formal terms how various responsibilities are fulfilled and by which postholders or groups.

Another important policy document was the management framework. This aimed to put into effect one of the principles, that of clarity of management responsibility, and it was vital both in distinguishing sequence of action and in assigning responsibility for each element of it. Adherence to the principles and to the management framework throughout the development of the partnership between Bath and Strode ensured that, well in advance of the formal course validation meetings of March 1993, discussions were held with all parties. These discussions established what was required by way of course validation documents, identified the course validation agenda and kept under review the inter-locking of the two related, but quite discrete, processes of course validation and institutional recognition of Strode College.

Following fulfilment of the conditions of course validation for the BSc in social sciences in late May 1993, a proposal was approved by the academic board of BCHE in late June to accord associate college status to Strode College. This completed a process in which evidence of readiness to offer higher education had been provided by Strode College and considered appropriate and satisfactory by BCHE, the validating authority. This was in the particular form of the social sciences degree at level 1 and also, in general, covering any future development.

It was important for the well-being of the partnership that the institutional dimension was checked with as much sensitivity and respect as with rigour. In this connection it was timely that Strode College, in common with all other colleges of further education, was approaching independent corporate status (April 1993) and making ready for this by the preparation of position papers. These papers often served a dual purpose: on the one hand, recording policies, management and academic structures, and procedures relevant to operations when incorporated; on the other, constituting evidence of readiness to embark on higher education provision. This conjunction facilitated discussion between the two institutions, in December 1992, regarding the recognition process for the 'institutional dimension'.

Following consideration of Strode's draft institutional papers in late January, a visit to Strode by a sub-committee (four members including an external) of the BCHE academic quality and standards committee was arranged. The visit took place in late February so that a report could be available for the course validation meeting. Most of the matters raised in what proved to be a positive report were addressed before the validation meeting and there was, therefore, confidence that the course was well supported at institutional level. Following the course validation it was a simple matter to forward the supplemented Strode institutional papers to the academic board of BCHE for recognition of Strode as an associate college in June 1993.

The principal practical advantage of association was that, in consideration of any future course, the appropriateness of the institutional dimension could be assumed as satisfactory, although always subject to the terms of any course-specific memoranda of cooperation. There was also an element of prestige for both institutions in association, because its accomplishment demonstrated the stature of each institution and comparability with respective FE and HE peers in the business of franchising.

Retrospect

In many respects the environment within which BCHE and Strode College developed the partnership, both the course and the institutional relationship, was unpromising. It was both strongly competitive and, as was increasingly obvious during the 1992–3 session, without any resource advantage for either partner. How then did the partnership manage to get off the ground?

Timing

The timing of the BCHE–Strode initiative is critical to an understanding of the way the partnership worked. Franchising was, in effect, at second generation stage by the autumn of 1992, so there was extensive evidence of how it operated elsewhere and clear lessons could be learned from good, and not so good, practice. Senior staff at BCHE made a careful trawl of local FE–HE partnerships to evaluate the experiences and perceptions of those involved. Outstanding among these was that some of the patronizing and paternalistic connotations of franchising were becoming not only less than welcome to the now confident FE colleges, but unacceptable as a basis for negotiation. It was clear to BCHE, at the point that it entered the franchising arena, that if it were to be successful it must proceed within the ethos of partnership. Joint course development proved to be feasible if carefully managed; and this was how Bath proposed to proceed with Strode. For jointness to be meaningful, franchising needed to be reconceptualized as partnership; and then partnership clearly articulated in all communications and consistently practised by both partners.

Late entry into the field of franchising had the advantage of enabling both colleges to adopt an up-to-date and appropriate partnership style. Had it been 12 months earlier, it is unlikely that there would have been such a high consciousness of the significance of partnership. This awareness served course development exceptionally well against a fairly tight valida-tion schedule. It also allowed the institutional relationship to consolidate in parallel with course planning, and this was invaluable in protecting the partnership when it was confronted by the threatening changes in funding.

The principal of Strode, reflecting on why BCHE was chosen as a partner rather than other HE institutions, pointed to the importance of both col-leges tackling franchising for the first time, and that this permitted an equal working relationship with both in at the beginning.

Scope

Late entry was the reason why the scope of BCHE's franchising remained limited. Certainly in 1992–3, in spite of promising possibilities for collabo-ration with a number of other FE colleges in a variety of subjects, no fur-ther franchise occurred, except in the development of INSET units within an already validated programme where core funding was available. Clearly the impact of the 1992 autumn statement cannot be underestimated as an explanation. Since that time, of course, the autumn statement in 1993, which reduced the marginal fee to £750, has effectively prevented any fur-ther increase in marginally funded numbers. A number of new initiatives inspired by the Strode model, and which in early autumn 1993 looked strong possibilities for growth, were, by November, dead in the water. A second obstacle was the capping of HE numbers in the financial year 1994–5.

However, it is also interesting to speculate on the extent to which Bath's scope in franchising was always likely to be modest, given the proximity of the University of the West of England, with its greater range of courses, including science and technology. It is perhaps even surprising that BCHE secured *any* place in the competitive world of franchising, given that it could not realistically have embarked on this activity earlier. The merger talks with the University of Bath had occupied senior staff, and degree-awarding powers were not secured until September 1992. It is important here to explain that the University of the West of England, in spite of its well known strategy to establish a regional network with FE colleges, did not set out actively to exclude BCHE. On the contrary, in any discussions between senior staff of the UWE and Bath about franchising, the UWE was always ready, on the one hand, to acknowledge that Bath may well be able to develop particular links with FE, and, on the other, to make readily available its franchising papers, including those on associate college procedures. In this way BCHE was aware in detail of the terms in which franchising closest to home had taken place and was still being developed, so that its approach to any potential FE partner was suitably informed and realistic. Interestingly, therefore, the huge disadvantage of complete exclusion from franchising that might have befallen BCHE did not materialize.

Dividends and mutual benefits

In the event, the Bath–Strode partnership emerged as the only successful major franchising initiative of 1992–3 and this was probably more significant for Bath as the HE provider. However, its significance was considerable in terms of dividends and mutual benefits. A list of dividends drawn from the comments of members of both institutions, not surprisingly, does not include financial gain. Resource issues were more to do with maintaining good faith between the two colleges in the apportionment of low fees and the practicalities of running the course effectively. Nor was there any prospect of significantly increasing student numbers into HE, and into BCHE in particular. Rather there remained the challenge of resourcing a cohort of fees-only students as it progresses through the course.

The benefits of the partnership are less tangible than those of financial profit and of increased student numbers. The addition of a new degree programme for BCHE and of degree level work for Strode was concrete enough at a time when it was particularly difficult to enlarge the portfolio of course provision. Other benefits were more to do with discharging institutional missions and being able to exemplify this convincingly. The partnership provided evidence for this against two principal corporate objectives, which were common to BCHE and Strode: one was access, or widening participation; the other was the importance of networking.

BCHE was committed in its mission statement to make increasing provision for mature, locally based students. Similarly, for Strode, the partnership was integral to its strategic development in making a material contribution to the provision of local higher education. Ninety per cent of the Strode students were aged 22 years or over, with 50 per cent over 30 years. These students were from a wide range of backgrounds, including family care and full-time and part-time work. At Bath a high proportion (64 per cent) came from school or college backgrounds and were in the 18–22-year -old age range. This suggests that the FE college did offer the course to a different population of students, who would not otherwise have had the chance to do justice to their academic abilities, or to test their vocational aspirations on the basis of an enhanced qualification, because they were unable to study away from home. These students also perceived the course as enhancing their life chances, with 81 per cent seeing better prospects for self-improvement or careers (Payne 1994). Of the 20 students who began the first year at Strode in 1993, only two chose not to carry on to the second year of the course at Bath, indicating that the opportunity to take an exploratory year locally had provided the confidence and determination to carry on.

Both colleges valued the network that the partnership provided. At one level this can be described in terms of staff development opportunities: a two-way learning experience in curriculum development and in pedagogy. Without the contribution of each partner, the course would have been different in both content and methodology; staff development plans were to continue and extend staff exchange, stimulating individual staff members' ambitions for their own further study. At another level, the network permitted each institution to become a part of another system and to be able to feature in the emergent FHE world; not easy for either when they are relatively small, and it is therefore all the more useful to be able to cite this achievement as one of the institutional goals.

Prospect

The short- and medium-term prospect for active partnership in undergraduate courses, for a small HE institution like BCHE, is not good. The complex changes to higher education funding made in the 1993 autumn statement, while partly protecting the limited franchise arrangements which were already in place, effectively terminated further franchising of HE work to the FE sector. While the autumn 1992 reduction from £1,800 to £1,300 left scope for continuing with brave and intelligent resource management, the 1993 reduction to £750 effectively closed the door on any attempts to run courses on marginal fees. Only the addition of HE core funding to the allocations of the FE colleges would allow any further developments. This is extremely limited to date. While some institutions may have prospects of attracting external funding for part-time courses, this potential at BCHE, with its preponderance of 'soft' courses in humanities, art and design and teacher education, is severely restricted. Only a major realignment of the institution's academic direction could enhance this prospect. It is self-evident that this is not possible in the current funding climate.

It was clearly government policy to curtail further developments and to stop the expansion of higher education in the medium term. The FEFC has also indicated that it will obstruct HE developments within resources that it has allocated for FE work in the form of plant, accommodation etc. For this reason, BCHE's late entry into the franchising arena has been disastrous. This is particularly dispiriting in view of the very positive response the college has received to its partnership approach to franchising. During the early part of the autumn term of 1993, a number of local FE colleges expressed enthusiasm to develop HE work with the college, much of this coming from their knowledge of the ways in which the partnership with

Strode College had developed, and the trust that FE staff were able to place in BCHE. A head of steam had begun to develop, and many possibilities for local mature students appeared to be about to open up. What is particularly damaging is the halting of the dynamic which came from the enthusiasm of the staff participating in the Bath–Strode partnership. As shown above, these people had worked rapidly, and ignoring material benefits, to develop an HE course that would serve the local community. To do this was effectively to work in the face of government intentions. Commitment to worthy causes can only go so far, and it could not possibly reach down to £750! The senior management of the college was bound to instruct its staff to continue no further with franchised or partnership arrangements at marginal costs.

However, as long as student demand for HE continues and tends to be more and more localized because of the reduction of student grants, the collaboration of FE and HE in localized HE provision will remain. Moreover, given the will to work across boundaries and the individual dynamic and flair to make a reality of the concept of partnership, links of sometimes an unlikely nature will surely happen. BCHE's model for partnership collaboration between HE and FE is in place and can move into action as soon as the funding climate improves. Strode College's plan for HE provision, while modest, extended beyond participation in level 1 of the social sciences degree. The college envisaged level 2 work, new courses in different curricular areas and links with other HE institutions. In December 1993 these developments were being actively considered, but all were subject to funding. The link with BCHE, while not exclusive, was prized not least because, with associate college status, course development would be able to flourish when the funding climate improved.

There is one further limit on the degree to which a small HE institution like BCHE can participate in local franchising. Again, given the severe curb on expansion in HE in the medium term, a small institution like Bath has to consider the benefits of relationships with FE colleges in the national context. The expansion of access and franchised arrangements inevitably increases the proportion of local student cohorts. With the reduction in student grants this might be advantageous. But where an institution has relatively small student numbers, there can be a danger that increasing the local recruitment will so reduce the proportion of national recruitment that it could lose its identity as a national, and then as an international, institution.

The BCHE–Strode partnership perhaps serves as a microcosm not only in highlighting some of the 'second generation franchising' characteristics, but also in suggesting future FE–HE agenda items. Independently, staff at Strode and at Bath identified broadly the same key issues, relative both to the specific course and to any other possible partnership developments.

1. The student experience. Can the student experience of HE in FE institutions ever match the traditional expectations of higher education, with

its notions of academic community, social learning and generous resource provision?

2. Equality of opportunity for full-time and part-time students. How can part-time students be supported, given the way modularization dismantles the distinction between full-time and part-time students?

3. Quality assurance at the FE–HE interface. What can and should be devolved from HE to FE? Can standards be maintained if quality assurance as well as quality control is decentralized?

4. Funding and its distribution. Costing start-up and ongoing partnership operation at the economic rate.

5. Staff development. What staff development is needed to meet the challenge of the changing FE–HE interface?

References

Bone, J., Enstock, N. and Macmillan, F. (1993) The validating university and associated colleges: the evolution of a relationship. In S. Brownlow (ed.) *Equal Outcomes – Equal Experiences?* Blagdon, The Staff College.

Gunn, R. (1994) *Franchising in Higher Education*, Universities Staff Development Unit Briefing Paper 5. Pontypridd: University of Glamorgan.

Payne, W. (1994) A comparison of the cohorts of BSc students at Strode College and Bath College of Higher Education. Unpublished paper, Strode College, Street.

10

The Development of a Franchised Part-Time Degree Programme: The Local Integrated Colleges Scheme

Alan Roff and James Lusty

Introduction

The development of franchised degree and diploma programmes has been well established in the United Kingdom for a number of years and even longer in some other countries, notably the United States of America. In the 1990s, however, the United Kingdom saw an explosion both in terms of the number of institutions participating and, more importantly, in terms of student participation. The topic of franchising itself has been the subject of a number of reviews (Bird *et al.* 1993; HEQC 1993) and journal articles, not all of them favourably disposed towards the concept. There are many reasons for the continued debate on the role of, and the relationships in, further and higher education partnerships:

- The perceived, and indeed the real, competition that these partnerships create for neighbouring institutions.
- The ability to monitor successfully the quality assurance processes.
- The role and remit of the parent institution (DFE 1994).
- The roles and responsibilities of both the franchisee and the franchiser.
- Possibly most importantly, the rights, responsibilities and opportunities these arrangements offer to students.

This chapter looks at the development of a regional partnership scheme, from its inception just over ten years ago to its current position, where it enrols over 2,000 students from over twenty regional colleges throughout Lancashire, Cumbria, Greater Manchester and Merseyside.

The network that started this initiative is known as the Local Integrated Colleges Scheme, abbreviated to LINCS, and has gone through several phases of development. This chapter looks in detail at each phase of development based on a mission- and access-oriented approach: the way in which the rapid expansion of student numbers was encouraged by both the government funding methodology and the manner in which the curriculum was delivered. The LINCS network has also been cited as an example of good practice in a number of instances, which will be explored in more detail in the ensuing sections. Initially, however, we need to look back twenty years or so to see how the network began.

The early years, 1974–1984

Formation of Lancashire Polytechnic

Preston Polytechnic was created as the last of the first wave of polytechnics in 1974. It was the thirty-first polytechnic to be designated and was selected from a number of possible contenders throughout Lancashire. By the early 1970s, Lancashire had a number of well established FEIs and HEIs but no recognized single focus for higher education. As county boroughs, towns had aimed to provide a broad range of FE provision, including some HE, in the local colleges. This was both a strength, in that each town had a tradition of high-level FE and HE provision, and a weakness, in that no concentration of activity had taken place at one college in the county. Bolton, Blackburn, Blackpool, Preston and other towns were anxious to develop their educational provision for the local population and also for the region. Hence each was able to present a case to be 'the last polytechnic'. In the event, the Secretary of State for Education designated the Harris College in Preston. The institution became Preston Polytechnic in 1974 and set about carving out for itself a distinctive mission and purpose. Perhaps because of the fact that it was the last designated polytechnic, and perhaps because of its original position, the polytechnic began to develop new links and consolidate existing links with neighbouring colleges of further education. With only several hundred HE students at its designation, Preston Polytechnic had both the opportunity and the challenge of developing higher education provision almost from scratch. During the 1970s it grew rapidly under the directorship of the late Harry Law.

The development of a regional commitment

The second director of the polytechnic, Eric Robinson, who took office in 1981, had spent many years promoting a distinctive concept for the polytechnics and began to lay the foundations for a new type of HEI, one that had links throughout the region and promoted a high level of opportunity for anyone who was able to benefit from higher education – not only those who were qualified for entry by traditional yardsticks. As part of the strategy, the name of the institution was changed to Lancashire Polytechnic in 1984 (it was to become the University of Central Lancashire in 1992). Not everyone was delighted with this change. The local people of Preston felt that the institution was turning its back on the town, some in Lancashire felt it was arrogant and others, particularly in Cumbria, believed it was yet another instance of being ignored by higher education. However, the timing and implementation of the name change was crucial. The polytechnic had publicly indicated that it was there to serve the higher education needs of Lancashire (and Cumbria, although it is difficult to see how this reference could have been included in the new title for the institution) and to develop higher education throughout the region.

Several other very important developments were in an embryonic form at that stage.

First, following the lead of the director, the academic board at the polytechnic had given a clear indication that it would seek to re-prioritize the polytechnic's resources and energies to maintain rather than shed its commitment to non-degree work. It also decided to increase its degree level provision across a broad curricular base, while at the same time enhancing and emphasizing access opportunities on to these courses. Such routes would be for mature students, who would not, in the main, have the traditional entry requirements.

Second, the academic board had reviewed the new mixed mode and flexible study routes that were being developed under the combined science and combined humanities schemes. These were beginning to attract external interest as well as internal departmental recognition. The polytechnic brought together these developments into a combined studies degree programme, which grew rapidly in the 1980s, forming a natural focus for radical developments, and which was later to develop into a full blown credit accumulation scheme. The scheme allowed departments to experiment with particular subject offerings and incorporate within these new and often, at that time, novel methods of teaching, learning and assessment.

Third, the polytechnic was starting to develop its mission statement, the first to be developed by any United Kingdom HEI. This statement remains virtually unchanged today and commits the university 'to encourage and enable individuals to develop their full potential', and particularly to 'enable those in the region of the [university], especially in Lancashire and Cumbria, to participate in and benefit from higher education in general and the [university's] provisions in particular, thereby taking part in the enrichment and development of the region's social, economic, cultural and recreational activities'. The emphasis on the regional dimension is striking.

Finally, and this will be pursued in more detail in the next section, the student was beginning to be seen as a 'customer'. These were early days and many staff – and students – objected to this business terminology and felt that the message that was being proclaimed was that students were not being treated as individuals. However, the real message was that customers have rights and can expect a good deal backed by a contract of purchase.

Firms such as Marks and Spencer had long thought of the customer as being central to the operation and not merely as the end of the line.

An additional initiative that occurred at this time was the formation of the Open College of the North West (OCNW) and this also gave a valuable boost to opening up access opportunities. The polytechnic was a co-founder of the OCNW and this provided an alternative route into higher education. However, LINCS was proving extremely popular because it guaranteed progression rights, something other schemes either could not, or did not, offer. From the student's point of view, particularly the part-time mature student, this was an attractive package. It allowed the student to map out a five- or six-year programme of study (or occasionally longer) with much more certainty than was offered by other access schemes. During this period the student was also guaranteed regular meetings with an academic counsellor, an opportunity to discuss other options (even the transfer to other institutions such as the Open University) at the annual progression exercise and the availability of different modes of attendance, such as part-time evening, part-time day or full-time.

Lancashire Polytechnic was beginning to become a distinctive institution, known throughout the UK for the different way it was approaching higher education provision. It espoused its values at every opportunity, and, by a series of important (often relatively young) staff appointments, equipped itself well for the next ten-year development that was to occur.

The development of LINCS

Continuing education

The polytechnic established a continuing education service in early 1984 to coordinate and develop further its access provision. The emphasis on coordination was significant in that the polytechnic expected *all* its departments to be active in developing continuing education provision as an integral part of overall provision. Continuing education was regarded as mainstream, not peripheral, provision and part of the polytechnic's commitment to the idea of 'lifelong learning'. As part of the commitment to widening access, staff from the combined studies scheme and the continuing education service undertook a number of initiatives and collaborated with a number of local colleges and regional organizations. To promote its position within the region as a major provider of higher education opportunities, the polytechnic devised a scheme to attract students to sample courses before they needed to make a commitment to the course. Under the Associate Student Scheme, a student could, at very little cost (£5, a fee which stayed in place until 1991), enrol for a course unit on the combined studies programme, and decide at the end of the year whether or not he or she would be examined in the course unit and thus whether or not it would count towards a final-year award. Although the scheme was never as successful as was hoped, partly owing to an already rapidly increasing full-time student intake and alternative part-time provision, it did serve at least two purposes.

First, it gave a valuable boost to the efforts of staff in the combined honours and continuing education service and gave them the institutional backing to persuade departments to offer part-time programmes for these students. Second, it put out a very strong message throughout the region that the polytechnic was trying to cater for the local population, providing places for as many part-time students as it could on a very easy 'sample and see' basis. This was further expanded by the successful validation of a 'foundation studies' programme, which runs from January to June and is essentially a part-time evening-only access course for the combined honours programme. It is divided into two parts. The completion of the first part of the course may lead to a recommendation of further study before the commencement of a degree programme. Those who successfully complete the entire course are guaranteed progression to the first year of the combined honours programme either through LINCS in one of the colleges or at the university in Preston.

It was against this background that Lancashire Polytechnic underwent a CNAA Quinquennial Institutional Review in 1984. The polytechnic undertook a commitment to foster 'a continuum of further education provision within the region' (CNAA 1985). Colleges throughout Lancashire had been watching these developments with interest. Indeed, the colleges were by no means passive in the developments and the good relationships enjoyed between the polytechnic and the colleges enabled rapid progress to be made in the ensuing months. In the academic year 1984–5 an experimental pilot franchise was launched with one of the Lancashire colleges at Nelson and Colne. This is now recognized as the first higher education franchise of this type (Robertson 1994). The two combined studies subjects offered at level 1 to the eleven students who had enrolled at Nelson and Colne College were economics and education studies, which, as part of the rationale for LINCS, were offered on a part-time evening-only basis. The name LINCS actually only surfaced in 1985–6 when there was considerable additional interest shown by another five Lancashire colleges, namely Blackpool and the Fylde College, W. R. Tuson College (later to change its name to Preston College), Blackburn College, Accrington and Rossendale College and Burnley College. All these colleges successfully negotiated their way through the polytechnic's rigorous validation procedures (likened at the time to the Spanish Inquisition and/or the early days of CNAA) and were able to offer combined studies subjects for their local populations.

Credit accumulation and transfer scheme

Meanwhile, at the polytechnic, the successful adoption by the combined studies degree programme of a credit accumulation and transfer scheme

(CATS) was having an enormous impact on curriculum development across the entire institution. The combined studies scheme underwent a major revalidation in early 1987 and the outcome was the adoption and validation of a number of new subjects on the programme. This brought to 24 the number of subjects on offer, which could, when they had successfully run for a year on-campus, be franchised at level 1 to the colleges.

Even this expansion proved insufficient for some of the colleges. Although the credit-based curriculum had enabled colleges to be more flexible in what they could offer, they felt that many of the more attractive disciplines were still not available. Many of the subjects on combined studies fell into two categories. Either they were available because recruitment to a single honours degree in the subject was difficult and they had joined the combined studies programme through necessity (such as electronics, chemistry and mathematics), or they were part of the large combined humanities programme which had been a forerunner of the combined studies programme (such as history, English and education studies). Recruitment to the latter group proved much easier than to the former group. However, many of the popular options of the day, such as business, accountancy and fashion, were not credit-based and could not in any easy way be franchised on a part-time evening-only basis. It was impossible to break up the course in a meaningful way which at the same time allowed the colleges to play to their strengths. In many cases colleges were unable to offer the full programme that would have been required for a single honours course and joint honours did not, and could not, under the structure current at that time, exist. These pressures from the colleges were duplicated by similar pressures in the polytechnic.

Such was the success of LINCS that by 1986–7 a total of 400 enrolments were recorded. A similar success story was being enjoyed by the combined studies programme on-campus, as the polytechnic continued to channel much of its growth into these areas. As a result of this, and other mission-related arguments, the polytechnic's academic board took the decision in 1988 to move to a polytechnic-wide credit accumulation system. Looking back, there were two extremely ambitious aspects associated with this debate. First, the polytechnic had adopted a five-year strategic plan which would see student numbers double from 8,000 to 16,000 over five years (this plan has now been achieved). Second, the academic board had decided to move to CATS 2, as it was affectionately known, using the 'big bang' approach. This resulted in a massive revalidation and validation programme between 1990 and 1992, which resulted in all departments revamping their provision to fit within the CATS. Because of the nature of the structure of the CATS it was necessary for all degrees to come forward with a subject base in the first year. This, and the growth plan, saw the total of subjects on offer increase from 24 in 1990 to over 70 in 1992. This was largely as a result of the polytechnic encouraging the departments' enthusiasm and opportunism in coming forward with a significant number of new named degree awards, which increased the degree provision by over 300 per cent. Since all the degrees were subject-based, all these subjects would, after a period used to gain experience, be available for the LINCS colleges. The scope for growth now became far larger and the need to look carefully at the purpose of the scheme correspondingly increased.

The LINCS network

The purpose of the LINCS partnership was to develop a regional network of colleges which would improve access opportunities throughout the area and provide the opportunity for progression to the polytechnic. It was summarized in a recent review of the programme (Abramson 1993):

- To increase, widen and deepen participation in higher education for adults within the north west region.
- To maintain (or better) academic standards, academic parity and academic integrity of franchised provision delivered in partnership with colleges.
- To encourage continuation of study to a higher level by guaranteeing progression into the polytechnic.

This last aspect was one of the real attractions and benefits of the scheme. Progression was guaranteed to any student, whether on or off campus. The whole basis of LINCS was that students, having completed level 1 of a degree course on a part-time basis at their local college, could progress to the polytechnic to complete their degrees on either a part-time or a full-time basis. The only caveat to progression was that the student had the ability to benefit. This was most easily identified through the assessment process and, provided the student had sufficient credit to progress, the right of progression was automatic. This has been modified recently, for planning reasons, in order to require students to declare their progression route for the following year in March of the current academic year. This has proved necessary as the polytechnic (and later university) has grown to over 16,000 students, and planning the course provision has become vital, not only at the institutional level but for the heads of department, the central services and the colleges.

While the guarantee of progression was a huge benefit and an excellent marketing tool, it also presented the colleges with some difficulties, particularly those furthest from the polytechnic site in Preston. However, they began to use this to their advantage and used the progression arguments to push the polytechnic into looking at higher level provision. While 80 per cent of LINCS students live within 25 miles of Preston, the students attending from West Cumbria College had to make a 220-mile round trip in order to progress to level 2 on the part-time or full-time programmes. This was recognized as a major issue in terms of retention and was referred to in the review of franchising (Abramson 1993). It seemed difficult to defend in terms of the access policy. During the early 1990s the polytechnic looked very closely at developing, in association with colleges such as West Cumbria College, open and distance learning packages based on its curriculum (Roff 1991). However, while this had some success and still operates for some subjects at West Cumbria College, it was never developed to any significant extent. Eventually other developments interrupted this initiative, and these are considered in more detail in the next section.

The LINCS partnership was growing throughout this time, attracting considerable attention as it did (Abramson 1988; CNAA 1989; 1990). By 1991, LINCS enrolments hit 800 and several cohorts of LINCS students who had commenced their study at a college had been awarded degrees (with results exceeding the average for traditional full-time students) by the polytechnic. An analysis of final-year degree classifications of students shows a higher proportion of first class and upper second class degrees from students who originated in LINCS colleges than seen within the cohort as a whole. Furthermore, the percentage of students who drop out of the programme after completion of their first year of study is much lower (about 30 per cent) than the national average for part-time students. The polytechnic's quality assurance processes (developed very much on CNAA terms) were rigorously applied to colleges (Roff 1991). Despite frequent political problems caused by the failure of courses to achieve validation, these processes were not varied and came to be accepted by colleges as part of the agreement associated with developing higher education provision. Indeed, many college principals were privately enthusiastic about the effect on standards of the rigorous procedures imposed by the polytechnic. Simultaneously, polytechnic staff involved in course development and validation learnt from some colleges about ways of dealing with mature students, which facilitated their learning. Overall, the exchange of cultures was mutually beneficial but not without difficulties.

While these developments continued apace, some of the colleges in Cumbria were seeking higher education provision of their own. In the absence of any government commitment – or even interest – a number of colleges contacted the polytechnic in order to join the LINCS partnership. A second pilot ran at the Workington campus of West Cumbria College (CNAA 1989). Cumbria County Council invited seven higher education institutions to tender to develop higher education provision in the country. The Lancashire Polytechnic tender, which involved the development of higher education provision (especially part-time provision) at each of the six colleges in the county, was selected by Cumbria County Council in 1990. The outcome was that a new grouping was established under the auspices of the Cumbria Degree Programme (CDP). Carlisle College, Furness College and Kendal College joined West Cumbria College, now including the Whitehaven site involving science, to form this new network. Specialist provision at Newton Rigg College (land-based) and Cumbria College of Art and Design in Carlisle was also facilitated under this programme. The scheme now included colleges throughout these two large counties with around

1,000 participating students. As a large scheme working from a large polytechnic it was ready for a further phase in its development.

Meanwhile, the University also had come through a period of rapid expansion, student numbers increasing from 8,000 to 16,000 between 1988 and 1993. This expansion, a major restructuring within the polytechnic to create new faculties and departments, the growth of franchise provision and the new curriculum developments had placed an enormous burden on staff. Students became more aware of their rights and the opportunities afforded by the credit-based system and by the partnership networks. The term 'customer' became acceptable as students were seen as individuals having rights and responsibilities. The ideas of business became influential in shaping the views of the polytechnic towards its 'customers'. Instead of concentrating on the product, it emphasized the student-centred approach to course design and delivery; the delivery was thought to be necessary at a place, time and mode that was convenient to the student. The net result of this was that the partnership networks expanded to take on some other non-combined honours courses and the college aspirations were fuelled still further.

Funding

Before we proceed to look at the current state of development, it is worthwhile to pause and consider the financial implications of the franchising arrangements. Many pious words have been written about franchising and, in the main, the opportunities for access and the integrity of such schemes remain true and valid. However, without sufficient funding, the colleges would neither have been able, nor have desired, to develop their higher education provision. The networks are funded by the University on the basis of credits linked to student numbers. The price per credit reflects the nature of the discipline, so that science and engineering subjects attract the premium rates whereas most humanities subjects are funded at the lower rate. In addition, given the sparsely populated nature of Cumbria, it was decided that these colleges should be funded at a slightly higher rate than the Lancashire colleges. This was to try to ensure that some of the classes run by colleges in Cumbria were economical to run even with fewer enrolled students. Funding support secured from Cumbria County Council under the terms of the successful tender helped to make up this differential in the early years. The funding methodology was open and transparent, so colleges did not feel they were being played off against each other. It is interesting to note that the differential payment that was introduced still exists for colleges in Cumbria compared to the Lancashire colleges. Although it is only a relatively small amount, it signals the university's commitment to encouraging higher education in Cumbria in terms of trying to ensure the viability of smaller cohorts of students and assisting colleges which often did not have the breadth of provision on offer.

Although targets were set for each college it was possible, during the late 1980s and the early part of the 1990s, to increase the student numbers without too much trouble. In fact, most colleges stuck to their targets, with only the most popular options in only one or two colleges over-recruiting. In recent years, with a very tight control of student numbers, this has continued to work well.

In addition to the polytechnic/university funding, the colleges also charged the students the fee for the subject, which was set at £15 per credit in 1990. (It is worth commenting that several colleges, particularly those close to the polytechnic, actually undercut it on their credit charge. Perhaps this was partly through poor communications and partly through the competitive spirit that exists within the network.)

Recent developments

At the beginning of 1992 the polytechnic (soon to be university) was facing, for the first time in its short history, a period of consolidation. There were already signs that the government was going to look for some way to curb the enormous growth that had occurred in higher education; the target participation rate of 33 per cent was going to be met long before the end of the decade. The university was in the fortunate position of having consolidated its student intake at around 3,000 new full-time students a year in 1991 as the physical development plan caught up with the increased intakes. However, such was the success of the franchising arrangements that, in addition to the courses which had been developed on-campus being franchised, some of the links had led to collaborative course development. An HND in forestry (with Newton Rigg College in Cumbria), a four-year BSc (Hons) in horticultural management (with Myerscough College near Preston) and a BA (Hons) in hospitality management (with Blackpool and the Fylde College) were all developed jointly using both university and college expertise.

College aspirations and proposals for validation continued to flood into the university for new courses and for subjects on the combined studies programme. Unfortunately, it was proving impossible to meet all of these aspirations. In some cases the university felt that the proposals were not viable, based on the college's expertise and ability; in some cases the increasing numbers would eventually have placed a considerable strain on the university in future years, given the university's guarantee of progression; in some instances the university did not believe that the academic basis was sound. Indeed, the reluctance of the university to validate courses beyond level 1 prompted some colleges to develop their own programmes and seek validation from other universities without such reluctance. Discussions within the university led to the view that it was necessary to formalize the relationship between the university and the colleges still further. In October 1992 the rector of the university, Brian Booth, sent a letter to the college principals explaining, at great length, the reasons why it had become necessary to review the current arrangements. In the letter he outlined two forms of agreement. Principals were asked to consider which, if either, of the relationships was the one most suited to their development plans. The two alternatives were licensed and associate college status.

In essence, opting for licensed college status implied very little change over the current arrangements that existed. The university was prepared to continue to franchise level 1 part-time provision to licensed colleges on an agreed course-by-course or subject-by-subject basis. Progression of students to other levels of work would take place at the university rather than at the college. Colleges opting for this arrangement would not be able to increase their student numbers much beyond their existing levels because no growth was implicated in the university's own numbers. No provision would be validated beyond level 1 and, even at level 1 full-time provision would not be validated. Licensed colleges would offer access routes into higher education but awards would require all the post-level 1 study to take place at the university.

Associate college status was the other alternative. The university was prepared to extend to colleges that chose this option the opportunity for increased involvement, going beyond level 1 franchising, with the possibility of sharing in any limited growth available in return for entering into a rolling three-year formal planning agreement. To become an associate college, the college had to agree to work exclusively with the university and to develop an HE programme covering a three-year planning cycle. This would enable the university to target its resources on the associated colleges, enabling the expertise of university staff to facilitate development at the colleges. The associate colleges in turn would be able to make long-term investment in a more confident planning environment.

This development naturally created both enthusiasm and some disquiet within the network. It formed the major discussion point in a number of meetings that took place during 1992 and 1993. The LINCS programme continued to recruit and, despite the fact that many colleges opted for licensed status, the recruitment figures continued to climb steadily. Initially four colleges opted to become associate colleges, but this has since risen to eight, including two of the major LINCS colleges. It was, perhaps, the idea of exclusivity that appeared threatening to several colleges. However, government pronouncements, culminating in the autumn statement in November 1993 and the HEFCE declaration in 1994, served to demonstrate the accuracy of the university's warnings in 1992 that the period of rapid growth was over. As other universities and colleges found existing partnerships under very heavy strain given the extent of the government's efforts to curb growth in higher education, the university found itself able to meet most of the (albeit reduced) aspirations for growth in its associate colleges.

Nevertheless, at the time the colleges felt that such a major development should have had further discussion, and that a period of consultation should have preceded any decisions that were taken. However, the university, faced with several instances where lack of exclusivity had resulted in course development teams seeing their work drift away, either to another HEI or directly to a validating agency such as BTEC, was convinced that the time was right to make such changes. In addition, it had anticipated curbs on growth by central government, which would inevitably force a reassessment of growth aspirations, and saw the need to act quickly. It did not, it is fair to say, predict the extent of ill will that was generated by a few of the colleges, which felt that the university had acted in a heavy-handed and dictatorial fashion. It is clear in retrospect (and was clear at the time) that a longer period of consultation would have been better for all parties, but it is equally clear now that, had the university allowed growth to continue at the same rate as before, there would have been far more damage caused to college links when the government changed policy in 1993.

The colleges decided according to their own perspectives, and either remained as licensed colleges or signed to become associate colleges of the University of Central Lancashire. It is interesting to note that not one college withdrew from the scheme at this time.

Since 1993 four more colleges have opted for the exclusive associate status, two of which have accepted that, in the current climate of consolidation, they will not see any development of full-time provision. Relationships between the university and the colleges are now generally believed to be better than ever before. The greater clarity of the university's position with respect to exclusivity and consolidation has helped all the partners.

At times, colleges have been openly critical of the university, particularly with respect to the scope and rate at which the university is prepared to franchise its material. In turn, the university has been critical of individual colleges, and nowhere is this more apparent than at pre-validation and validation events, where on occasions the college aspirations have outstripped both the ability to deliver and the resources available to fund the higher education programme. There have been times when the lack of clarity and guidance from the university has caused problems and some ill feeling. However, the open nature of the relationship and the improved clarity of communication routes have assisted in reducing the misunderstandings and helping forward planning. This also means that the more difficult decisions, which could cause some disquiet, such as withdrawing or cancelling a validation, are taken earlier. The timescales that have now been set and agreed require colleges to declare an interest in courses or subjects about eighteen months before the course commences. This is done openly at the January meeting of the academic board sub-committee that is responsible for partnership activities, the academic partnership committee. This has led to a much higher degree of trust, which has strengthened the partnership.

Within the university there is increased respect for the achievements of the colleges and their students. Within the colleges there is a greater appreciation of the commitment of the university to widen access and to provide opportunities across the region. There is also greater confidence in the colleges because of the longevity of the links with the university and the fact that colleges were not sacrificed when the period of expansion ended.

Retrospect

Over twenty colleges remain within the partnership network. They recruit almost 2,000 students between them and of those over half belong to LINCS, which was formed out of the merger of the old Lancashire and Cumbria networks. The LINCS coordinators continue to meet regularly and staff development days and events are organized throughout the year. In the early days the staff development sessions were focused on operational issues and on the delivery vehicle – CATS. In the recent period the sessions, particularly the two-day residential meeting, have been much more focused on strategic issues, such as the overlap and integration of vocational and academic programmes.

There still remains some tension between the associate and licensed colleges and also, perhaps more surprisingly, between the LINCS network colleges and the rest of the partnership network. To some extent this is understandable. The staff involved in combined honours and the LINCS coordinators have, over a number of years, developed a comprehensive, well documented, well structured partnership network with a well organized and well supported staff development programme, including one-day events, conferences, residential sessions and even quiz nights. They, as a group, seem reluctant to give up the lead role that has developed in Lancashire, but has also been highly commended nationally as an example of good practice. This system provides a support structure for staff involved in the colleges, who are given opportunities to exchange ideas with subject colleagues in other colleges as well as those at the university. However, it also places demands on the participants. At times those not in LINCS look with envy on the support structure. At other times, those in LINCS look with envy at the apparently looser and more moderate networking demands placed on non-LINCS participants. It is as well not to be too sensitive about any of these tensions, which are perhaps closest to those arising from comparisons made by staff in universities between 'their' department and others. Is it possible even to imagine an educational institute without such tensions?

In the early years of partnership activity the colleges played a more subservient role. In many ways this was to be expected as the university's experience and knowledge of HE programmes was much greater than that to be found in the colleges. As the colleges developed, so did the partnership. A franchise board operated at the university between 1989 and 1993, when it was replaced by a new committee, which was a sub-committee of the university's academic board; it is known as the academic partnership committee. College staff, and particularly the college principalship, play an increasingly influential role in areas such as admissions, quality assurance and policy and planning of the regional network.

Funding the partnership still remains both an important and a complex aspect of partnership work. Some colleges are intent on developing their higher education routes through part-time courses, while others are looking to develop a much stronger full-time portfolio. Most colleges remain committed to developing both full- and part-time provision. This is partly about economies of scale and cost-effectiveness. The recent developments in part-time HND provision have accelerated this process, as has the fact that most colleges, like the university, have a strong desire to run a balanced programme for both full- and part-time students. In 1994–5 two colleges have indicated their desire to withdraw from the scheme, but the work currently offered by these colleges has been taken up with enthusiasm by two associate colleges in close geographic proximity. So although the number of college links may decline, the provision and certainly the number of students remains constant and even shows signs of increasing.

The strong links that currently exist augur well for the future and many new initiatives are being promoted and initiated by the colleges.

Prospect

The network has survived upheavals created by expansion, consolidation and the advent of exclusivity within the network. It has continued to thrive and increase both in student number terms and the number of colleges. While it is unlikely that the growth experienced over the past ten years will ever be repeated, the network remains committed to providing opportunities to students throughout the region. In 1995–6 some 2,500 students will be studying on courses at associate or licensed colleges, thereby creating a vast range of hitherto non-existent opportunities, primarily for the people of the two large counties. Ten years ago even the most enthusiastic advocate of LINCS would not have envisaged anything approaching this level of activity. In looking forward to the next ten years, therefore, we must be wary of overstating our ability to foretell the future.

There are several initiatives that could now affect the network. Some of these, though representing the very essence of access and flexibility, could in themselves deliver a severe blow to the partnership network. For example, there are very strong arguments that Cumbria should have its own higher education centre. Cumbria will soon be the largest rural location in England without a university. A federal University of the Lakes, which was recently proposed (Campbell-Savours and Mahon 1989), could serve the population of the county, but its location will no doubt be the subject of considerable infighting. An alternative University of Carlisle has a larger single conurbation to draw from, but nevertheless has several major drawbacks. Would students in Barrow find it any easier to travel to Carlisle than to Preston? Will a centre be better than the current network that encourages access, albeit only to diploma level awards before a student must transfer to the university in Preston?

Other developments could be beneficial to both the network and the people of Lancashire and Cumbria. A more supportive financial climate for part-time students could lead to an upsurge in demand in the two counties, and would allow the benefits of the network to be more fully realized.

The really exciting developments in the future must reside somewhere between the centralized approach of a new university and the current networking arrangements. In historical terms, the partnerships between the university and the associate colleges are very young, yet they have already led to significant achievements. Developing these partnerships, taking a long-term view of the staff development and taking advantage of new technologies could widen access yet further. For example, the advent and application of new technology could create the new centres desperately sought by rural or isolated communities. These centres could be limited to and draw support from the university and its partner colleges. The 'virtual college' has become an attainable goal. Interactive satellite broadcasting and the use of land-based cable networks are not new, and have made it possible to deliver and interact with several audiences at once. The university is currently undertaking a pilot project with Furness College, which is sponsored by British Telecom and aims to deliver programmes of study from the Preston campus. It is not only the delivery of lectures and seminars – although that in itself is a giant step forward – but all the associated staff development programmes that are run at the university, linked to teaching and learning, that will be open to staff at the college. The current cost of the technology is high; the returns are low; the student experience is in question. However, the possibilities are enormous and the implications for the university and the colleges are considerable. The network exists and could be developed to move to the next phase of responsive, customer-oriented, higher education provision. Whether such technology can be funded in the near future, whether it is cost-effective, even in comparison to a new university, whether the student experience can be enhanced; all of these remain to be seen.

The next ten years could, after all, see a second explosion in the LINCS network. Ultimately the only certainty even in a period of consolidation is that developments will continue. By opening the Pandora's box of LINCS ten years ago the university unleashed aspirations in individuals, communities and colleges which it will be impossible to contain. Ultimately this was, and remains, the key achievement of the network.

References

Abramson, M. and Grannell, M. (1989) *Forging Higher Education Links with an Isolated Community. London, CNAA.*
Abramson, M. (1988) *The Lancashire Integrated Colleges Scheme (LINCS): Widening Access with Advanced Standing.* London, Royal Society.

Abramson, M., Ellwood, S. and Thompson, L. (1993) *Five Years of Franchising.* Preston, University of Central Lancashire.

Bird, J., Crawley, G. and Sheibani, A. (1993) *Franchising and Access to Higher Education: a Study of HE/FE Collaboration.* Bristol, University of the West of England/ Department of Employment.

Campbell-Savours, D. and Mahon, J. (1989) *The Case for the University of the Lakes.* Privately published.

CNAA (1985) *Institutional Report, Lancashire Polytechnic, November 1994–March 1995.* London, CNAA.

CNAA (1990) *Briefing Paper Number 23.* London, CNAA.

DFE (1994) *Circular ACL 4/94.* London, HMSO.

HEQC (1993) *Some Aspects of Higher Education Programmes in Further Education Institutions.* London, HEQC.

Robertson, D. (1994) *Choosing to Change: Extending Access Choice and Mobility in Higher Education.* London, HEQC Report on Credit Accumulation and Transfer.

Roff, A.E. (1991) *Franchising: Assuring the Quality of Student Experience.* Coombe Lodge Report. Bristol.

11

Post-16 Compact in Birmingham: School and College Links with Higher Education

Stephen Bigger

Introduction

This chapter describes a particular model of links between HEIs and post-16 institutions. The overriding purpose is to enhance the motivation, aspirations and achievement of able students who might not otherwise consider higher education as a viable option for themselves because of personal circumstances or background. The setting is inner-ring Birmingham, and the focus is on schools and colleges serving areas of physical deprivation, high unemployment and a broad ethnic mix.

In Birmingham, action was set in train in 1987–8 to raise pupils' general motivation about their education within the 14–18-year-old age group in the inner city. It was part of the Department of Employment's 'Compact' initiative, and had its prime focus on 14–16-year-olds (Bigger 1994a). After the first year, as schools with sixth forms were expressing interest in Compact, the decision was made to plan for continuity by developing a 'post-16 Compact', also involving two FE Colleges and one sixth form college. Birmingham Polytechnic, now the University of Central England (UCE), became a close partner: a Compact agreement was signed at the highest level. Although recruitment was their initial motivation, this quickly fell into the background. UCE is situated in the inner city, in areas of need and of low aspirations: its mission stresses the importance of becoming more involved with the local community. Motivating local youngsters to aspire to higher education might mean that they secure places in other institutions, but this still is viewed as success.

Compact

The word 'Compact' has been widely and broadly used over the past decade to signify an agreement that is not binding like a contract but still demonstrates substantial commitment. Both the HEI and the Compact applicant promise to take specified actions: the applicant to develop certain strengths and broaden its experience and skills; the HEI to offer experiences of higher education and to consider successful students for a place. Various models are examined in Bird and Yee (1994).

Compact does not refer exclusively to HE/post-16 links; it also builds links between pupils and a broad range of employers and training providers. It was, in the 1980s, the favoured term for education–business partnership in the USA, which attempted to raise motivation, attainment and skill levels among inner-city youngsters against the guarantee of employment or training for successful youngsters. Boston Compact was a prime example, attempting to create a positive employment climate to counteract inner-city despair.

The Compact model was adopted by the Department of Employment (DOE) for similar reasons. The context in the mid-1980s was a buoyant economy with the prospect of a shortage of young employees in the 1990s owing to demographic trends. Companies in this early stage viewed Compact as a way of enticing able youngsters by guaranteeing employment to appropriate and suitable youngsters. The first Compacts were in the inner cities: Birmingham Compact emerged during the second wave in 1987–8 (BITC 1991). Today Compacts are widespread in cities, towns and rural areas. The first inner-city Compacts tended to set the standard for those developed later, although each Compact is locally negotiated and idiosyncratic, not structured within a national scheme. A national evaluation by the National Foundation for Educational Research (NFER) is ongoing (Saunders *et al.* 1993a, b) and Compact remains important among DOE strategies (DOE 1994).

The funding and management of Compact was first linked with the Birmingham Heartlands Urban Development Corporation (UDC): it was called Birmingham Heartlands Compact, and operated in or around the Heartlands development area. From 1990 the strategy was adopted elsewhere in Birmingham, with the support of Technical and Vocational Education (TVE). The name was at this point changed to 'Birmingham Compact'. Funding was provided through Birmingham Training and Enterprise Council (TEC), with some advisory teachers provided by the LEA and a marketing team seconded from local industry. Birmingham Compact merged with the Birmingham Education Business Partnership in 1993. Compact, built on the principle of partnership, brought together a range of individuals and institutions with an interest in the education and development of young people: schools, colleges, employers, training providers, the careers service, HEIs and so on. Wherever possible, the views of each were taken into account in policy, planning and the production of materials.

Although Compacts were conceived and born in a buoyant economy, they were weaned in greatly altered circumstances, with employment scarce and with companies struggling and shrinking. Employment guarantees became more of a vain hope than a reality. Nevertheless, Compacts thrived: although conceived as an employment strategy, Compacts were developed as an educational strategy to enhance the motivation of pupils and the relevance of the curriculum (Birmingham Compact 1992, 1993a, 1994a). Informing and motivating youngsters about higher education became part of this, particularly in schools which had no tradition of pupils securing HE places.

The obligations at the heart of Compact are expressed as goals. In Birmingham, goals were set for students, schools and employers: they were the result of widespread consultation, focusing on the question of what is meant by a good student. The first lists of goals were cumbersome, with over twenty individual goals. They soon became consolidated into four more easily remembered groups of goals. Birmingham's pre-16 goals were not untypical of Compacts as a whole, focusing on: attendance and punctuality; coursework completion; involvement in work-related activities; the development of personal skills and qualities.

Compact has from the beginning been for all pupils, achievable across the ability range. Students meeting all goals are awarded a Compact certificate, presented in Birmingham in very high profile events. The certificate is the main motivator, representing a record of a kind of personal attainment not measured by academic examinations – whatever his or her ability, the Compact certificate shows a pupil to be a good student, reliable, hardworking, broad in outlook and concerned to develop skills and potential. Schools and employers are also set goals, which have at their heart their commitment to support pupils and to help them succeed.

In Birmingham and across the country, Compact has operated mainly with 14–16-year-olds. Career choices for 16–18-year-olds involve jobs, training or higher education. Post-16 Compact seeks ideally to provide a framework for all post-16 pupils, whatever their eventual destinations. The HE route is important, but not the sole reason for post-16 Compact's existence. The goals are not dissimilar to those of pre-16 Compact, but show progression. Students are asked to prepare appropriately for post-16 national qualifications (this includes attendance, punctuality and coursework completion): to develop core skills to the best of their abilities; to research a career plan; to complete a work-based assignment satisfactorily; to participate in a higher education experience.

The post-16 Compact pilot was restricted by the fact that only one HEI was involved, and not with every faculty. Students nominated themselves to take part only if applying to those faculties. Schools and colleges, all in areas of urban deprivation, involved only small cohorts at post-16 level. After considering how to set aside quotas for Compact students, UCE opted finally, in 1992, for crediting the post-16 Compact certificate as being equivalent to six A level points – the equivalent of a grade C – as long as specified requirements about qualifications and core skill levels were met. These were set out on 'descriptor sheets' and varied from course to course. This decision, more than any other, raised the credibility of the whole process in the eyes of pupils and school/college staff. It also simplified admission processes within UCE, as there was no need to balance applicants to quotas. Post-16 Compact became recognized as an appropriate qualification for HE entry since it made additional demands on students. The first Compact students entered UCE in October 1993: initial reports indicate that, where these have been tracked, tutors are delighted with their ability and progress.

Expansion and consolidation, 1992–1994

An evaluation of the post-16 Compact pilot in 1993 (Birmingham Compact 1993b) led to a strategy of expansion. Two interrelated problems were identified with respect to the HE route: the need for more HEIs to become partners; and the need for more pupils to take post-16 Compact seriously. The strategy in Birmingham was to bring all five HEIs into the partnership: Aston University, the University of Birmingham, Newman College and West-hill College as well as UCE. All were very supportive, seeing their involvement with the local communities as important. The strategy was not seen primarily as a recruitment exercise: HE expansion was in the process of halting, and there were real concerns about HEIs being swamped with applicants (although this has not proved to be the case). The decision to credit post-16 Compact with six A level points was resisted by the other Birmingham universities, who preferred to see the Compact certificate as an additional qualification able to increase the likelihood of an offer being made and perhaps a lower offer. The willingness of the HEIs to support post-16 Compact was demonstrated in a formal ceremony on 24 March 1994 in The Council House, Birmingham, when each HEI signed a declaration of support (Birmingham Compact 1994a).

Other Midlands HEIs were also approached, with a view to them recognizing the Compact certificate in their own admissions process. Many had a particular interest in supporting able inner-city pupils. It was considered important not to restrict applicants in any way; HEIs were against the notion of exclusive compacts which forced applicants to restrict their choice if they wished to benefit from the agreement. Four other institutions recognized post-16 Compact in this way, three offering six points credit. They were interested in local partnership in their own areas, while working towards a national network in which the certificate is recognized. The Midlands Compact Group, made up of individual Compacts from Derbyshire to Gloucestershire began to negotiate common Compact goals and standards and by 1994 approached HEIs. A national network is still some way off.

The number of schools and colleges using post-16 Compact also increased. More 11–18 age-range schools had developed pre-16 Compact and were invited to adopt Compact in the sixth form; many pre-16 Compact youngsters went to college, and three more colleges asked to become involved. The broader participation has not in practice been fully realized in 1994–5 because of other pressures on schools and colleges.

A major result of the 1993 evaluation was to formalize three levels of post-16 Compact according to the qualifications studied, and these are still used. The advanced certificate requires students to take A levels, advanced GNVQ or BTEC National certificates: these students can participate in the

HE route. The intermediate certificate supports one-year courses, at AS level, intermediate GNVQ or BTEC First Certificates. The foundation certificate is offered alongside the GNVQ foundation and comparable courses. This breadth is becoming increasingly important as the staying-on rate into post-16 courses rapidly increases, as it has done for the past five years: it presently (1995) stands at 66 per cent.

Compact should weld together existing provision rather than bolting on a new scheme. It links a range of non-assessed but important components, such as careers education, work experience, the National Record of Achievement, core skills and vocational visits, into a cohesive, tradeable certificate. It is designed to help schools and colleges develop quality by focusing on student motivation, and the 1993 evaluation revealed that, where Compact was seen as a key element in strategic planning, it was successful and highly regarded. Where it was isolated to a few individuals, it was much slower in having an effect in the institution. The support of senior management has proved crucial.

Compact quality development has the potential to help institutions to meet the external demands made by the Office for Standards in Education (OFSTED) and the FEFC. Standards regarded as ideal and unreachable in 1990 are more taken for granted today; for example, the monitoring of attendance and punctuality and the assessment of core skills. Institutions with scarcely a dozen candidates in the pilot were considering using Compact with the whole cohort of, in some cases, several hundred students to help them consolidate their general programmes. Only a proportion are advanced level students, and not all of these are HE applicants; but larger numbers do have an effect on HEIs' response to Compact applications in a contracting HE market. It is also worth commenting that quality is never straightforward: schools and colleges are not finding it easy to translate good intention into secure practice, so consolidating the Compact process is currently high priority.

Compact contains the seeds of its own redundancy. When quality standards are reached routinely they need refining or replacing. One interesting example is provided by the GNVQ developments that began in Birmingham in the third year of post-16 Compact. Birmingham has opted into GNVQ in a big way, with Birmingham TEC providing funding for training. By 1995–6 around 40 per cent of the city's post-16 cohort will be registered on GNVQ programmes, in both schools and colleges. GNVQ embedded many of post-16 Compact's quality standards: action planning, core skills, attendance requirements and work placements. The real challenge for post-16 Compact was what it could add to already quality-conscious programmes: the answer lay in student motivation and the development of quality systems. In the post-16 world, Compact assumes and develops student initiative, confidence and responsibility, each crucial for GNVQ success.

A key issue has been to assure HEIs of the quality of the certificate. Compact has required schools and colleges to develop a system of monitoring to provide evidence of a student's success, evidence which is open to external scrutiny. This requirement helps to create sound systems of record keeping and encourages judgements to be made on evidence rather than opinion. A formal committee, the Compact Monitoring Group, scrutinizes the evidence in deciding on the award of certificates. Thus, recommendations for the award are made by pupils' own institutions, based on systematic evidence that has to satisfy Compact as the awarding body.

The partnership makes demands upon HEIs. The HE experiences proved, in the pilot, to be the most demanding, largely because at this stage only UCE was involved. These experiences ideally involve Compact students in interactive activities in the HEI. Each HE experience involved large numbers of potential applicants, requiring organization and participation by the HEI staff – based largely on goodwill, as it is seen as a recruitment event. These turned out to be significant learning experiences for HE staff, and there have been particular frustrations when pupils clearly had no intention of applying for UCE courses. Ideally, pupils should be directed to attend an HEI to which they intend to apply.

The principle underlying the HE experience is to give pupils a brief taste of an HEI and the work that would be expected, meeting staff and students in the process. There are many other ways of achieving this, some involving small groups visiting a specific department, or larger groups coming to a sixth-form conference. Post-16 Compact asks for one such experience, but would encourage pupils to go to a range of open days that are routinely on offer. When a range of HEIs provide opportunities for such visits, the pressure on any one becomes more reasonable. A broader range of events allows pupils to select what interests them, providing groups of interested and focused youngsters. In a sense, HE experience provides a helpful model of liaison between HEIs and post-16 institutions.

Another demand on HEIs is to track Compact applicants through the admissions process. In the pilot in UCE, this was done through close liaison between the Compact director and the central university registry, ensuring that admissions tutors were aware and that appropriate offers were made. Since Compact certificates are not awarded until May in year 13, offers made are conditional on success. An offer of grades CCC at A level plus Compact would be equivalent to grades BBB without Compact; a requirement for an advanced GNVQ pass with Compact might become a merit without Compact. In the early stages, we found that management information systems required some modification in order to cope with the new demand. There have proved to be reciprocal benefits to HEIs (for example, through formal and informal staff training and development in areas such as GNVQ, records of achievement and core skills); in addition, HEIs have found closer links with schools and colleges helpful.

Targeting and positive action

Why should some students be so favoured and not others? In over-subscribed courses, it is an issue with admissions tutors to consider a CCC plus

Compact alongside a straight BBB – it is easy to favour the higher grades, particularly where there are pressures from A level points league tables. The broadening of advanced level qualifications is causing this whole area to be reviewed. Substantial issues are raised by positive action, particularly in the United States of America (see the *Economist* no. 7910, April 1995: 21–3). There is an uneasy tension between Compact's functions of raising educational quality through pupil motivation and equalising opportunity by targeting deprived areas. Deprivation in Birmingham is different from deprivation in rural Herefordshire. The common thread is to encourage able pupils, who would not normally aspire to HE, to consider taking a degree. Compact resources are therefore focused on areas of need; Compact quality standards are relevant everywhere.

Post-16 Compact in Birmingham has been targeted on schools and colleges serving inner-city areas where the rate of application to HE was low. These areas are also ethnically mixed, and suffer from high unemployment. Compact is marketed as an additional qualification worth credit. It assesses the extent to which an applicant is a good, committed and reliable student. For those students who are capable of succeeding in HE, this provides the flexibility to compensate for aspects of particular disadvantage, such as operating in English as a second language. No student in these institutions is refused post-16 Compact on the grounds of a targeting policy – it is virtually impossible for judgements to be secure. Any particular observations about individual candidates can be addressed, as they are at present, through the reference.

Compact is part of a broader equal opportunities agenda (Birmingham Compact 1991). A level scores are a crude measure of ability: they favour pupils from affluent families who can provide resources, enrichment experiences, extra tuition and academic schools; grades may reflect the talent of the teacher as much as the ability of the applicant; candidates with high grades might be bright but unreliable. A measure of other qualities adds greatly to the picture of the potential student available to the HEI. The post-16 Compact certificate also sets an agenda for pupils, encouraging them to develop their qualities and skills, providing good preparation for HE: thus Compact helps to equalize opportunity, helping to provide a playing field that is more level and fair. In Birmingham, Compact was associated with other initiatives which targeted particular groups, such as one based in Newman College encouraging ethnic minority students into teacher education.

Consultation: February 1994

A consultation on post-16 Compact was held in Birmingham in February 1994, bringing together a hundred practitioners from post-16 institutions, HEIs (35 delegates from 21 institutions) and other Compacts (see Bigger

1994b). A report was published (Birmingham Compact 1994b), which includes a detailed analysis of questionnaire returns made by delegates.

There were returns from 13 HEIs. All reported that their mission included statements of working with the local community. By way of clarification, delegates reported: priority application schemes for access students; a role in adult education and training; projects involving the local community, such as student tutoring and placements; and a variety of outreach schemes, access programmes and compacts. Compacts in this context often mean individual agreements with particular schools and colleges rather than a wider consortium such as described in this chapter.

Asked about their policies on access, especially in relation to applicants from underrepresented groups, all declared a real commitment to widening participation in HE. They reported: a range of recruitment schemes; a good practice document for interviewers; monitoring of recruitment patterns; involvement in the validation and design of access and foundation courses; designated access staff and units; and direct entry through the accreditation of prior experiential learning (APEL).

Asked about the importance of A levels in admission decisions, the HEIs represented felt that admissions tutors were interested in the whole student profile, in which A levels play an important part for students who take them, with other qualifications and qualities being considered. GCSE results were felt to be important markers of potential for young applicants; together, GCSE and A level are straightforward markers. Much depends on how competitive the subject course is: asking for 27 points or so may be the clearest way of thinning out the applicants. A number of HEIs reported more flexible approaches, through portfolios, motivation, commitment and other indications suggesting a good and interesting applicant. A number looked forward to a radical review of post-16 qualifications.

Over two-thirds (69 per cent) felt that the National Record of Achievement (NRA) is not commonly brought in by students, and no institution found it to be extensively available. Most reported that the NRA seemed difficult to give due weight to in the time available for the interview. They noted that many are offered places without interview; that applicants often repeat sections in their Universities and Colleges Admissions Service (UCAS) application form; that interviewers need some training; that the NRA needs to be more selective; and that it can show a great deal about the applicant's broader personality. One respondent felt that many applicants brought their NRA with them, but few interviewers looked at them. Post-16 Compact provides a means of summing up the NRA in quality terms. To have been awarded the certificate means that quality thresholds have been met in personal reliability, in core skills, in appropriate experience and in having an informed and thoughtful approach to career choice.

The consultation raised a range of issues more fully analysed in Birmingham Compact (1994b). Many relate to HE links.

Is HE equipped to support the kind of students that Compact encourages?
Post-16 Compact is not providing backdoor entry to less able students but

encouraging all students involved to raise their skills and personal self-discipline, and encouraging able students from disadvantaged backgrounds to give serious consideration to HE. Nevertheless, some HE departments may need to address internal issues arising from the broadening in the character of the student body.

Can there be a better match between what students achieve and what HE needs? Traditionally, HE courses have decided what is appropriate to their course needs, so applicants need to research their application properly. Much is having to be reconsidered in the wake of GNVQs. In this rethinking, departments could consider what expertise they require rather than what qualification they demand. This expertise may be demonstrable in ways other than A level. More clarity in HE prospectuses would help applicants to decide on their post-16 courses. A difficulty might emerge if different institutions demand different qualifications for the same course, making choices difficult for post-16 students: stating the expertise (rather than the qualification) required would provide enough flexibility to prevent this.

How is student choice communicated to HE? This is done through UCAS. In Birmingham, liaison between Compact and the HEIs helps to identify Compact students. Offering post-16 Compact does not restrict an applicant's choice in any way.

Although breadth is important, focus should not be understated. The career planning process in post-16 Compact requires students to identify what qualifications they require for the courses they are selecting. This allows them to select properly focused courses, perhaps at A level or advanced GNVQ, at the beginning of their post-16 course.

Where do descriptor sheets fit in? Compact asks students to give their best effort and make progress in relation to their capabilities. The descriptor sheet provides the benchmark of minimum qualification and experience for particular courses. In some cases, sufficient information is given in the prospectus. Both help students to research their career plan.

It is important to sell the idea to admissions tutors. Admissions tutors have the difficult task of sifting applications. Although they routinely look for deserving cases, their time is limited. A post-16 Compact certificate provides a shorthand marker of quality, if the tutor recognizes what it is. The more nationally common Compact becomes, the easier this will be.

Compact could increase the demand for HE places against a background of HE intake restrictions. In Birmingham, we took a long-term view, although in the early days expansion was part of the agenda of all HEIs. The approach has been to equalize opportunity and broaden HEIs' perspectives of quality, whatever the political climate. Compact seeks to open up opportunities; it does not guarantee places. Whether an application is successful may depend on the competition.

What part should Compacts play in management? Some HEIs have dedicated access and Compact staffing, but these are concerned only with students interested in their institution. In a city such as Birmingham, a consortium of post-16 providers and HEIs provides a greater coherence. Many areas in

Great Britain have Compacts, funded through TECs, which could help with a coordinating role. Coordination between Compacts is also important: Birmingham worked particularly closely with Walsall and Shropshire as part of the Midlands Compact Consortium.

It is important not to lose local partnership. Compact begins with the notion of local partnership, helping to develop and refine local links. This is also helpful to HEIs, enabling staff to keep up to date in areas such as GNVQs, Records of Achievement, core skills and so on. It helps them to get to know the local schools and colleges that feed a number of students to them. There is potential for a range of projects between HEIs, schools and colleges, which could be mutually helpful. Successful Compact achievers will further act as role models, encouraging younger students to consider HE as an option.

Can HEIs guarantee places to compact achievers? Guarantees are already made by some faculties, but they are not usually possible. To motivate students to find post-16 Compact worthwhile, some benefit needs to be seen; but guarantees should only be given if they can be honoured. Schools and colleges should be stressing that post-16 Compact is an additional certificate which could help them to obtain an HE place.

How important are core skills for HE courses? It is important to note that Compact encourages general progress in qualities and skills. HE benefits by having students who know the basics of information technology, maths and study skills. The descriptor sheet can stipulate benchmark levels required for particular courses, and may well indicate that some core skills are only required at beginner level.

It is good to use existing systems rather than inventing new ones. Compact seeks to merge into a coherent form a wide range of existing systems: careers education, Records of Achievement, action planning, work experience and coursework monitoring, alongside national academic or vocational courses. Its strategic underpinning lies in having student motivation as the quality strategic objective, encouraging students to make full use of what is available and to build up the self-discipline of giving their best effort. Compact should support existing systems, and not impose new and different agendas.

It is important to track youngsters through HE. Tracking individual students through HE is important in demonstrating that they have proved to be students of quality, and in determining whether they complete courses successfully. It is possible in a local partnership to compile sufficient information to do this. There is a danger that over-zealous tracking will single a student out as being different: given the motivation that Compact should have engendered, it is not necessary to assume that Compact students enter university with minimum grades.

A national accreditation system should be encouraged. It is hard to see how this could be achieved without it being expensive and bureaucratic; and a national system could destroy local partnerships. Common standards of goals and quality assurance would, however, be helpful.

Retrospect

Since it began in 1987, Compact in Birmingham has provided a carefully worked out strategy of partnership involving not only schools, colleges and HEIs but also employers, training providers and a range of organizations involved in the education and guidance of 14–18-year-old students. By 1994, post-16 Compact certificates with higher education links had been developed in a handful of Compacts. Birmingham, Walsall and Shropshire worked particularly closely in the Midlands.

Compact certificates that offer profiles of personal skills and qualities of potential applicants have interested the Midland HEIs involved. HEIs have been further motivated by the strategy of raising aspirations among inner-city pupils. Some inner-city schools and colleges are beginning to build up a tradition of HE entrance, which helps to create an expectation among younger pupils that HE might be a viable career choice.

Student quality and potential can be measured not only by academic grades at GCSE and A level, but also by their core skills, breadth of perspective, reliability and responsibility for their own learning. Post-16 Compact provides a convenient summary statement of achievements.

Quality assurance is vital, but should be part of the overall drive for quality within schools and colleges, stimulated by OFSTED and FEFC. Institutions with sound monitoring and reporting strategies should not find Compact an added burden; those without should find Compact helpful in developing quality, based on the strategy of pupils' involvement, motivation and responsibility for their own learning. The road of establishing quality is, however, never smooth. External monitoring through the central Compact Monitoring Group helps to ensure comparability of standards between institutions.

Compacts are part of the local Education Business Partnerships, funded by the DOE through TECs. The staffing and finance for these are not large, and not particularly secure or uniform. Without central coordination it is hard to be confident about partnership and comparability of standards.

Prospect

Post-16 Compact is a simple idea with a challenging agenda: to raise achievement and aspiration by enhancing motivation. This produces a drive for quality which requires effort and enthusiasm in all staff. Its effectiveness is strategic and requires support at the highest level through the institution's mission, vision and strategic plan. Some schools and colleges have found this difficult, so the philosophy of the programme is not regularly matched by the reality of implementation: post-16 agendas can reflect survival rather than quality. Looking forward, therefore, the priority is to support institutions in developing quality processes.

There is a parallel process in HEIs that is equally significant: to perceive the continuity between the post-16 and HE student experience and enhance progression; to offer a variety of opportunities to welcome post-16 students into HEIs, and equally to encourage HE staff and students to visit schools and colleges; and to view an applicant's quality through the wide lens of overall achievement rather than taking a narrow view based only on specific qualifications.

The post-16 Compact certificate represents these joint processes. The potential exists for it to be offered and coordinated nationally while retaining its local flavour through partnership: however, future funding is precarious. Compact funding has been attached, in the main, to enhancing the motivation of 14–16-year-olds; post-16 Compact funding is at the margins of what is already a small post – often no more than £5,000 per school or college. In Birmingham, specific funding for post-16 Compact never exceeded £1,000 per institution. Yet Compact acts as a catalyst, providing a strategy based on motivating students which enhances quality development. There can be a degree of leverage since Compact helps to focus a range of provision (from the LEA, DFE or DOE, for example) for the enhancement of quality.

The inner-city pupil sits in the middle: it is to the long-term advantage of inner-city communities that the schools and colleges serving them develop expectations that pupils can and will succeed; and a tradition of HE entrance will develop that will give encouragement to younger pupils. This cannot be done without effort; but there will be gains not only in quality but also in broadening the pool of young people who regard HE as an important ambition.

References

Bigger, S. (1994a) Compact in Birmingham: supporting young people, *Business and Connections*, January.

Bigger, S. (1994b) Making a difference, *Access News*, 18, March.

Bird, J. and Yee, W.C. (1994) *From Compacts to Consortia: a Study of Partnerships Involving Schools, Colleges and HEIs*. Bristol, University of the West of England/ Department of Employment.

Birmingham Compact (1991) *Birmingham Compact: Equal Opportunities Policy*. Birmingham, Birmingham Compact.

Birmingham Compact (1992) *Improving Practice in Work Related Activities: Quality Prompts*. Birmingham, Birmingham Compact.

Birmingham Compact (1993a) *New Ideas for Compact Tutors*. Birmingham, Birmingham Compact.

Birmingham Compact (1993b) *Post-16 Compact Evaluation*. Birmingham, Birmingham EBP.

Birmingham Compact (1994a) *Motivating Students: Birmingham Compact 1988–94*. Birmingham, Birmingham EBP.

Birmingham Compact (1994b) *Making a Difference: Post-16 Compact*. Birmingham, Birmingham EBP.

BITC (1991) *The Compacts Directory: a Directory of Achievements in the First Two Years*. London, Business in the Community.

Saunders, L., Morris, M. and Schagen, I. (1993a) *National Evaluation of Inner City Compacts: Annual Overview 1992* . Slough, NFER.

Saunders, L. Morris, M. and Schagen, I. (1993b) *National Evaluation of Inner City Compacts: Supporting Students' Needs through Compacts.* Thematic Report 1992. Slough, NFER.

12

Agreement on Association: Partnerships between the University of Bradford and Bradford and Ilkley Community College

Colin Mellors and Peter Chambers

Introduction

This chapter analyses the process by which two established higher education institutions, one an 'old' university and the other an associated college of the CNAA, previously separated by a variety of organizational and ideological imperatives, found common cause in anticipation of the demise of the CNAA. It describes how, despite the major cultural differences that existed, shared interests were identified and how, facilitated by the adjacent location of the two institutions, recognition of these mutual interests has been fostered and sustained. The case study highlights the ways in which informal negotiations have been translated into formal agreements and procedures to create a framework that is intended to encourage the development of collaborative academic provision across a developing range of agreed areas. While acknowledging that practical and political difficulties still constrain the process of collaboration between the two institutions, it describes the development of a real partnership in which the university and the college make joint and separate provision of courses leading to university awards, the majority of which are full-time. Ultimately, it concludes that formal statements of intent, however laudable, must be reconciled with the deep structure of discourse that underpins them.

Cultural and organizational context

The pursuit of enlightened self-interest is a powerful motivation for organizational collaboration within democratic capitalist economies (Gray 1991).

Such an interpretation certainly appears valid for an understanding of the dynamics that have brought together FEIs and HEIs, institutions that were often quite separate and even divergent in their missions. More than a simple marriage of convenience, but falling short of comprehensive integration, collaboration across the two sectors reflects a desire to secure mutual benefit at minimal risk. Links are potentially symbiotic, bringing equal, if not identical, rewards to each partner. Managed carefully, such arrangements probably most benefit the recipients of the extended and more flexible provision that comes from bridging the two sectors. However, creating and sustaining cross-sector collaboration is beset with difficulties: ideological, organizational, political, financial and practical. Not least, the linking of two disparate academic cultures remains a significant challenge to all who wish to make the collaboration work and develop.

The introduction of market forces into educational planning is now an accepted feature in even the most elite and pure groves of academe, but, at the same time, the involvement of such forces illustrates the different traditions of the two sectors. In the further education sector – always short of money or, at least, lacking guaranteed sources of long-term funding – entrepreneurial approaches to educational practice, although undesirable to many, are well embedded. They exist not just in each college's strategic planning processes, but are evident in the communications used to legitimate the resources required and to justify the end products of the academic process. That rhetoric has created a culture and habit patterns for staff and students that influence FE college decision-making procedures and particularly movements towards collaboration or partnership with other agencies, or 'providers' to use the terminology of the market place. By contrast, setting aside medieval practice, when professors refused to teach until students had placed sufficient fees in the leather bag before the dais, higher education has sometimes appeared to distance itself from the world of trade and been accused of creating a culture in which the values of academic freedom and pursuit of knowledge for its own sake are placed firmly above relevance and applicability. To redress this balance, much weight has been attached in recent government policy statements to the notion that HEIs should be seen to contribute to wealth creation and to the quality of life. As a consequence, much effort has recently gone into demonstrating the very real and practical impact that higher education makes to the well-being of national and local economics.

This portrayal of the two sectors is, of course, a parody, and is unfair to both sectors. It fails to recognize the enormous economic benefit (either intended or simply fortuitous) that emerges from teaching and research in higher education and vocational training in further education. It is certainly an inaccurate representation of the two institutions discussed here. Nevertheless, it serves to indicate how institutional cultures can develop, how they affect organizational and decision-making procedures, how they shape the habitual responses of their members and, thus, how they determine definitions of 'enlightened self-interest'. When collaboration between members of diverse cultures is sought, the meanings of 'enlightenment' must be reconciled to ensure that the 'self-interest' of both parties is satisfied. Moreover, that reconciliation has to be sought through negotiation in a politically directed and financially driven context, one that continues to legitimate historical differences in power and expectations, that is accountable above all to market forces, yet has to be conducted through the language of educational discourse.

In the attempt to understand the framework in which cross-sector institutional collaboration is being sought (and, therefore, to appreciate both the potential and the limiting factors involved), it may be useful to draw on earlier studies of collaborative ventures. One such study considered how local education authorities brought different partners together to bid for funds for the Technical and Vocational Education Initiative (TVEI) against a background of tight resources and a political requirement for innovative practice (Chambers 1986). In this case, in the exercise of gaining collaboration, four key dimensions were identified – financial, political, institutional and educational – although they were not, of course, discrete. The allocation of finance for education is manifestly political and the power to allocate funds relates to the place of institutions in the perceived hierarchy. When the academic cultures are as different as has been suggested, all four dimensions must be explored, fully and honestly.

In the TVEI bid, differences in levels of institutional resourcing, an industrial dispute with the teachers' unions and competition between the LEA's advisory service and the college's in-service department for a lucrative training market combined to affect the workings of the group responsible for coordinating the bid. The participants rarely acknowledged their individual agenda or their different power bases, and the group dynamics were strongly influenced by variations in the political and bargaining skills of the members. Nevertheless, the externally imposed imperative to collaborate ensured that these difficulties were surmounted, with the key actors combining their political and instrumental effectiveness to create a successful bid. Different priorities and levels of accountability remained, but they did not prevent a collaborative partnership finding ways of reconciling conflicting interests expressed as educational values and concepts in a dynamic dialogue. They did, however, create a new agenda for educational development. Financial concerns, competition for power and influence, and institutional cultures rapidly persuaded the partners to incorporate these agenda into their subsequent discourse and negotiations. They influenced the dialogue by shaping what was seen to be in each partner's self-interest.

Most of these factors can be observed in any potential collaborative venture, since underlying the desire to join forces in a particular area, or for a specific venture, is the recognition that, together, the institutions will be able to perform better than either one can alone. This is a central tenet that underpins any form of collaboration or coalition. Success will depend upon a variety of factors: the assessment of the potential rewards and risks of collaboration; the ease with which the two institutions match their organizational and decision-making structures; the strategic priorities and timescales of the potential partnership; the perceived results of previous experiences of collaboration, either with each other or with other institutions; and, not least, the level of respect and trust between the chief actors. As the TVEI bid revealed, collaboration is a *process* and not a single *event.* Successful collaboration in one area encourages experimentation in another, producing a form of functional spillover.

The institutional setting

Both the college and the university have common origins in the Bradford Technical School, which was set up in 1878, but their subsequent development has been parallel, and sometimes divergent, rather than coordinated.

Bradford and Ilkley Community College was established in 1982, bringing together the 1975 merger of the Bradford College of Art and Technology and Margaret McMillan College of Education, with Ilkley College, itself a merger of teacher training colleges. It continued a process launched in the White Paper *Education: a Framework for Expansion* (DES 1972), in which the new institution was encouraged to extend its programme of higher education for full-time students beyond teacher training to include a number of programmes for preparing to work with people. It did so with a clear vision that such programmes would extend access to a wide variety of students not traditionally associated with further or higher education, so that it would become a genuinely comprehensive higher education institution offering real progression to any student who could benefit.

Perhaps the most crucial element of the college's history for the present partnership has been its independent existence as a substantial provider of higher education, within a mission to establish itself as: 'a comprehensive college of further and higher education, and to provide a range of courses that would meet the needs of the urban, industrial and multicultural community of Bradford' (Bradford College 1977).

It has become just such an institution: a 'mixed-economy' college (HEFCE 1994) funded directly by both the FEFC and the HEFCE, explicitly committed to serving the needs of the Bradford community. Its 40,000 enrolments cover adult education, further education and higher education in a uniquely comprehensive range of programmes of study. Over one-third (35 per cent) of its work is funded by the HEFCE for a student population of almost 3,000 full-time students with a further 1,000 following part-time courses that include postgraduate programmes. The College's higher education programme includes art and design, business studies, community studies, health-related education, management education, social work, teacher training and youth work. Academic programmes are organized into five schools: adult and general education; art, design and textiles; business and professional studies; science and technology; and teaching and community studies. Each programme is vocationally orientated. From its platform as a substantial provider of adult and continuing education, and from its place both as one of the largest institutions funded by the FEFC and as the largest mixed economy college funded by the HEFCE, Bradford and Ilkley Community College offers a uniquely comprehensive provision of further and higher education. It allows unimpeded progression to any student who can benefit from its diverse range of vocational and professional programmes.

With its common ancestry, the University of Bradford, like the college, traces its origins back to the mid-nineteenth-century movement for technological and scientific enlightenment. A former college of advanced technology, it was granted university status in 1966 following the Robbins Report (McKinlay 1991). Since that time, the university has more than doubled in size, and now has nearly 6,000 full-time undergraduate students, approximately 250 part-time and associate students on undergraduate programmes and approaching 2,000 full- and part-time postgraduates. Many programmes are interdisciplinary and, befitting its motto 'making knowledge work', almost all have an applied or area- or problem-based focus. Many first degree programmes are four years in duration, involving work placements or their equivalent. The Faculty of Engineering offers professionally accredited courses in civil and environmental, electrical and electronic, and mechanical and manufacturing areas, and an interdisciplinary first degree programme in technology and management. It is also the home of the Electronic Imaging and Media Communications Unit (EIMCU) which, with the college, runs a novel programme focused on the production of audio and visual images, in conjunction with the National Museum of Film, Photography and Television. The Faculty of Natural and Applied Sciences includes a number of health-related departments (biomedical sciences, optometry and pharmacy) as well as archaeological sciences, computing, environmental sciences and mathematics. The largest faculty, social sciences, spans humanities (languages, human studies), social sciences (applied social studies, European studies, development and project planning, peace studies, social and economic studies) and business and management studies. In addition to this portfolio, the university offers post-experience provision to some 8,000 participants each year.

The university is strongly committed to innovation. Its courses in European studies and environmental sciences were among the first in Britain. Others, such as peace studies and electronic imaging and media communications, remain unique. It combines close links with the city, with an international outlook through its Development and Project Planning Centre, which is renowned for its specialist training for overseas public officials. The university, like the college, operates a number of overseas programmes – in the Netherlands, Malaysia, Pakistan, the Far East and Japan – in areas such as management and engineering. At any one time, students from approximately eighty countries will be present in Bradford.

This brief description of the two institutions indicates some of the contextual features that encouraged collaboration between the university and the college. They include: the complementary rather than competitive nature of programmes of study; potential progression routes for students in many areas (particularly engineering and management); an adjacent location that lends itself to shared teaching and support services; a mutual commitment to the application of teaching and research; and a common interest in contributing to the reputation and well-being of the City of Bradford. The arrival of a new vice chancellor at the university in 1988, committed to extending access opportunities, encouraged the two institutions to look for ways in which they could exploit these features through partnership.

Prior to recent developments, links between them have been surprisingly limited, despite their close proximity and their common origins. During the period of expansion of higher education (1957–75) there had been separate, but parallel, developments, but these were followed by a period of diverging allegiances (1976–90) (White 1978). As a consequence, while some common student welfare provision was shared, relatively little was done to explore, or to exploit, further potential common interests. The college, still under local authority control, and committed to its comprehensive values, pursued its distinctive mission, and the university, still relatively new, was intent upon making its mark in the university sector. The trigger for a re-evaluation of these positions came with the college's need to seek an alternative source of validation for its degree programmes. The neighbouring university was an obvious solution.

The mechanisms for association

In 1990, following relatively constructive negotiations between the two institutions, the respective governing bodies committed themselves to an agreement of future association. The agreement left unspecified some aspects of the association, but clearly signalled the intention of both institutions to work towards common processes for course approval and review, which would ensure the quality of provision and, subsequently, achieve a common modular structure. It was intended to be more than simply a validating arrangement. At the heart of the association have been the processes through which university and college seek to promote: 'the joint commitment to strengthening the processes of academic collaboration and institutional partnership and to confirming the shared responsibility to enhance the quality of provision of further and higher education in Bradford' (Bradford and Ilkley Community College/University of Bradford 1994).

The relationship has built upon the experience that both sides have brought to the association and, encouragingly, each has been willing to learn from the other. The college brought to the association experience of peer group review and validation through the CNAA. This experience was particularly relevant at a time when the university sector was about to face the processes of external quality audit and, subsequently, assessment. Such sharing has also been facilitated by the good personal relationships that have existed between many of the key actors.

Importantly, senior members of the university respected the distinctive mission and achievements of the college, and the culture it represented, and expressed confidence in the college's quality assurance procedures. They also drew upon the expertise of college members in developing their own academic audit processes and, significantly, a senior member of the college was chosen to lead the team that took the university through the final stages of its preparation for academic audit. The successful audit visit, and the report that followed, certainly benefited from the collaboration during the preparatory stage. The relationship was two-way and, therefore, when the college was preparing for the early rounds of the subject assessments by the HEFCE, a senior member of the university reviewed the written submission and took part in the college's internal preparations. The outcome was successful – the college's own assessments of 'excellent' for applied social work and 'satisfactory' for business and management were confirmed by the HEFCE.

The association was intended to be of mutual benefit. The university believed that it could profit from the college's experience in preparing itself for the changing culture of quality assurance in higher education. In turn, the college recognized the advantages to be gained from association with an institution that has a rich research and teaching culture, and had sufficient confidence in the quality of its own provision and trust in its relationship with the university to accede to an agreement that left it inevitably subordinate to the statutes of the university. That trust is a feature that continues to colour the development of the association and should be seen as an important aspect of this case study.

In order to give momentum and strategic direction to the association, a joint policy and planning group was established, comprising the senior management teams of both institutions. The group meets termly and reports to the senior academic bodies of the university and college, senate and academic board respectively. However, the core of the process of academic association rests with the board of collegiate studies, a body comprising six members of each institution, and chaired by the university's pro-vice chancellor responsible for academic policy. Recently, it has been agreed that, in future, a senior member of the college staff nominated by its academic board will chair the board of collegiate studies. The board performs a role similar to that of the university's three faculty boards in respect of the college's degree programmes and reports in parallel to the college's academic board and to the senate via the university's academic policy committee. In addition, there is significant cross-membership in lower tier sub-committees and working groups, and college and university staff (admittedly usually drawn from a small and senior group of staff) are enmeshed in the academic work of both institutions.

What the university has done in this respect has been to acknowledge the quality of the college's procedures and their previous endorsement by the CNAA. It is an important acknowledgement of trust and mutual understanding. The college adjusted its joint accreditation position and the university accepted that its involvement was to replicate the functions of the CNAA. Thus validation and course review arrangements remained those developed by the college, with CNAA representatives replaced by university members. In turn, the college substituted university arrangements for the appointment of external examiners and the conduct of examination boards. It is a partnership that is intended to allow both college and university to expand their provision overseas without compromise on quality or standards.

Widening participation and protecting standards

Institutional mechanisms and procedures are, of course, means rather than ends. The purpose of the university–college partnership is to help both to rise to the challenge of increasing participation while retaining standards. A central concern has been to create effective progression routes into higher education, a genuine ladder of opportunity, for a diverse range of students, many of whom rarely aspire to futures at college or university. At the same time, both institutions had to ensure that this combination of provision had currency and credibility as 'proper' higher education, both in the public eye and in the judgment of peer groups. No matter how laudable the aim, standards and quality could not be allowed to be compromised in the interests of access, progression and opportunity.

One indictment of higher education is that, despite efforts to change, the social mix of the higher education population has scarcely altered. Improvements in the gender balance and increases in the participation rates of mature and access students have not been matched by the involvement of many more students from working-class backgrounds or, indeed, from minority groups. It is not a uniquely British characteristic. Notwithstanding the efforts of federal and state governments in the United States, social differentiation continues to shape both educational opportunity and take-up. The problem is, in many ways, self-sustaining, and the starting point must be to increase awareness of, and aspiration to, higher education among those groups that are currently underrepresented. The challenges are particularly salient for the two institutions in this case study, given their stated missions and their location in a geographical area that does not perform well in terms of the numbers who achieve national educational and training targets. Both the university and the college recognize their responsibilities in this respect. The university, for example, has organized one of the first part-time evening degree courses outside London, in social studies. Over 27 per cent of students are mature. The college has developed a still wider response to less traditional students. Twenty-two per cent of its students on mainstream courses are of minority ethnic backgrounds and the majority of its students are mature. Both the university and the college programmes have achieved national recognition for their contributions to increasing access to adult learners.

In establishing and operating the relationship, the college and the university have, in common with other institutions, had to face the implications of a situation which is dominated by publicly accountable measures of academic 'quality' and funding regimes that do not always give positive steers to HEIs about how they can best please their political superiors, their paymasters and their markets. The diverse audiences to whom they have to appeal have conflicting values and standards. Entry standards to higher education and, consequently, alternative qualifications – or, more importantly, alternative evidence to justify entry – have to be considered in this context of diversity and conflict. HEIs have the equivalents of school league tables and all their attendant consequences for marketing and recruitment. Their position in the table is not only affected by their recruitment and access policies, but also depends on the quantity and quality of research activity and related income generation. Reputation and prestige depend on these matters, and on the quality of students attracted. In these circumstances, a positive attitude towards the underrepresented can remain, regrettably, a lower priority. The strength and legitimacy of these concerns still affect the association and even, on occasions, pulls the two institutions in different directions, but they remain an integral objective of the partnership.

What of standards? Traditionally, it has sometimes been implicitly believed that standards were ensured by the limited number of higher education places available and by the selective, and sometimes elitist, process of choosing candidates. The so-called 'massification' of higher education has therefore sent enormous ripples throughout the system. 'More' cannot be allowed to mean 'worse', but it certainly must mean 'different', and revisiting two of the traditional 'input' and 'output' measures used in higher education (standard entry qualifications and degree classifications) may well be part of that difference. A further aspect of the new approach will be new pressures on HEIs to receive the much expanded output of further education colleges, where qualifications will, of necessity, be 'new' NVQ-type awards.

The premise that 'more inevitably means worse' is, of course, applied to all educational levels. Thus, the increasing numbers of GCSE and GCE passes are often used to assert that there has been a lowering of the standards of assessment rather than an improvement in the standards of achievement. If expansion produces comparable levels of achievement measured by the previous assessment indicators, then it is asserted that the indicators are being less rigorously applied. The processes described above are designed to ensure that this is demonstrably not the case at Bradford. The university– college partnership, therefore, aims to extend opportunities, especially to previously underrepresented groups, without undermining quality and standards.

Creating new programmes and pathways

This description of the partnership established between the university and the college has intentionally focused on the institutional framework. The overriding aim has been to create a structure, and an organizational environment, that encourages the extension of complementary courses and programmes rather than presenting staff at both institutions with a fixed agenda. In that sense, the relationship is seen as progressive and dynamic. One aim of the exercise has been to create a portfolio of HE provision in Bradford that exploits the different strengths of the two institutions. Hence the college focus has been towards art and design, teacher training and youth and community work, while that of the university has been towards engineering, health-related studies and the social sciences. With this context in mind, some specific examples will illustrate the range of collaborative programmes that have been established. The first, an innovative degree in electronic imaging, is a genuine joint programme developed out of the university's Department of Electronic and Electrical Engineering with the college's School of Art, Design and Textiles. Staff from both institutions teach on the programme. A second example is the agreement to develop comparable undergraduate programmes in business studies that allow both college and university students to follow modules offered by either institution. The development of the programmes is the subject of regular planning meetings. In the area of engineering, the college and the university together have for several years planned and delivered a foundation programme leading to entry into the university's undergraduate engineering courses. In so doing, they have opened a pathway into professionally accredited courses for students who would not otherwise have qualified. Perhaps most innovative, and reflecting the real attempt to achieve collaboration at all levels, the two institutions have jointly designed and launched a Postgraduate Certificate of Higher Education. This part-time programme is taught by staff from the college's Department of Teaching Studies and the university's Teaching and Learning Development Unit. Although aimed at all those in higher education, it serves a particularly important staff development function for the college, the university and a local college of health. The symbolism of a scenario in which groups of staff being taught by those from the other institutions illustrates the way in which genuine partnership is being developed. Such examples of formal provision are supported by many smaller opportunities for shared teaching; for instance, in law and women's studies.

Retrospect

The agreement signed in 1990 was, strictly, an agreement of future association, and it was assumed that this would be translated into a more formal arrangement in due course. By 1993, a review was begun with the intention of formalizing the earlier agreement. This process has revealed how the four dimensions of dialogue referred to earlier – financial, political, institutional and educational – have shaped the developing partnership.

A full exploration of these dimensions is inappropriate to a published case study, but continues to take place through the machinery of interinstitutional dialogue. However, it can be acknowledged that the different levels of resourcing, some competition between departments for a declining pool of students and the ramifications of a protracted industrial dispute over college lecturers' contracts have combined to produce difficulties in the relationship, mirroring those reported in the study of the TVEI bid referred to earlier. However, parallels also exist between the two cases that have allowed potential difficulties to be overcome. For example, the process of developing partnership has been made easier by the establishment of separate arenas in which each of the different dimensions has been addressed in order to establish trust prior to the more formal and public discussions. The part played by informal contacts should not be ignored. Because preparatory meetings have maintained awareness of the financial, political, institutional and educational dimensions that influence the process of negotiation, progress has been relatively quick and smooth. Nevertheless, it has often been apparent that each side has brought its own values to the decision-making process. Those values are hard to break down, and attempts to do so might not be considered necessary or even desirable, provided that acknowledgement of their distinct values opens ways to smoothing the path to progress.

Predictably, the political dimension of the collaboration was soon manifest. Members of the university senate did not hesitate to express their concern at the conduct of the processes of preparation for academic audit and their impact on the university's *modus operandi*. Likewise, staff and students of the college informed the academic board that some aspects of university regulations appeared to disenfranchise them. Productively, at both college and university it was possible to demonstrate the mutual benefits, and the careful preparation that had gone into the negotiation of the association promoted the advantages of collaboration, minimized potential areas of conflict and consigned financial considerations to the respective finance officers. Indeed, the financial memorandum was not drafted until after the revised agreement in 1995. Although this has been a source of frustration, and led to a number of unsatisfactory 'local' agreements, it has meant that pre-eminence has been given to the establishment of institutional and educational dimensions.

The progress report of November 1993 described the association as 'one of the success stories for both the college and the university'. In a period of rapid growth in both institutions, during which the university responded with enormous success to the process of academic audit and the college proceeded securely through the process of incorporation, the needs of students were kept at the forefront, their opportunities were extended and, independently, each institution succeeded in demonstrating the quality of its provision. Together, they have developed semester-based modular programmes with the intention of increasing choice and extending flexible learning opportunities.

It is, however, a process that has been described as 'harmonization' rather than 'integration'. This pragmatic choice of words is intended to reduce the threats to institutional autonomy, while stressing the concord needed in partnerships. However, it also means that there are limitations to serious joint action: parallel activities are still more likely to be found than integrated strategic planning.

Fortunately, since the portfolios of the college and the university tend to be complementary rather than competing, this has only created minor problems, notably in areas where provision overlaps (e.g. business studies and social work), but even here potential problems have been resolved by careful negotiation. Pragmatism is necessary, but is clearly not the most effective way of exploiting the full potential of the two institutions' combined resources. What the agreement of association started was a process of acculturation, and the joint policy and planning group has encouraged that process. It has steered conduct rather than exercised authority to direct the partnership to ensure the achievement of the association's objectives.

Nevertheless, even if progress has been measured rather than urgent, the achievements have been solid and contrast with the volatility of much of the higher education scene in recent times. The integration of the college's programmes within the university's teaching, examination and validation processes has come about smoothly and in ways that have preserved the college's own quality assurance procedures. The transfer of validation arrangements and the creation of collegial structures were remarkable: students moved from CNAA-approved courses to university-validated courses without a hitch. The support of the university registry, and the ease with which regulations were adapted and embedded, reflected the real commitment to making the arrangement work. There was *de facto* accreditation of the college as a suitable institution to offer courses leading to degrees of the university. College members have valued the support and goodwill of the university members who participated in the committees established. University members have valued the contribution college members made to university committees. However, it has to be recognized that much of this cooperation has taken place at senior levels of both institutions, while at other levels cooperation is willing and supportive, but much less structured and coordinated. Initiatives have tended to be *ad hoc* and isolated, and no structural mechanisms have yet been established to consolidate arrangements for more systematic collaboration.

The college and the university are now reviewing the progress made and groups have been identified to consider different areas (non-academic as well as academic) where further progress might be possible. So far, officers of both institutions judge the association to have been a success and to be meeting its objectives. Validation and review procedures for college programmes have been established smoothly and effectively in a way that has enhanced the quality of higher education available to students of each institution. Both institutions have benefited from examination and adaptation of their respective quality assurance procedures. Arrangements for modularization and semesterization mean that the two institutions now operate in parallel, so opening the way for any further academic programmes that might be considered desirable. The plethora of collaborative initiatives within a very solid framework of association has created a strong and permanent alliance, which has become the basis for the stronger agreement of association now approved.

The standard and quality of the provision remains paramount. National quality assurance systems assert emphatically the importance of institutional missions and the context within which individual students complete their programmes. The college and university have, therefore, combined to make such a statement. Quality is an institutional value and its determinants – excellence, fitness for purpose and success in realizing customer aspirations – are generalizable only as far as the association's mission acknowledges the normative assumptions of the system. What the association is establishing is creative opportunities based on those assumptions. It is designed to exploit the talents of those students that the present (and traditional) educational and training opportunities have often failed to exploit. At the same time, however, there are areas where collaboration has been limited – usually reflecting the separate cultures and agenda of the two institutions and the sensitivities about even appearing to threaten the autonomy of either institution. As a consequence, the role that each institution can play in the other's strategic planning processes remains marginal. This is likely to remain the case in the foreseeable future.

Prospect

The way forward for the association is to build with caution on the trust created and the achievements thus far established. Both the college and the university remain conscious of the need to protect their separate identities and reputations and recognize that, in doing this, they may be led towards divergent goals. Divergence may be further encouraged by the different funding arrangements for HE students in the two sectors at a time when full-time student numbers are capped. This was well illustrated by the difference in tone of the responses of the two institutions to the recent HEFCE consultation about the funding of HE students in colleges (HEFCE 1994).

There are other factors that continue to discourage a closer alliance. Recent university planning has been much influenced by the imperatives of the 1996 research assessment exercise, which will affect both its finances and its reputation. While the university is anxious to underline and enhance its research ethos, the college, denied access to research funding by HEFCE, seeks mainly to gain recognition. Research at the college is largely the preserve of individual academic departments and lecturers, is funded on the back of successful income generation or bidding for research projects and takes place in a culture that gives greater priority to teaching and learning. These different emphases do not deny that research and teaching go hand in hand; but for those, in both institutions, who remain sceptical about the relationship, they are easy to portray as mutually exclusive cultures. More-over, when they are related to the imperatives of the external funding agen-cies, the threat of competition can inhibit efforts to exploit the benefits of collaboration.

Notwithstanding these pressures, there are also influences that encour-age further collaboration. Given the current low HE participation rate by school-leavers from the Bradford district, it is clearly in the interests of both institutions to expand 'ladders of educational opportunity', especially if the expected trend towards more locally based student recruitment takes place in future years. Similarly, in the field of continuing vocational education (CVE), there may be more opportunities for the institutions to work together rather than in competition. The university's Management Centre and the college's Business Studies department, for example, already cooperate in a first-level supervisory management programme run on behalf of the Royal Mail. There are also powerful external forces that require greater coopera-tion. In the field of technology transfer, for instance, both European Union and UK government funding is increasingly being allocated in a way that encourages local and regional collaboration within, and across, HE and FE sectors. Since Bradford qualifies for European Regional Development Fund Objective 2 status, this provides a clear incentive for the two institutions to work together in securing grant aid.

Nor has the need to respond to the rising costs of providing mass higher education, by extending access to full-time education through the modular-ization of programmes and the semesterization of attendance, escaped the college and the university. Both institutions have modularized their full-time HE programmes within a common framework and the scheduling of semesters has been harmonized. So far, few undergraduates have exploited the opportunities being opened up, but the first common curriculum will be available to them in 1995–6, when the college's law modules, designed for its business studies students, will be offered to business studies students at the university. If the suspicions and anxieties about separate cultural identities are not allowed to inhibit such opportunities, the prospects for full-time students will be significantly enhanced and the pressures on funding eased, but it will require courage and imagination from members of the college and the university. The new agreement of association indicates that neither the courage nor the imagination is absent in the corporate vision.

Nevertheless, the present position of the association is at a crossroad – the movement to open up access, to collaborate more closely, to accept the parity of college provision and to change practices may be challenged by the policies of research selectivity and the publicity accorded to the rankings that are constructed as a consequence. The tension is real, but the sensitive handling of the association over the past five years has demonstrated how apparently conflicting aims can be reconciled in the interests of educational innovation and the needs of students. The academic community created by the association between Bradford and Ilkley Community College and the Uni-versity of Bradford is responding, as necessary, to the needs of the market, to the challenge of market forces and to the quality requirements of its own academic values. It illustrates how, with goodwill and the occasional steer, enlightened self-interest can find ways of overcoming financial differences, political difficulties and institutional imperatives to make educational sense for a greater variety of full-time students. In so doing, it points to the clear benefits to both institutions of translating mere coexistence into real collaboration.

The views expressed in this chapter are those of the authors and do not necessarily reflect those of their respective institutions.

References

Bradford College (1977) *Academic Policy Statements.* Bradford.

Bradford and Ilkley Community College/University of Bradford (1994) *Joint Policy and Planning Group Review.* Bradford, BICC/University of Bradford.

Chambers, P. (1986) TVEI-related INSET (TRIST). In *Proceedings of the British Educational Research Association.* Bristol, BERA.

DES (1972) *Education: a Framework for Expansion,* Cmnd 5174. London, HMSO.

Gray, J. (1991) *The Moral Foundations of Market Institutions.* London, IEA Health and Welfare Unit.

HEFCE (1994) *Funding the Relationship.* Bristol: Higher Education Funding Council for England.

McKinlay, R.A. (1991) *The University of Bradford.* Bradford, University of Bradford.

White, D. (1978) *100 Years of Technical Education in Bradford.* Bradford, Bradford College.

Part 3

The Future of Partnerships

13

Beyond Franchising: The Future of Partnerships

Mike Abramson, John Bird and Anne Stennett

Introduction

One of the main aims of this book was to look beyond franchising. While franchising was, for some time, the dominant relationship between further education and higher education, there is now a wide variety of second-generation partnerships, which include increasing numbers of partnerships involving schools, joint courses, validation and articulation agreements. What is perhaps most important now is that there is a two-way flow between FE, schools and HE, whereas, in the past, HE was often the dominant partner. This two-way flow occurs because there is an increasing recognition that all members of partnerships have something to offer, and that there is strength in their diversity. Put another way, we are moving to a situation in which hierarchies in post-16 education are less and less the order of the day and more parity of esteem is emerging. There is, for example, collaboration in quality assurance, in course design and delivery, in staff development and in research.

Given that we have moved beyond franchising, what is the future of partnerships likely to look like? Given the difficulties of predicting future policy on education and the current problems attendant upon FE expansion, HE consolidation and the funding of students, what does the future hold? What follows in this chapter falls into two sections: first, a series of bullet points which effectively summarize the predictions that have been made by each contributor; second, some more detailed discussion, often speculative but also informed, of the future for partnership. Futurology is, doubtless, a failed scientific exercise but, none the less, we think it will prove useful and interesting to draw out a possible picture of partnerships as they develop into the next century.

Prospects

Resources and capacity

See, for example, Chapters 1, 3, 9 and 10.

- A single funding system for FE and HE to enhance collaboration.
- Following this, a move from *ad hoc* to secure funding for collaboration.
- Funding by module rather than funding for courses.
- Better support for part-time students, but within a reformed system of student funding.
- Joint use of resources, including staff and plant.
- Joint strategic planning to facilitate ease of progression through post-compulsory education.

Structure and delivery

See, for example, Chapters 5, 7, 8, 11 and 12.

- Greater use of articulation agreements on the Scottish model.
- Increasing numbers of FE–FE and FE–HE mergers; the possibility of FE–sixth form college mergers.
- More European and international links, with quality enhanced through technology.
- A continuous system of post-compulsory education which includes schools, colleges and HEIs.
- The development of community colleges on the United States model.
- An increase in associate college status with exclusivity agreements.
- More joint courses and straight validations.
- Local and regional strategic planning to enhance progression.
- New universities or university colleges in isolated areas.
- Increasing partnerships between FE and schools.
- Franchising of BTEC and other FE work to schools.

Teaching and learning

See, for example, Chapters 1, 4 and 6.

- Greater use of multimedia and resource-based learning; development of electronic libraries through JANET, superJANET and other online facilities.
- The delivery of level 2, and possibly level 3, of degree programmes in FE, hence minimizing progression difficulties.
- More flexible and part-time delivery; more sympathetic timetabling, including weekends, summer schools and third semesters.

- Customized programmes through the credit accumulation and transfer scheme and modularization.
- More competency-based teaching and learning to articulate with NVQs and GNVQs.

Quality

See, for example, Chapters 5 and 7.

- A single quality and funding body.
- More degree awarding powers to members of collaborative networks.
- Greater acceptance of colleges' own internal quality assurance systems.
- Greater stress on the strengths and distinctiveness of FE and HE, i.e. the recognition of distinctiveness with reference to fitness for purpose.
- Greater emphasis on student rights and entitlements, including induction, delivery, assessment, progression and after-sales care.

Students

See, for example, Chapters 2 and 6.

- Clearer entitlements.
- Greater student responsibility for their own programmes.
- More individual, customized programmes.
- Greater demand for complete award bearing programmes to be delivered locally.
- Guaranteed progression to the HEI, where necessary, to complete awards.
- Greater access to learning technology networks, e.g. CD-ROM.
- Some increase in the dystopian side of FE; for example, greater size and increased student numbers.

Discussion

FHE institutions, schools and expansion

While there is, at present, a consolidation of HE together with an expansion in FE, the targets for proportions of 16–19-year-olds entering HE by the year 2000 – some 40 per cent – suggest that expansion is on the long-term agenda. It is hoped that only in the short-term will there be a disjuncture in the expansion of FE and HE with the possible structural strains that this can produce; for example, pressure on FE to expand HE provision when HE finds it difficult to do so. Perhaps the most important aspect of future expansion relates to the nature of the student population: it will be from more diverse backgrounds and will have new qualifications, such as GNVQs.

This will put pressure on FHE to innovate in curriculum terms; to provide different, more flexible and more customer-designed courses, modes of assessment and delivery.

The increasing diversity in the student population will also tend to make global, sector-wide, solutions more untenable. For example, however much the virtual university makes sense, it will only serve the needs of some students, and may serve the needs of some students only at certain points in their academic careers. Put another way, there is no magical, technological solution in the development of a mass FHE system. New technologies of teaching and learning (see Chapter 4) are only appropriate to the extent that they meet student needs and enhance the quality of the student experience. It is not unduly Luddite to question the assumption, embodied in a variety of forms of technological determinism, that technology *is* the panacea.

Moreover, from listening to students, it is clear that many of them now opt to study in FE because it is local and relatively small. As FE expansion proceeds these advantages may, for some students, be lost. They may face the prospect of studying in institutions that are much bigger than they expect, and in which access to staff and to learning resources becomes as difficult as in some large HEIs. Mergers of FEIs may exacerbate the problems for students if some of them lose access to a local, and relatively accessible, institution.

Finally, there are some interesting things happening to bring closer links between FHE and schools (see Chapter 11). Compacts and other forms of partnership that involve schools are likely to increase in number and in significance. In many ways, links with schools – especially where these involve students from 11 years old – are probably among the most effective ways of increasing the demand for post-compulsory education. Such partnerships are likely to prosper and are, therefore, likely to place great pressure on FEIs and HEIs to offer places to suitably qualified students from an increasing diversity of backgrounds.

The quality debate

The debate about quality is, in part, a debate about whether quality issues and funding issues should be dealt with by one body or two. There is no second guessing the results of this debate, other than saying that it is more likely that, in the future, there will be a single body.

More important for this volume is the issue of quality fears. It is far from clear that FHE partnerships are replete with quality problems. While there may be problems with some collaborative ventures, the whole movement for collaboration is no more likely to produce poor quality education than any other attempt to link sectors. As Lines and Clarke argue in Chapter 8, international links are no more subject to quality problems than are national ones. The future agenda will need to include more research than there has been; research that will codify those aspects of collaboration which ensure the best quality of provision. It is also important here to acknowledge that the issue of quality is a profoundly political one. There is every reason to assume that the agenda of the HEQC, HMI, OFSTED and, of course, the *Times Higher Education Supplement* are politically driven. The lesson from this volume is that there is no one thing called quality. There is a diversity of institutions with a diversity of missions delivering a diversity of programmes. There is, as Chapters 1, 2 and 5 indicate, strength in this diversity, a strength which will not be developed and enhanced if quality is seen only to reside in the practices of one type of institution, which then becomes the model for all.

There is a final issue with reference to quality, which is the much thought about, but hardly mentioned, idea that quality is *not* being maintained, in large measure because the expansion of student numbers in FHE has not been met by commensurate increases in staffing and learning resources. While staff in FHE are doubtless flattered by the notion that they can maintain standards in such an environment, it is far less clear that the quality of what the students are receiving is perceived by them as of uniformly high quality (see Chapter 6).

Collaboration or exclusivity

There is a drive for collaboration and a drive for exclusivity. The former is found in partnerships where a number of FHE institutions and schools collaborate to plan provision. The latter occurs where associate college arrangements tie one HEI to a number of FEIs to the exclusion of other HEIs; this may include tying of students to single exits into the HEI.

Whether the drive for collaboration or the drive for exclusivity will be victorious is a complex issue. While we can say that competition between institutions in some sectors (FE–HE, HE–HE) is part of the grain of education policy, there are regional and local factors that favour institutions going against the grain and developing a new geography of partnership (see Chapter 1). These factors will include whether, historically, there has been cooperation and whether there are structures that will favour cooperation; that is, whether there are existing consortia that can be sustained. Again there will be parts of the country where existing cooperation may be threatened; for example, those faced with the establishment of unitary authorities. However, there will also be parts where existing consortia – based on open college networks and TVEI consortia – will survive. In addition, there are curriculum changes – the introduction of GNVQs – that may favour cooperation between schools and FEIs and between these and HEIs. As the Further Education Unit has indicated, 'who shares wins'. That is, there is a partnership imperative with sound financial, political and social groundings. Partnerships can yield mutual benefits and, as Chapter 12 suggests, may be based on enlightened self-interest.

New institutions: mixed-economy colleges, mergers and community colleges

If there are, as some would argue, too many FEIs and HEIs, then mergers are likely. To the extent that they are mergers of local institutions, this will not necessarily be a bad thing. What will these merged colleges look like? They are likely to be mixed-economy colleges delivering both sub-degree/diploma and degree/diploma programmes. They are likely to be comparatively large, with both the benefits and difficulties associated with size; for example, a wider range of programmes delivered with larger class sizes. They may, as suggested earlier, take provision further away from some more isolated communities. Some of the mergers will involve HEIs and specialist colleges which now deliver nursing, art or agriculture related programmes. These specialist colleges are likely to become new faculties or campuses of HEIs. Finally, we may see the development of community colleges on the US model, since, in many senses, they are a model for much of the good practice identified in this volume. They are user-led in the sense of developing curriculum responses to diverse groups of students. Because they provide a modular programme and are semesterized, they allow greater flexibility. Students may start at a variety of points in the year, gaining credit in one college that will be recognized by others, including local, state and Ivy League universities. Community colleges also have close links with local state universities, often including university involvement in their governance. Finally, they offer a great variety of provision, from the vocational to the academic and from supplementary language provision to degree work. In some ways, then, community colleges resemble the best of the links that, in the past, existed between polytechnics and their local FEIs.

Processes by which FEIs and HEIs move closer together are central to the partnership agenda. However, it is by no means clear that all universities will move in this direction, and there are processes which may mitigate against commitments to serve local communities. It is by no means certain that all the former polytechnics will maintain their distinct missions to serve their communities and to specialize in teaching. On the contrary, many may become – or at least try to become – more like traditional universities, with an emphasis on more research and more postgraduate provision. Some aspects of the HEFCE research assessment exercises and the relationships which exist – or are believed to exist – between teaching and research may exacerbate this. Taking a pessimistic view, we would need to ask whether the pursuit of research and postgraduate provision works against the social mission of these institutions.

The mutual benefits of partnership

It is important that institutions do get benefits. To the extent that there is no hierarchy of institutions, then the benefits should accrue to all those involved, be they schools, FEIs or HEIs. As suggested earlier, mutual benefits will often go hand in hand with enlightened self-interest. Joint courses between FE and HE or between FE and schools can benefit both students and institutions, especially if no one institution can provide such programmes on its own, owing to, for example, lack of staff, resources or expertise.

The future is, therefore, likely to see partnerships extend beyond the provision of courses to include collaboration in teaching and learning, in research, and in staff development; for example, staff may be exchanged between institutions. The important thing here is not only that benefits accrue to all those involved, but that the calculation of benefits in simple income terms becomes too limited. If, in the past, there was resistance to partnerships on the grounds that they did not generate any, or sufficient, income, such resistance will, it is hoped, decline as the wider benefits become obvious.

The participation debate

The participation debate is, in part, a debate about numbers; it includes targets for the numbers of 16–19-year-olds who are to go into HE. It is also, however, a debate about raising aspirations among those who would not normally see HE as a possibility; that is, it is about widening access as a positive action strategy. It is in this context that US-style community colleges are so successful.

Some of the things that collaboration achieves – part-time study, modularization, local study, guaranteed progression, progression for those with GNVQs – can enhance participation and progression for underrepresented groups. However, these things are not sufficient to guarantee wider participation. What is needed is a curricular response within HE to diversity, in order to enhance the quality of the student experience for new client groups. This is another way of saying that collaboration is a dynamic relationship and not simply a functional one, and one in which there are mutual benefits, recognition of strengths and weaknesses and, as a result, mutually agreed changes.

Curriculum change

There are two main themes here: first, the development of new qualifications; second, the related issue of credit frameworks. Both the FEU and the Robertson Report, *Choosing to Change*, have said much about both of these.

Robertson recommends three things that are particularly important for the future of partnerships: a national credit framework, an associate degree (with dual accreditation at GNVQ level 4) and a credit-based system of funding. As Chapter 7 indicates, Scotland is already some way towards such a common credit currency, with a recognition of the mutual benefits for institutions and students within the SCOTCATS and SCOTVEC systems. The reactions to Robertson in England have been more negative, in part because of the sensitivity of HEIs to what they see as outside interference and the relative lack, when compared with Scotland, of interest among employers in the vocational side of HE provision.

Conclusion

What have been suggested above are some of the features of a future that goes beyond franchising towards greater partnership and, hence, mutuality. Already, partnerships have significantly affected institutional relationships in the post-16 sector, and the concept and practice of partnership are deeply embedded in many institutions. Partnerships have the potential to produce a genuinely mass system of higher education.

While it would be naive to ignore the possibility that partnerships are not all mutuality – to deny that there are private, institutional agendas – the real conclusion to this volume is very simple: *partnerships work for HE, FE and schools.*

Appendix: The Literature of Partnership: A Bibliographical Critique

Mike Abramson

Introduction

In 1993 two well known British educationalists, in articles cited fully below, bemoaned the dearth of published material on franchising and other forms of cross-sector collaboration. Maggie Woodrow (1993) described franchising as a 'quiet revolution' bereft of analytical or policy-oriented publications, while Mantz Yorke's (1993) contribution could only 'draw from the relatively meagre extant literature'. These complaints are not well founded, since the literature of partnership is already extensive, and continues to grow. They do, however, indicate that no collation of the emerging literature of this relatively new academic area has yet been undertaken; hence this critical bibliography.

The current literature may be seen to take two forms: first, official papers and reports that provide the new political, financial and educational landscape in which partnerships have emerged; second, the many forms of publication which directly focus on partnership initiatives and, in particular, explore rationales, forms and nature of collaboration and the quality debate surrounding further education and higher education enterprises.

In the volatile environment of further and higher education, it would be foolish to say that what follows is exhaustive or definitive. It does, however, attempt to garner all the key publications and provides brief critical comment on the issues they raise. Since the literature is often free-ranging, and does not easily fall into generic themes such as funding, quality, etc., headings based upon the type of publication have been adopted. Where appropriate, however, in order to sustain or elaborate a point, and to avoid extensive cross-referencing, the main headings include sources from other categories.

Official reports and papers

While they do not explicitly address further and higher education partnerships, three government White Papers are important in their provision of a new political dynamic which enabled such partnerships to emerge. *Higher Education: Meeting the Challenge* (1987), HMSO, Cm. 714 outlined the need for strategies to increase participation in higher education, including a new emphasis on the admission of mature, non-traditional applicants and a revised policy on access routes. *Higher Education: a New Framework* (1991), HMSO, Cm. 1541 totally reformed higher education at a stroke by dismantling the binary line between universities and polytechnics. *Education and Training for the 21st Century* (1991), HMSO, Cm. 1536 gave FEIs independence from LEAs and provided colleges with directions into the 1990s.

As the first 'official' survey of new FHE networks, the HMI Report, *Higher Education in Further Education Colleges: Franchising and Other Forms of Collaboration with Polytechnics* (1991), Department of Education and Science Reference 228/91/N5, is a milestone publication that went some way to allay elitist fears as to the quality of HE in FE and to provide official sanction. This balanced and objective report expressed concerns over the provision of equipment and information technology in the colleges, found staff development variable and believed college libraries to be 'generally inadequate'. However, the report revealed that the operation of quality assurance procedures was vigorous, that college students benefited from better quality teaching accommodation and from 'the relatively small numbers in many classes'. It also believed that 'access to higher education has been widened by this collaboration' and that the 'quality of much of the teaching and learning is comparable with similar work found in the polytechnics'.

In part, the vigorous quality assurance procedures noted in the HMI Report may have benefited from the 1988 *Handbook* of the Council for National Academic Awards (CNAA), which first acknowledged the importance of emerging cross-sector partnerships in an amended Section B10 (validation, approval and review of courses offered in collaboration between institutions). This introduced, for the first time, quality guidelines, including the form of a memorandum of cooperation and regulations governing the franchising of courses to overseas institutions. These were later complemented by *Good Practice Guidelines in Franchised Courses with Special Reference to Law* (1992), CNAA. Accepting the popularity of HNC/D franchises, BTEC also produced *Franchising: a Guide to Partnerships in Programme Delivery* (1991), BTEC. Although now overtaken by licensing agreements, the guide is still useful for the checklist of actions to be undertaken by franchiser and franchisee.

In pursuit of its mission 'to contribute to the maintenance of and improvement of quality, at all levels, in institutions of higher education in the United Kingdom', the HEQC has made significant contributions to the literature of partnership. *Some Aspects of Higher Education Programmes in Further Education Institutions* (1993), HEQC, is a clear and useful study, though its findings are based upon visits to only seven HEIs and eight FEIs. The three main sections of the report (initiation and planning; validation and approval; and quality assurance and quality control) are refreshing in their identification of important contextual considerations, factors which appear to underpin good practice and problem areas which are a cause of some anxiety. This study is ably complemented by *Aspects of FE/HE Collaborative Links in Scotland* (1995), HEQC. The introduction to this survey insists that:

> Many of the organisations . . . who assisted the HEQC with this study felt that the uniqueness of further and higher education links in Scotland were not always understood by those within and without the country who were not closely associated with them. They felt that there was always the danger of research and practice originating from other parts of the UK being applied uncritically to Scottish higher and further education partnerships.

The survey is at pains, therefore, to provide the distinctive national context underpinning Scottish partnership, including the role of SCOTVEC, SWAP, SCOTCATS and the Scottish Quality Management System (SQMS). What emerges is a country which, by consensus, has moved further down the path of a national post-compulsory credit framework than England and Wales (see Robertson Report, below), and which can therefore develop articulation agreements, as against franchising, as the dominant form of collaboration. The report discusses Scottish approaches to such collaborative working and good practice in general, and concludes with clearly itemized areas for further consideration.

Comparisons are further explored in J. Gallacher and M. Osborne (1991) Differing national models of access provision: a comparison between Scotland and England, *Journal of Access Studies*, 6(2), 147–64. Also valuable for Scottish perspectives are J. Gallacher (1994) Widening access to higher education in Scotland: a discussion of the contribution of the Scottish Wider Access Programme, *Scottish Journal of Adult and Continuing Education*, 1(2), 6–17, and J. Gallacher, H. Alexander, J. Leahy and W. Yule (1995) *A National Study of FE/HE Links in Scotland*, Glasgow, Caledonian University.

Learning from Collaborative Audit: an Interim Report (1995), HEQC, is a balanced but more controversial report altogether, which synthesizes the outcomes of a limited number (14) of published collaborative audits, and finds issues of concern. It is important to note, however, that all but one of these audits were based upon pre-1992 universities. Since partnership activities have largely been dominated by the former polytechnic HEIs, the findings of the report may not, therefore, be representative.

The first part of the report puts collaborative audit into context, and the second summarizes the observations of audit teams. It is at pains to applaud good practice but also notes 'considerable variation in the strength of practice in a number of areas' (p. 10). Such concerns prompted the Chief Executive of the HEQC to make the following point in his introduction:

The study concludes that while there are examples of good practice, some universities have yet fully to come to terms with the quality assurance demands of their collaborative activity. This is seen most clearly in the whole area of monitoring and review but it also applies, to a lesser extent, at other stages as well. Unless institutions are able to bring at least the same degree of consistency and rigour to the quality assurance of their collaborative provision as they apply to the 'internal' provision for which they are wholly responsible, there must be a risk that collaboration in all its forms will come to be seen as 'second best'. Since collaboration is a means of responding more suitably and flexibly to external demands on the system, this would be a considerable setback not only for the students and employers concerned, but also for British higher education as a whole.

Learning from Collaborative Audit was quickly (and selectively) exploited by the educational press. See, for example, C. Sanders (1995) Second best degree risk: universities warned, *THES*, 28 April, 1, which omits to mention good practice. A critique of HEQC collaborative audit is also provided by M. Harrison (1995) Complex debate spoiled by hype, *THES*, 5 May, 15, and P. Walking (1995) Partners for better not worse, *THES*, 26 May, 14. At the time of writing (June 1995) the quality debate continues to rage. The HEQC's *Guidelines on the Quality Assurance of Credit-based Learning* (1995), HEQC, contains a significant section on collaborative quality assurance, which may be a positive contribution to this debate.

The need for a national credit framework is a core recommendation of *Choosing to Change: Extending Access, Choice and Mobility in Higher Education. The Report of the HEQC CAT Development Project* (1994), HEQC. This *opus magnum*, containing 104 main recommendations and 1,105 sub-sections, and summarized into a separate *Executive Statement and Summary* (1994), HEQC, is disappointing in its slim treatment of FHE partnerships (see Sections 567–576). However, the report's far-reaching key recommendations, including the creation of an associate degree, which would also attract dual accreditation as a GNVQ level 4, the development of credit-based funding through a system of credit-led vouchers and the creation of a single post-compulsory CATS framework, are of direct relevance to the future of FHE partnership. Indeed, the report recommends 'much closer working relationships between higher and further education' and believes that agreements on franchising and its quality assurance 'may have profound consequences for the effective operation of a national credit framework' (Section 570).

Choosing to Change is a controversial, far-reaching and (some would argue) wildly ambitious document that has already engendered much debate and critical appraisal, and will continue to do so in the years to come. Several responses are already in print. See, for example, R. Allan (1994) *A Staff Developer's Briefing on the HEQC Report: Choosing to Change*, University Staff Development Unit, Briefing Paper No. 10; and M. Abramson (ed.) (1994)

The New National Agenda for Student Flexibility and Choice: towards a Credit Based Culture, University of Central Lancashire, which explores the issues raised by Robertson within the published proceedings of a national conference held in October 1994. It provides in full the presentations of three keynote speakers (including a frank insight into the history and impact of the report by Robertson himself) and concludes with its own ten-point national agenda.

Supplementing the work of the HEQC, the Further Education Unit has published several bulletins and reports which pre-date Robertson in their advocacy of a national CATS framework as a means of enhancing learner motivation and widening participation, and which display a strong commitment to the value of FHE links. R. J. Mackenzie (1989) *Partnership in Continuing Education,* FEU Project RP 371, is an early and now largely forgotten report which was 'intended to provide stimulus to debate rather than draw firm conclusions'. Focusing on partnerships between adult and further education, and exploiting fieldwork examples, the project 'set out to address the issues inherent in the rhetoric on collaboration and competition which exists in much educational provision for adults', and makes the still very current statement that 'the arguments for collaboration are compelling, but are in contention with deep-seated drives towards competition and resistance to co-ordination. Collaboration needs time and understanding: it is also a process which needs nurturing' (p. vii).

Open College Networks: Participation and Progression (1993), FEU, based upon a research project of the Unit for the Development of Adult Continuing Education (UDACE) provides insight into FE–FE partnerships and explores the motivation of adult returners, particularly underrepresented groups, and their academic ambitions to progress further. *Challenges for Colleges: Developing a Corporate Approach to Curriculum and Strategic Planning* (1993), FEU, is a substantial report offering a series of challenges for FE, based upon case studies of seven colleges and containing a valuable section on HE collaboration. More influential has been *Approaches to Partnership: Who Shares Wins* (1994), FEU. This innovative discussion paper, based upon the findings of the FEU's project *Collaborative Arrangements Post-incorporation* (RP765) is directed squarely at FE college managers and partnership co-ordinators, and, via the use of case studies, focuses on FE–schools collaborative arrangements. The paper also contains two candid sub-sections on tensions and issues (e.g. the competition/collaboration debate) and dos and don'ts (e.g. 'do ensure accountability on both sides', 'don't assume that collaboration is, of itself, a good thing').

A Basis for Credit? Developing a Post–16 Credit Accumulation and Transfer Framework (1992), FEU, is a quite daring case for an overarching post-16 CAT framework, offering a common language for expressing achievement across a range of subject/vocational areas covering FE, adult education (AE) and HE and with potential alignment with the National Curriculum. Following 'an exceptionally high number of responses' to this paper a second paper of the same name, subtitled *Feedback and Developments* (1993), FEU, was produced a year later and outlined new initiatives and developments. Enhancing both is *A Framework for Credit: a Common Framework for Post-14 Education and Training for the Twenty-first Century* (1995), FEU, which gives key specifications and definitions to support its primary concern of 'outlining a vision for the future'.

Another recent FEU bulletin, *General National Vocational Qualification and Progression to Higher Education* (1995), FEU, is derived from research undertaken by the UCAS and NCVQ. The bulletin describes the potential of the new GNVQs, sometimes called 'vocational A levels', to facilitate progression from schools or FE into higher education and offers sound advice and guidance as to how cross-sector articulation agreements can be reached.

Also of value is *The Impact of Incorporation on Partnership Arrangements* (1995), FEU (RP911), which suggests that the 'heightened sense of competition post-incorporation' has not adversely affected the forging of new partnerships. Indeed, the report finds 'strong evidence of colleges' continuing involvement in a range of partnership activities'; however, 'post-incorporation, colleges would seem to be much less prepared to commit energies and resources to partnership activities which lack specific (measurable) outcomes'.

R. Gunn (1994), *Franchising in Higher Education*, USDU Briefing Paper No. 5, provides clear and concise notes on rationales for franchising, functional processes and key issues, and is particularly valuable on the implications for staff development. Gunn advocates 'the organisation of awareness-raising seminars' for staff involved in all levels of franchise operation and specific skills training in areas such as negotiation, costing and pricing and mentoring.

Official pronouncements (or even unofficial, for that matter!) on the funding of HE in FE have been conspicuous only by their absence. A welcome addition to the literature, therefore, is a report of the HEFCE entitled *Higher Education in Further Education Colleges: Funding the Relationship* (1995). This report provides substantial background on the nature of the FE–HE interface and explores funding policy through a series of questions. Should the HEFCE be more even-handed its funding of higher education in the colleges? Should the council give special treatment to the small group of 'mixed-economy' colleges? Should the council be proactive or reactive in its influence over franchise arrangements? It is disappointing that the report makes no attempt to answer these questions. Nor does it make any specific recommendations, since its explicit purpose is to stimulate discussion and to seek responses 'in order to develop further its policies on the funding of provision in FE colleges'. A more pragmatic approach to funding can be found in R. J. T. Wilson (1991) Financial considerations in franchising, within a Coombe Lodge Report, 22(10), cited in full below.

Research surveys

Since the late 1980s several excellent surveys have appeared. Some of the earliest focus was on what some regard as the initial propellant fuel of partnership, increasing participation rates within higher education. O. Fulton and S. Ellwood (1989) *Admission to Higher Education: Policy and Practice* (Department of Employment) is the product of a Training Agency funded project to map existing admission policies and to assess strategies in the move towards a mass higher education system. It views franchising as one of the more 'radical developments' and recommends that all HEIs 'should (be encouraged to) form or join regional access consortia including FE as well as HE providers, with opportunities not only for credit transfer on a case-by-case basis but also for collaborative course provision' (p. 15). Franchising also figures briefly in the mass education strategies within A. Smithers and P. Robinson (1989) *Increasing Participation in Higher Education*, BP Educational Service, and the Polytechnics and Colleges Funding Council (PCFC) (1992) *Widening Participation in Higher Education: Report of a Study of Polytechnics and Colleges of Higher Education in England*, PCFC.

C. Ball (1990) *More Means Different: Widening Access to Higher Education*, RSA/Industry Matters, is an influential and provocative case for wider participation, though its 31 recommendations are hampered by the political correctness of its day. Ball's insistence that the 'traditional model of university education is an impediment to expansion' (p. 6), his support for the massive expansion of part-time higher education (p. 31) and his case for the local marketing of 'user-friendly' higher education (p. 39) implicitly support the move to partnership. More explicitly, he notes (p. 39) that in Wales it was suggested that

> higher education must learn 'to reach out from the institution to the village hall' . . . Many wished to see stronger links between further education and higher education, suggesting wider use of franchising agreement . . . They proposed that, for many of the new students, a pattern of local, highly relevant, part-time foundation courses should be developed (where they do not already exist).

A. Baxter and J. Bird (1991) *Franchising and Associate College Arrangements in the PCFC Sector*, University of the West of England, was the product of a short PCFC funded project which began the task of gathering systematic data on partnership arrangements. Based upon information gained from questionnaires distributed to all PCFC funded institutions and to all FEIs and LEAs in England, the authors concluded that (at the time of writing) franchising was dominated by four larger polytechnics and focused on providing the first level of degrees to mature students. In 1991–2 they estimated a total of 4,605 students on franchised courses but predicted a 300 per cent increase in that number over the next three years.

The major issue for Baxter and Bird, however, was 'widening access to higher education, and whether franchising is an appropriate vehicle for widening access. The response to the question of student type would not, in this context, support this view: most arrangements were targeting mature students rather than post-access students' (p. 27). Other research findings (Abramson *et al.* 1993 and Bocock and Scott 1994, cited below) paint a somewhat more optimistic picture, but the Baxter and Bird Report was very useful in opening the debate over the issue of FHE links *widening* as well as merely *increasing* participation in the HE experience. More sustained research, including longitudinal progression analysis, is clearly needed in this area.

A more influential, oft-cited research report is provided by J. Bird, G. Crawley and A. Sheibani (1993) *Franchising and Access to Higher Education: a Study in HE/FE Collaboration*, University of the West of England/Department of Employment. The report gives an in-depth analysis of partnership arrangements and issues, places a refreshing emphasis on student opinion (e.g. 'We would prefer to stay here [the college] for three years') and makes clear recommendations on good practice. Moreover, the report was the first to drive the HE in FE quality debate into less archaic and more meaningful directions by recognizing 'that FEIs and HEIs are different and have their own strengths . . . following this, a simplistic view that quality in HE can be reproduced exactly in FE, is misleading' (p. 24). 'Commonality', the report insists later, 'usually means FE following HE; the pursuit of a common identity between HE and FE is a chimera' (p. 45). The report is usefully summarized by J. Bird, and G. Crawley (1994) Franchising and other further education/higher education partnerships: the student experience and policy, in S. Haselgrove (ed.) (1994) *The Student Experience*, SRHE and Open University Press, 37–43.

Access and Community Services (ACES) within the University of North London has been a regular contributor to the literature of partnership via its research reports, conference proceedings and newsletter, *Access News* (see below). G. Grindlay *et al.* (1992) *Report of the Access News Franchising Survey*, ACES, is a basic analysis of returned questionnaires from 92 institutions, divided roughly equally between FEIs and HEIs, presented in user-friendly graphical and tabular form. This report was a preliminary to L. Sims and M. Woodrow (1992) Franchising for Wider Access, ACES, which offers a no-nonsense precis of the main issues through sections headed 'partnership in practice', 'funding for franchising', 'what staff think', etc. Its conclusion emphasizes the positive value of franchising in 12 key statements.

The interim report by J. Bocock and P. Scott (1994) *Re-drawing the Boundaries: Further and Higher Education Partnerships*, Centre for Policy Studies in Education, University of Leeds, is another cogent and penetrating examination of the partnership phenomenon. Within the brisk nine-point executive summary (pp. 1–2) there is an optimistic insistence that FHE partnerships are 'here to stay'. It argues that although 'recent reductions in tuition fees may undermine the short-term viability of some courses funded on a fees only basis, the development of partnerships is driven by more deep-rooted phenomena – the broadening of university missions and the dynamics of the FE and HE curriculum' (p. 1). The summary also points to 'a lack of co-ordination between the HEFCE's and the Further Education Funding Council of England's (FEFCE's) current approaches to quality assessment which makes it difficult to assess F/HE partnerships' but supports the previous conclusions of the Bird, Crawley and Sheibani research, which see difference as a strength in terms of quality. 'It is unreasonable', the summary states, to expect the traditional HE experience simply to be replicated. 'FE colleges offer their students a different but equally positive experience based upon closer attention to learning support, the development of core skills, and so on' (p. 2).

A national evaluation of the impact of school Compacts, conducted by the NFER, has resulted in a series of informative reports and briefing papers. See, for example, M. Morris and I. Schagen (1993) *Motivation for Success? A Cohort Study of Young People Involved in Urban Compacts,* NFER Briefing Paper No. 1; and, by the same authors, *Compacts and the Work-related Curriculum,* NFER Briefing Paper No. 2 (1994), and *Students at Risk: the Impact of Compacts,* NFER Briefing Paper No. 3 (1994). Compacts are explored further in a more widely focused survey by J. Bird and W. Yee (1994) *From Compacts to Consortia: a Study of Partnerships Involving Schools, Colleges and HEIs,* Department of Employment/University of the West of England. In mapping the variety and extent of such partnerships during May/June 1993, the survey indicated 'that 25 HEIs now have Compacts with from three to 47 schools and colleges, and a further 30 have prioritized the development of Compacts' (p. 9). Addressing rationales for partnerships, the survey notes that there seems to be, 'two faces to partnerships: that which is more *public* and includes reference to access, progression and serving the community; and that which is more *private*: for HEIs, filling under-recruiting courses, and for schools, improving their DFE ranking' (p. 25).

From Compacts to Consortia also includes valuable guidelines for action (pp. 29, 30) and a section headed '36 things you can try in School/College/HE Partnerships' (p. 31).

The Association for Colleges (AfC) survey (1994) *The Higher Education Role of Colleges of Further Education,* AfC, is a brief but powerful case for HE in FE. Based upon a questionnaire survey of all AfC members in England and Wales (though with no indication of response rate), the survey examines the nature and expansion of FEI participation in HE work and (more importantly) focuses on the effects and wider significance of reductions in funding and the capping of HE student numbers following the 1993 autumn statement. The survey is enhanced by valuable and clear statistical tables and charts.

The AfC survey reveals that reduction of tuition fees and the freeze on HE expansion were 'perceived as a double blow' by colleges. They were 'emphatic that this was not a response to any fall in demand. Rather the situation was the reverse . . . Some bitterness in circumstances like these is perhaps understandable' (p. 5). However, like Bocock and Scott (1994), it reveals a gritty optimism in the face of adversity and an indication of the resilience of most FHE partnerships:

Discussions about franchised provision in response to reductions in funding and HE student numbers followed no particular pattern and were obviously an indication of the relationship between FE and HE 'partners' . . . There were only a few examples of arbitrary action on the part of HE institutions . . . On the whole, however, given the pressure on both sectors, FE/HE partnerships seem to have survived with remarkably little acrimony.

In a somewhat colder financial climate colleges will therefore 'seek to develop flexible arrangements with universities which will overcome the barriers prescribed to [them] by the changes in funding'.

The survey's positive conclusions make it clear that 'FE colleges now perceive higher education work as an integral part of their curriculum offer, whether provided independently or in conjunction with HE partners. The inclusion of higher education work is viewed as not a form of academic drift, but as being complementary to, as distinct from in conflict with, their expanding portfolio of further education provision' (p. 11). This assertion is supported by the colleges' 'consciousness of their local role and the relevance of their higher education work to this', their strong commitment to meeting the needs of mature students with regard to local delivery of HE, and their belief in a distinctive FE formula for higher education, focusing on the more vocationally oriented areas of science, technology, engineering and business studies. However, fulfilment of this vision requires 'greater clarity about the sources of funding for FE based higher education' and an end to 'the GO/STOP policies towards higher education' (p. 12).

Published conference proceedings

The rapid growth and development of FHE links over the past five years in the UK has been supported by many staff development seminars and national conferences, the outcomes of some of which have been published.

One early report of a conference organized by the National Association of Teachers in Further and Higher Education (NATFHE), entitled *Franchising and Access: Towards an Identification of Good Practice* (1991), NATFHE, contains useful contributions from BTEC, CNAA and PCFC as well as some valuable case studies and a summary of workshop outcomes. In her introduction to the conference, Judith Summers, the 1990–1 President of NATFHE, sought to assess the balance between the positive and negative features of franchising. Franchising, she noted, 'may pose a challenge to the traditional view of a full-time residential degree course targeted at a relatively small 18+ cohort or it may be seen as further extending invidious funding distinctions. Perhaps, most importantly for us, it may offer a key to extending access to low or non-participant groups' (p. 1). Further outcomes are summarized in G. Melling (1991) Franchising and access: towards a definition of good practice, *NATFHE Journal*, 16(2), 14–16.

S. Leather and S. Toogood (eds) (1991) *Franchising in Post-16 Education*, Coombe Lodge Report 22(8), The Staff College, arose from a seminar for principals at the Staff College, Blagdon, in April 1991. Formally produced in short book form, it contains three valuable chapters which explore an area on which little has been published so far (i.e. BTEC franchises to schools). From the experience of Bedfordshire, Brian Cue (pp. 779–94) notes that 'the culture clash between schools and colleges – still very real despite all the changes – makes it hard to agree definitions of quality'. Barbara Molog (pp. 785–96) explains a BTEC franchise scheme coordinated across an entire LEA, the London Borough of Brent, based on the pragmatic need to stem the tide of student exports to colleges outside the LEA. Robert Hughes (pp. 797–802) uses Preston Manor High School to provide a case study of the Brent initiative, arguing a need to increase student retention and to make the most cost-effective use of resources.

G. Blake *et al.* (1991) *Franchising: Assuring the Quality of the Student Experience*, Coombe Lodge Report 22(8), The Staff College, is the product of a joint CNAA and Staff College conference of the same name held in January 1992. Published in short book form, its chapters contain material on policy, funding and learning support, together with an interesting comparison by Geoff Blake (cited fully elsewhere) of academic franchising in the UK with commercial franchising in the United States of America.

ACES organized two partnership conferences in 1992: *Taking Franchising Forward* (March 1992) and *A Formula for Franchising* (November 1992). Although presentations were not formally collated, various useful papers are available from ACES, including L. Wagner (1992) Franchising: good or bad news for higher and future education?, given at the November conference.

M. Abramson (ed.) (1994) *FHE Partnership and Quality: towards a National Agenda*, University of Central Lancashire, provides in full the keynote presentations of three national speakers representing the perspectives of HE, FE and the National Union of Students (NUS), summarizes outcomes of workshop sessions and concludes with a ten-point national agenda. Reinforcing the quality themes explored in Bird, Crawley and Sheibani (1993) and Bocock and Scott (1994), this agenda insists, among other things, that 'FE partnerships are best judged in terms of "fitness for purpose" as determined by the needs of the student body' and that 'quality frameworks for FHE partnerships must accept the differences and diversity within FE and HE as a strength and not as a weakness'. M. Abramson (1994) Ten years of franchising, *The Lecturer*, October, 11, provides a useful summary of this ten-point agenda.

The proceedings of two important conferences have appeared as Mendip Papers. S. Brownlow (ed.) (1994) *Equal Outcomes – Equal Experiences*, Mendip Paper No. 059, Staff College/SRHE, was the product of the 1993 joint annual conference of the Society for Research into Higher Education and the Staff College. Focusing on franchising, the 'programme was designed to shift the emphasis away from the 'nuts and bolts' of franchising arrangements and onto the student experience' (p. 1), and contains several valuable contributions, including that of David Morris, which explains the difference between 'first' and 'second' generation franchising (pp. 10–12).

An outcome of the following (1994) annual joint conference was S. Brownlow (ed.) (1995) *Managing Quality Assurance at the FE/HE Interface*, Mendip Paper No. 080, Further Education Development Agency. These proceedings include an enterprising resumé of key issues by Anne Stennett (drawn from delegate responses prior to the conference), papers from three quality 'regulators' (HEQC, FEFC and BTEC) and presentations from institutional practitioners at the 'sharp end' of quality assurance. Key issues from conference workshops are also usefully summarized to 'provide an agenda for future research and development' (p. 45).

Books and journal articles

Given the emerging nature of partnerships it is not surprising to find that no single text, apart from this one, has yet been dedicated to cross-sector collaboration. E. Robinson (1968) *The New Polytechnics*, Cornmarket, London, was remarkable in its efforts to chart a distinctive role for the emerging polytechnics, and, in part, laid the foundations upon which FHE collaboration was built, with such statements as 'the polytechnics should fulfil a regional or area function for the education service and the community at large' (p. 131) and 'they should open up new routes to the bachelors' degree ... establish a ladder of steps towards it' (p. 125). Other prophetic collections, however, including C. Ball and H. Eggins (eds) (1989) *Higher Education into the 1990s*, SRHE and Open University Press, and I. McNay (ed.) (1992) *Visions of Post-compulsory Education*, SRHE and Open University Press, are disappointing in their complete omission of partnership developments.

Articles within the scholarly journals are now emerging and should be read in parallel with the literature of CATS, modularity and access which make frequent appearances in publications such as the *Journal of Access Studies* and the *Journal of Further and Higher Education*.

D. Warner (1992) Classless study, *Education*, October, 330–1, gives a very brief but clear outline of the nature and forms of partnership and provides concise rationales from the perspective of FEIs, HEIs and students. He concludes that

> perhaps the most important long-term consequence of collaboration will be the elimination of the old 'class' system in education. Already the binary division between universities and polytechnics has been removed ... The next division to fall must be that between HE and FE and collaboration is doing much to blur the edges. Finally, the division between HE/FE and schools may also go.

Observations drawn from the findings of several recent national surveys and a critique of the exclusivity debate are to be found in M. Abramson (1994) Franchising, access, quality and exclusivity, *Journal of Access Studies*, 9(1), 109–14. Two other articles draw interesting comparisons between private sector franchising and higher education partnerships. From the perspective of the Leicester Business School at de Montfort University, A. Palmer (1992) Franchised degree teaching: what can educators learn from business?, *Journal of Further and Higher Education*, 16(3), 76–85, believes that the 'uncertain start to higher education franchising mirrors the early days of private sector franchising, but like the latter, it has the potential subsequently to achieve rapid mutually beneficial growth' (p. 77). This optimism is later reinforced in the statement that

> Public sector franchising initially found little favour with users of a service, but once the issue of consistent standards had been addressed effectively, it was accepted as routine. Franchised delivery of education is currently going through the process of establishing its credibility – with commitment from all parties involved in the process, the next decade could see franchising becoming as normal as it is now for privately provided services.

This intelligent and important article is complemented by D. Morris (1993) The business of franchising, *Journal of Further and Higher Education*, 17(1), 57–60. In a comparison of commercial and academic franchising, based upon initiatives within the Coventry University Business School, Morris explains the criteria for successful franchising, explores the concept of mutual benefit and (most importantly) isolates ten principles of 'general good practice for further growth and development'.

Another contribution which relates to business format franchising is M. Yorke (1993) Quality assurance for higher education franchising, *Higher Education*, 26(2), 167–82. This balanced and thoughtful study draws on the franchising experiences at Liverpool John Moores University and includes a valuable section on the under-published area of international franchising. The article's central concern, however, is to address the 'general principles underpinning the development of quality systems for franchising' (p. 181). Yorke insists that he has 'limited' his article to these principles, since the next step

> is to develop these principles into a quality system of a clarity and a robustness which could achieve a widespread recognition – perhaps through registration to the relevant part of British Standard BS 5750 or to the International Standardisation Organisation ISO 9000 Series . . . Good quality assurance does not come cheap, and is probably rather more expensive than many currently believe. However, from the franchiser's point of view (at least) it may be significantly less economical to run franchises with so light a touch on the quality assurance tiller that the franchise ship runs on the rocks.

M. Woodrow (1993) Franchising: the quiet revolution, *Higher Education Quarterly*, 47(3), Summer, 207–20, is another considered contribution from an experienced practitioner. Woodrow discovers the origins of franchising – a 'revolutionary activity', which was 'breathtaking' and 'astonishing' in its speed of development – in 'American parents of doubtful compatibility', i.e. commercial franchising and the community college movement, which both boomed in the 1970s (p. 208). However, it was not until the late 1980s, she argues, that conditions in Britain (the new enterprise culture, together with government demands for higher participation rates) provided a favourable take-off environment. The article is also particularly illuminating on the wider impact of franchising, which, even if the boom period is over, 'has permanently altered perceptions of the relationship between further and higher education institutions' (p. 220).

D. Brady and M. Metcalfe (1994) Staff and Student Perceptions of Franchising, *Journal of Access Studies*, 9(2), 271–7, provides the interim findings of a questionnaire survey of FE staff and students engaged in franchise activity. Curiously, staff regarded 'higher level teaching' as the most significant benefit of franchising, but cited 'increased preparation for classes' as the biggest disadvantage. Students gave local commitments as the most important reason for opting for a franchised course and perceived 'lack of social interaction with other higher education students' as the most serious drawback.

It is pleasing to note that a substantial body of work is already in print on library support for the off-campus learner, and continues to be published. Until recently this work was dominated by non-European authors. See, for example, D. Barron (1990) The use of distance education in United States library and information science, *Education for Information*, 8, 325–39; C. Crocker (1991) Off-campus library services in Australia, *Library Trends*, 39(4), 495–513; and A. Slade (1991) Library support for off-campus and distance education programmes in Canada: an overview, *Library Trends*, 39(4), 454–78. An early British insight is provided by R. K. Fisher, (1991) Off campus library services in HE in the United Kingdom, *Library Trends*, 39(4), 479–94.

These international perspectives were a valuable contribution to British librarians when they were formulating their own FHE partnership agenda. The Library Association (1992), for example, in *Library Provision for Franchised Courses*, provides guidelines for library support and argues a role for librarians at all stages of the partnership process, including strategic decision-making and course approval. Examples of institution-specific guidelines can be found in P. Brophy (1992) *University of Central Lancashire Franchised Courses: Guidelines for Franchised Courses*, University of Central Lancashire, and Sheffield City Polytechnic (1991) *Franchised Courses: Guidelines on Library Provision*, Coombe Lodge Report 22(10), cited in full above.

Several more articles and reports explore the role of the library in collaborative delivery, and in particular the need for higher levels of user-education. Of these, P. Brophy (1993) Franchising higher education: the library's role, in C. J. Jacob (ed.) *The Sixth Off-campus Library Services Conference Proceedings*, Central Michigan University, is one of the most thorough and important. Brophy provides an appraisal of British franchising, drawing upon the University of Central Lancashire's Partner College Library Network as an example of good practice. 'The basic concept', he argues, is to view Library services as a network of resources, with a wide range of delivery points, which is accessible to every franchised course student. While it will take time to achieve a high level of cross utilization of resources, the aim is to operate the libraries of all participating institutions as open resources for higher education students on . . . franchised courses.

Brophy also introduces the Libraries without Walls' Project, funded by the European Commission over the period February 1994 to July 1995, and involving the University of the Aegean (Greece), Dublin City University and the University of Central Lancashire, which is coordinating the project through its Centre for Research in Library and Information Management (CERLIM, see below). The aim of the project is to research and demonstrate techniques for providing access and delivery of library materials and services to users based at a distance from the physical library (particularly those in the less developed EU countries) and to disseminate interesting and good practice throughout the EU.

Surveying related issues and themes are P. Brophy (1991) Franchising courses: the library in distributed higher education, *COPOL Newsletter*, 56, 58–61, P. Brophy (1992) Distant libraries: the support of HE students who study off-campus, *Library Management*, 13(6), 22–3, and P. Brophy, D. Goodall and P. Wynne (1995) Library services to distance learners: research and operational developments in a UK and European context, in E. F. Watson (ed.) (1995) *Library Services to Distance Learners in the Commonwealth: A Reader*. Vancouver: Commonwealth of Learning.

Brophy's work is complemented by two case studies and another major research project. C. B. Linkman (1993) *A Study of the Learning Resource Implications of Higher Education*, Wigan and Leigh College, is a candid needs analysis from the perspective of an FE college with almost 20 per cent of its course portfolio devoted to HE. L. Unwin (1994) I'm a real student now: the importance of library access for distance learning students, *Journal of Further and Higher Education*, 18(1), 85–91, draws upon the research findings of a University of Sheffield project, which analysed questionnaires from 350 part-time masters students at four English universities. Like Brophy, she advocates a network solution to the 'considerable difficulty' faced by many off-campus students. 'This research', she asserts, 'demonstrates the need for a systematic national review of the library provision for distance learning students . . . In the light of the end of the binary divide, there is urgent need for adequately funded reciprocal agreements covering the whole of higher education in the UK' (p. 90).

While a research fellow within CERLIM at the University of Central Lancashire, Deborah Goodall undertook a two-year research project (1993–5), Library Support for Franchised Courses in Higher Education, funded by the British Library Research and Development Department. The interim findings of this thorough and imaginatively researched project, which have already appeared in several journals, reveal much dissatisfaction by librarians in the part they play (or do not play) in the development and delivery of FHE partnerships. For example, D. Goodall (1994) Franchised courses in higher education: implications for the library manager, *Library Management*, 15(2), 27–33, reveals that 'formal mechanisms enabling the library to input into the franchising process were few, or were still being established. The overwhelming impression was that, in practice, much of the library's impact within the colleges depended on the strength of informal networks and working with individuals' (p. 28). Similar frustrations emerge in D. Goodall (1994) Franchised courses, library resources: the view from both sides, *Library and Information Research News*, 18(61), 22–8; D. Goodall (1995) Franchised courses: the university library perspective, *Education Libraries Journal*, 37(3), 5–20, and D. Goodall (1995) The impact of franchised HE courses on library and information services in FE colleges, *Journal of Further and Higher Education*, 19(3). However, the last of these does itemize the positive benefits to FE libraries of becoming involved in HE work, including the improvement in stock (particularly journals), extended opening hours, computerized cataloguing, new services such as short loan and inter-library loan, and the use of JANET to access university holdings, together with online and CD-ROM provision. In all, therefore, college libraries generally felt that partnership developments had 'raised the status of the library within the college'.

D. Goodall (1994) Use of diaries in library and information research, *Library and Information Research News*, 18(59), 17–21, also provides insight into one way of conducting research into library usage by franchise students.

Literature on the 'information superhighway' and the electronic library is fast emerging. Appendix K (pp. 129–42) of the Dale Campbell-Savours case study on Cumbria, cited fully below, applies such developments to the concept of a 'distributed' university, and utilizes examples from several European initiatives, including de Montfort University's Electronic Library Project (ELINOR). See also J. Jackman (1994) En route to the super-highway, *THES*, 22 July, which provides information on a British Telecom funded project, based at the University of Central Lancashire and aimed at evaluating the use of Integrated Systems Digital Network (ISDN) as an aid to distance learning at Burnley and Furness Colleges.

Case studies

Many references to individual partnership schemes appear in conference proceedings and as examples in other reports, and a few receive more complete treatment. See, for example, I. Tunbridge (1991) Franchising higher education activity at Polytechnic South West, in the Coombe Lodge Report, 22(10), cited in full above.

Separately published case studies are thinner on the ground, in part because many internal papers have not yet found their way into the public domain. FHE collaboration in Lancashire and Cumbria, however, has been the subject of several reports and articles. M. Abramson and M. Grannell (1989) *Forging Higher Education Links with an Isolated Community: West Cumbria College as a Case Study*, Lancashire Polytechnic, is the result of a research project funded by the CNAA. Running to over 150 pages, this report charts the institutional context within which links were forged between what was then Lancashire Polytechnic and an isolated FE college on the West Cumbrian coast, and provides an in-depth analysis of two early cohorts (1984–6) of franchise students. A summary of the full technical support appeared as CNAA Briefing Paper No 23, June 1990, with the same title. Also of interest are M. Abramson (1992) Quality through partnership: franchise and collaborative course initiatives in Lancashire and Cumbria, *Promoting Education*, June, 12–14, and M. Abramson (1993) Franchising and Fitness for Purpose, *Access News*, June, 12–13.

A more wide-ranging survey of franchising in the North West is found in M. Abramson, S. Ellwood and L. Thompson (1993) *Five Years of Franchising: an Analysis of the Profile, Performance and Progression of LINCS Students 1985–90*, University of Central Lancashire, based upon a research survey of the Lancashire Integrated Colleges Scheme (LINCS), one of the earliest and largest franchise networks in the UK. The report analyses statistical data over a five-year period and via a 22-page questionnaire to all LINCS students within the 1989–90 cohort (which received a 75 per cent response rate), and provides qualitative conclusions. For a review of this report see H. Woolf (1993) Making LINCS work, *Access News*, 16 June, 16.

R. Bray (1989) *The Cumbria HE Research Project (CHERP). Final Report to the Director of Education*, Cumbria County Council, is an early investigation of the demand for higher education in Cumbria and how such demand could be met. Its conclusions are criticized by D. Campbell-Savours (1995) *The Case for the University of the Lakes*, privately published, for 'some general conclusions drawn upon small samples that, in some cases, had very low response rates'. Centrally, CHERP is flawed, he argues, in that it 'seriously underestimated local demand for higher education because it did not take into account social and cultural factors that are particularly strong in Cumbria, and which inhibit Cumbrians from leaving the County' (p. 26).

The Case for the University of the Lakes is an ambitious and extensively researched report which promulgates a 'distributed' or federal university for Cumbria aimed at the social, cultural and economic revitalization of the region. Campbell-Savours is emphatic that

Cumbria needs an integrated institutional approach to higher education. I believe that this can best be achieved by instituting a new Cumbria-wide, multi-sited, University of the Lakes, building on and embracing provision in existing institutions of further and higher education in the County . . . Specific 'Schools', or 'Colleges' of the University would be unapologetically designed to foster the development of particular sectors of the local economy in energy, agriculture and tourism.

Only time will tell whether such a daring vision can be realized.

More real, but less daring, are the HEQC's institutional reports of collaborative audit, which are gradually being published. Though somewhat formulaic and overly genteel in their isolation of 'issues for further consideration', they do provide valuable context and background to specific partnership ventures.

Newspaper and periodical press

FHE partnerships have occasionally interested the education correspondents of the national broadsheets. For some of the more interesting pieces see T. Reed (1992) Extending choice and access for students, *The Independent*, 18 June, D. Ward (1992) The red rose graduates, and A trip down memory lane, *The Guardian*, 15 December, and L. Heron (1993) Outposts of better learning, *The Independent*, 20 May. Barry Hugull's (1994) article in *The Observer*, 12 June, University degrees under fire amid sleaze allegations, made a front page headline out of the controversial aspects of overseas franchising.

The *Times Higher Education Supplement* (*THES*) has chartered the vicissitudes of cross-sector collaboration in a journalistic and sometimes provocative fashion over several years, and reflects the national debate on such activities. See, for example, C. Sanders (1992) Quality fear in franchise boom, *THES*, 5 June, countered by M. Woodrow (1992) Franchised courses built on firm foundations, *THES*, 2 October. A third salvo was fired by C. Sanders (1993) Franchising hopes hit the buffers, *THES*, 19 February. Issues of quality and learner support, which have been a focus for the partnership debate, form the basis of T. Tysome (1993) FE colleges lag on libraries, *THES*, 19 March, and C. Sanders (1994) Quality call on foreign links, *THES*, 20 September. I. Nash, (1994) Funding to consolidate or confuse, *THES*, 20 January, examines the impact of funding cuts and HE consolidation on collaborative ventures, despite burgeoning demand for such local provision.

Access News, the tri-annual magazine of ACES, has long featured brief policy articles and updates on new regional initiatives on franchising and other forms of collaboration. Of particular value are issues No. 11 (December 1991), which contains eight separate pieces on franchising, No. 12 (March 1992), which provides four articles, No. 13 (June 1992), which contains another four items, including a valuable editorial by Maggie Woodrow, and No. 14 (December 1992), which gives a perspective from Leslie Wagner.

Conclusion

It is hoped that the above collation reveals the rich and diverse nature of the extant literature of partnership and how it has already contributed to the wider debate on the nature, funding and quality of post-compulsory education as it approaches the twenty-first century. Whatever their strengths, however, current publications also indicate omissions and weaknesses. For example, there has been an over-emphasis on franchising, the earliest form of FE partnership, at the expense of more mature forms of collaboration, such as joint courses, articulation agreements and validations. There has been little serious analysis of partnership with schools, and, apart from a few sensational exposés in the press, there is 'virtually no public information regarding franchising to private institutions within the UK and to organizations beyond the UK' (Yorke 1993: 2, cited above).

Moreover, the claim that partnership has widened participation in HE has yet to be substantiated by thorough, empirical, case study research. Longitudinal cohort research into partnership students who need to progress to the host HEI to complete their programme of study is also lacking. Partnership literature would undoubtedly benefit from more prophetic vision, especially if focused on institutional and curricular merger, future funding methodologies and the life expectancy of the current quality agencies.

Hence, while this bibliography suggests that the partnership 'revolution' was, and is, not as 'quiet' as once believed, there is still room for much more noise. Future researchers and practitioners are encouraged to make it.

Index

Page numbers in italic indicate tables.

The Society for Research into Higher Education

The Society for Research into Higher Education exists to stimulate and coordinate research into all aspects of higher education. It aims to improve the quality of higher education through the encouragement of debate and publication on issues of policy, on the organization and management of higher education institutions, and on the curriculum and teaching methods.

The Society's income is derived from subscriptions, sales of its books and journals, conference fees and grants. It receives no subsidies, and is wholly independent. Its individual members include teachers, researchers, managers and students. Its corporate members are institutions of higher education, research institutes, professional, industrial and governmental bodies. Members are not only from the UK, but from elsewhere in Europe, from America, Canada and Australasia, and it regards its international work as among its most important activities.

Under the imprint *SRHE & Open University Press*, the Society is a specialist publisher of research, having some 60 titles in print. The Editorial Board of the Society's Imprint seeks authoritative research or study in the above fields. It offers competitive royalties, a highly recognizable format in both hardback and paperback and the world-wide reputation of the Open University Press.

The Society also publishes *Studies in Higher Education* (three times a year), which is mainly concerned with academic issues, *Higher Education Quarterly* (formerly *Universities Quarterly*), mainly concerned with policy issues, *Research into Higher Education Abstracts* (three times a year), and *SRHE News* (four times a year).

The Society holds a major annual conference in December, jointly with an institution of higher education. In 1993, the topic was 'Governments and the Higher Education Curriculum: Evolving Partnerships' at the University of Sussex in Brighton. In 1994, it was 'The Student Experience' at the University of York and in 1995, 'The Changing University' at Heriot-Watt University in Edinburgh. Conferences in 1996 include 'Working in Higher Education' at Cardiff Institute of Higher Education.

The Society's committees, study groups and branches are run by the members. The groups at present include:

Teacher Education Study Group
Continuing Education Group
Staff Development Group
Excellence in Teaching and Learning

Benefits to members

Individual

Individual members receive:

- SRHE: News, the Society's publications list, conference details and other material included in mailings.
- Greatly reduced rates for *Studies in Higher Education* and *Higher Education Quarterly*.
- A 35 per cent discount on all SRHE & Open University Press publications.
- Free copies of the Proceedings – commissioned papers on the theme of the Annual Conference.
- Free copies of *Research into Higher Education Abstracts*.
- Reduced rates for conferences.
- Extensive contacts and scope for facilitating initiatives.
- Reduced reciprocal memberships.
- Free copies of the *Register of Members' Research Interests*.

Corporate

Corporate members receive:

- All benefits of individual members, plus
- Free copies of *Studies in Higher Education*.
- Unlimited copies of the Society's publications at reduced rates.
- Special rates for its members e.g. to the Annual Conference.
- The right to submit application for the Society's research grants.

Membership details: SRHE, 3 Devonshire Street, London WIN 2BA, UK. Tel: 0171 637 2766. Fax: 0171 637 2781
Catalogue: SRHE & Open University Press, Celtic Court, 22 Ballmoor, Buckingham MK18 1XW. Tel: (0280) 823388.

HUMAN RESOURCE MANAGEMENT IN HIGHER AND FURTHER EDUCATION

David Warner and Elaine Crosthwaite (eds)

The major element of the budget of all educational institutions is spent on people. Their management and motivation is a prime concern of educational managers. At a time of unprecedented changes, this book provides the first ever comprehensive coverage of the key aspects of human resource management – central to the success of every educational institution.

Human Resource Management in Higher and Further Education has been written by a team of senior educational managers, academics and external experts. They examine the current major issues and future challenges; reflect and explore the trend toward greater managerialism; and include helpful case studies as well as analytical accounts of the topics covered. This is an essential guide to all the important areas of human resource and personnel management as they relate to further and higher education institutions.

Contents
Setting the scene – Managing change – Developing a human resource strategy – Managing diversity – The learning organization – Effective communication – Managing and rewarding performance – Executive recruitment – Essential employment law – Making educational institutions safer and healthier – Developing managers – Industrial relations strategies and tactics – Managing information – Bibliography – Index.

Contributors
Jo Andrews, David Bright, Elaine Crosthwaite, Emily Crowley, Diana Ellis, David House, Peter Knight, Elizabeth Lanchbery, Patricia Leighton, John McManus, Geoffrey Mead, Rebecca Nestor, Jennifer Tann, Elizabeth Walker, Roger Ward, David Warner, David Watson, Bill Williamson.

224pp   0 335 19377 3 (Paperback)   0 335 19378 1 (Hardback)

MISSION AND CHANGE
INSTITUTIONAL MISSION AND ITS APPLICATION TO THE MANAGEMENT
OF FURTHER AND HIGHER EDUCATION

Graham Peeke

Graham Peeke reviews critically the concept of institutional mission in higher and
further education, and evaluates the claims made for its use. Through case studies
he analyses different methods of establishing objectives, provides guidance on how
to operationalize missions so that they are more than just rhetoric, and links institutional change with the development of a strategic perspective in education management. He argues that it is essential to adopt participative methods in mission
development, that procedures for operationalization are crucial, and that broad
dimensions of mission need to be agreed with the core of the organization. However, given the plurality of educational organizations, he also argues that autonomy
is necessary for significant groupings throughout the institutions. This is essential
reading for all policy-makers and managers in higher and further education, and
for researchers into the management of higher education.

Contents

160pp   0 335 19338 2 (Paperback)   0 335 19337 4 (Hardback)